THE BOOK OF CAMPING AND WOODCRAFT

THE BOOK OF CAMPING AND WOODCRAFT

A GUIDEBOOK FOR THOSE WHO TRAVEL IN THE WILDERNESS

BY

HORACE KEPHART

KALPAZ

ISBN: 978-93-5128-802-2

First Published in 1906
Indian Reprint in 2017

Published by

Kalpaz Publications
C-30, Satyawati Nagar,
Delhi – 110052
E-mail: kalpaz@hotmail.com
Website: kalpazpublications.com
Ph.: +91-9212142040

Cataloging in Publication Data—DK
Courtesy: D.K. Agencies (P) Ltd. <docinfo@dkagencies.com>

Kephart, Horace, 1862-1931, **author.**
The book of camping and woodcraft : a guidebook for those who travel in the wilderness / by Horace Kephart.
pages cm
"First published in 1906"—Title page verso.
ISBN 9789351288022

1. Camping. 2. Outdoor life. I. Title.

GV191.7.K3 2017 DDC 796.54 23

"This is the forest primeval. The murmuring pines and the hemlock,
Bearded with moss, and in garments green, indistinct in the twilight,
Stand like Druids of old, with voices sad and prophetic,
Stand like harpers hoar, with beards that rest on their bosoms."

LONGFELLOW.

CONTENTS

CHAPTER		PAGE
	Foreword	xi
I	Outfitting	1
II	The Sportsman's Clothing	11
III	Personal Kits	22
IV	Tents and Tools	37
V	Utensils and Food	52
VI	A Check-List—Packing Up	62
VII	The Camp	70
VIII	The Camp-Fire	82
IX	Marksmanship in the Woods	92
X	Dressing and Keeping Game and Fish	100
XI	Camp Cookery	114
XII	Pests of the Woods	165
XIII	Forest Travel. Keeping a Course	179
XIV	Blazes—Survey Lines—Natural Signs of Direction	194
XV	Getting Lost—Bivouacs	207
XVI	Emergency Foods—Living off the Country	217

CHAPTER PAGE

XVII EDIBLE PLANTS OF THE WILDERNESS . 232

XVIII AXEMANSHIP—QUALITIES OF WOOD AND BARK 256

XIX TROPHIES, BUCKSKIN AND RAWHIDE . 277

XX TANNING PELTS—OTHER ANIMAL PRODUCTS 290

XXI ACCIDENTS: THEIR BACKWOODS TREATMENT 300

ILLUSTRATIONS

"The Forest Primeval" . . *Frontispiece*

Facing page

In Still Waters 20

A Proud Moment 32

Real Comfort in the Open 46

Starting a Lean-to Shelter . . . 72

The Fixed Camp 72

A Good Day's Shoot 98

An Ideal Camp-Fire 98

The Camp in Order 122

Just Starting Out 122

Crude, but Comfortable 182

Down the Snow-white Alleys . . . 182

The Old, Old Story 218

But a Good Day's Luck Lands Them . . 218

A Stray Goose Wanders Near . . . 230

Where Lurks the Lusty Trout . . . 230

FOREWORD

MY one aim in writing this little book is to make it of practical service to those who seek rest or sport in the wilderness, or whose business calls them thither. I have treated the matter of outfitting in some detail, not because elaborate outfits are usually desirable, for they are not, but because in town there is so much to pick and choose from. Thereafter, the body of the book is mainly given up to such shifts and expedients as are learned in the wilderness itself, where we have nothing to choose from but the raw materials that lie around us.

As for camps situated within easy reach of towns or supply-posts, every one, I suppose, knows best how to gratify his own tastes in fitting them up, and prefers to use his own ingenuity rather than copy after others. Real woodcraft consists rather in knowing how to get along without the appliances of civilization than in adapting them to wildwood life. Such an art comes in play when we travel "light," and especially in emergencies, when the equipment, or essential parts of it, have been destroyed. I am not advising anybody to travel with nothing but a gun and ammunition, a blanket, a frying-pan, and a tin cup; but it has been part of my object to show how the thing can be done, if necessary, without serious hardship.

Woodcraft may be defined as the art of getting along well in the wilderness by utilizing nature's storehouse. When we say that Daniel Boone, for example, was a good woodsman, we mean that he could confidently enter an unmapped wilderness, with no outfit but what was carried by his horse, his canoe, or on his own back, and with the intention of a protracted stay; that he could find his way through the dense forest without man-made marks to guide him; that he knew the habits and properties of trees and plants, and the ways of fish and game; that he was a good trailer and a good shot; that he could dress game and cure peltry, cook wholesome meals over an open fire, build adequate shelter against wind and rain, and keep himself warm through the bitter nights of winter—in short, that he knew how to utilize the gifts of nature, and could bide comfortably in the wilderness without help from outside.

The literature of outdoor sport is getting us used to such correlative terms as plainscraft, mountaincraft, and even icecraft, snowcraft, and birdcraft. This sort of thing can be overdone; but we need a generic term to express the art, in general, of getting on well in wild regions, whether in forests, deserts, mountains, plains, tropics or arctics; and for this I would suggest the plain English compound *wildcraft*.

In the following chapters I offer some suggestions on outfitting, making camps, dressing and keeping game and fish, camp cookery, forest travel, how to avoid getting lost, and what to do if one does get lost, living off the country, what the different species of trees are good for (from a camper's viewpoint), backwoods handicrafts in wood, bark, skins and other raw materials, the treatment of wounds and other injuries, and some other branches of woodcraft that may be of service when one is far from shops and from hired help. I have little or nothing to say, here, about hunting, fishing, trailing, trapping, canoeing, snowshoeing, or the management of horses and pack-trains, because each of these is an art by itself, and we have good books on all of them save trailing.*

* This would seem an impossible subject to treat in a book; but any one who reads German may come to a different conclusion after studying a work by Eugen Teuwsen and Carl Schulze, entitled, *Fährten und Spurenkunde* (Tracks and Trailing), published in 1901 by J. Neumann of Neudamm, Prussia. This describes the tracks made by the red deer, moose, fallow deer, roebuck, chamois, wild boar, hare, rabbit, squirrel, bear, wolf, dog, fox, wildcat, badger, otter, woods marten and stone marten, polecat, various weasels, and of the capercailzie, black-cock, hazel-grouse, moor-hen, quail, pheasant, curlew, bustard, crane, stork, heron, swan, wild goose, and wild duck. The text is accompanied by capital woodcuts, mostly life-size, showing with more than photographic exactness the tracks made by these animals in the various paces of walking, running, and jumping. A similar book for American game is much to be desired; not that it would make a good trailer out of anybody, but because it would give a beginner a clear idea of what to look for and what to avoid.

I have preferred to give full details, as far as this book goes. One's health and comfort in the wilds very often depend upon close observance of just such details as breathless people would skip or scurry over. Moreover, since this is not a guidebook to any one particular region, I have tried to keep in mind a variety of conditions existing in different kinds of country, and have suggested alternative methods or materials, to be used according to circumstances.

In the school of the woods there is no graduation day. What would be good woodcraft in one region might be bad bungling in another. A Maine guide may scour all the forests of northeastern America, and feel quite at home in any of them; but put him in a Mississippi canebrake, and it is long odds that he would be, for a time,

> Perplexed, bewildered, till he scarce doth know
> His right forefinger from his left big toe.

And a southern cane-cracker would be quite as much at sea if he were turned loose in a spruce forest in winter. But it would not take long for either of these men to "catch on" to the new conditions; for both are shifty, both are cool-headed, and both are keen observers. Any man may blunder once, when confronted by strange conditions; but none will repeat the error unless he be possessed by the notion that he has nothing new to learn.

As for book-learning, it is useful only to those who do not expect too much from it. No book can teach a man how to swing an axe or follow a trail. But there are some practical arts that it can teach, and, what is of more consequence, it can give a clear idea of general principles. It can also show how *not* to do a thing—and there is a good deal in that. Half of woodcraft, as of any other art, is in knowing what to avoid. That is the difference between a true knot and a granny knot, and the difference can be shown by a sketch as easily as with string in hand.

If any one should get the impression from these pages that camping out with a light outfit means little but a daily grind of camp chores, questionable meals, a hard bed, torment from insects, and a good chance of broken bones at the end, he will not have caught the spirit of my intent. It is not here my purpose to dwell on the charms of free life in a wild country; rather, taking all that for granted, I would point out some short-cuts, and offer a lift, here and there, over rough parts of the trail. No one need be told how to enjoy the smooth ones. Hence it is that I treat chiefly of difficulties, and how to overcome them.

This book had its origin in a series of articles, under a similar title, that I contributed, in 1904-6, to the magazine *Field and Stream*. The original chapters have been expanded, and new ones have been added, until there is here about double the matter that appeared in the parent series. I have also added two chapters previously published in *Sports Afield*.

Most of these pages were written in the wilderness, where there were abundant facilities for testing the value of suggestions that were outside my previous experience. In this connection I must acknowledge indebtedness to a scrap-book full of notes and clippings, the latter chiefly from old volumes of *Forest and Stream* and *Shooting and Fishing*, which was one of the most valued tomes in the rather select "library" that graced half a soap-box in one corner of my cabin.

I owe much, both to the spirit and the letter of that classic in the literature of outdoor life, the little book on *Woodcraft* by the late George R. Sears, who is best known by his Indian-given title of Nessmuk. To me, in a peculiar sense, it has been *remedium utriusque fortunæ;* and it is but fitting that I should dedicate to the memory of its author this humble pendant to his work.

HORACE KEPHART.

Dayton, Ohio
March, 1906.

CHAPTER I

OUTFITTING

"By St. Nicholas
I have a sudden passion for the wild wood—
We should be free as air in the wild wood—
What say you? Shall we go? Your hands, your hands!"
—*Robin Hood.*

IN some of our large cities there are professional outfitters to whom one can go and say: "So many of us wish to spend such a month in such a region, hunting and fishing: equip us." The dealer will name a price; you pay it, and leave the rest to him. When the time comes he will have the outfit ready and packed. It will include everything needed for the trip, well selected and of the best materials. When your party reaches the jumping-off place it will be met by professional guides and packers, who will take you to the best hunting grounds and fishing waters, and will do all the hard work of paddling, packing over portages, making camp, chopping wood, cooking, and cleaning up, besides showing you where the game and fish are "using," and how to get them. In this way a party of city men who know nothing of woodcraft can spend a season in the woods very comfortably, though getting little practical knowledge of the wilderness. This is touring, not campaigning. It is expensive; but it may be worth the price to such as can afford it, and who like that sort of thing.

But, aside from the expense of this kind of camping, it seems to me that whoever takes to the woods and waters for recreation should learn how to shift for himself in an emergency. He may employ guides and a cook—all that; but the day of disaster may come, the outfit may be destroyed, or the city man may find himself some day alone, lost in the forest, and compelled to meet the forces of nature in a struggle for his life. Then it may go hard with him indeed if he be not only master of himself, but of that woodcraft that holds the key to nature's storehouse. A camper should know for himself how to outfit, how to select and make a camp, how to wield an axe and make proper fires, how to cook, wash, mend, how to travel without losing his course, or what to do when he has lost it; how to trail, hunt, shoot, fish, dress game, manage boat or canoe, and how to extemporize such makeshifts as may be needed in wilderness faring. And he should know these things as he does the way to his mouth. Then is he truly a woodsman, sure to do promptly the right thing at the right time, whatever befalls. Such a man has an honest pride in his own resourcefulness, a sense of reserve force, a doughty self-reliance that is good to feel. His is the confidence of the lone sailorman, who whistles as he puts his tiny bark out to sea.

And there are many of us who, through some miscue of the Fates, are not rich enough to give *carte blanche* orders over the counter. We would like silk tents, air mattresses, fiber packing cases, and all that sort of thing; but we would soon "go broke" if we started in at that rate. I am saying nothing about guns, rods, reels, and such-like, because they are the things that every properly conducted sportsman goes broke on, anyway, as a matter of course. I am speaking only of such purchases as might be thought extravagant. And it is conceivable that some folks might call it extravagant to pay thirty-five dollars for a thing to sleep in when you lie out of doors on the ground from choice, or thirty dollars for pots and pans to cook with when you are "playing hobo," as the unregenerate call our sylvan sport.

Nor can we deny that a man with an axe and a couple of dollars' worth of cotton cloth can put up in two or three hours as good a woodland shelter as any mere democrat or republican needs between the ides of May and of November; and if he wants a portable tent he can generally buy very cheaply a second-hand army one that will meet all his requirements for several seasons. Tin or enameled ware, though not so smart nor so ingeniously nested as a special aluminum kit, will cook just as good meals, and will not burn one's fingers and mouth so severely. Blankets we can take from home (though never the second time, perhaps); and a narrow bed-tick, filled with browse, or with grass or leaves where there is no browse, in combination with a rubber blanket or poncho, makes a better mattress than the Father of his Country had on many a weary night. A discarded business suit and a flannel shirt, easy shoes and a campaign hat, are quite as respectable in the eyes of woodland folk as a costume of loden or gabardine, and they do not set one up so prominently as a mark. Grocery boxes make good packing cases, and they have the advantage that they are not too good to be broken up for shelves and table in camp. As for duffel bags, few things are more satisfactory than seamless grain bags that you have coated with boiled linseed oil. Such a bag, by the way, is a good thing to produce now and then to show your friends how ingeniously economical you are. It helps out when you are caught slipping in through the back gate with a brand-new gun, when everybody knows that you already possess more guns than you can find legitimate use for.

If one begins, as he should, six months in advance, to plan and prepare for his next summer or fall vacation, he can, by gradual and surreptitious hoarding, get together a commendable camping equipment, and nobody will notice the outlay. The best way is to make many of the things yourself. This gives your pastime an air of thrift, and propitiates the Lares and Penates by keeping you home o' nights. And there is a world of solid comfort in having everything fixed just to suit you. The only way to have it so is to do the work yourself. One can wear ready-made clothing, he can exist in ready-furnished rooms, but a ready-made camping outfit is a delusion and a snare. It is sure to be loaded with gimcracks that you have no use for, and to lack something that you will be miserable without.

It is great fun, in the long winter evenings, to sort over your beloved duffel, to make and fit up the little boxes and hold-alls in which everything has its proper place, to contrive new wrinkles that nobody but yourself has the gigantic brain to conceive, to concoct mysterious dopes that fill the house with unsanctimonious smells, to fish around for materials, in odd corners where you have no business, and, generally, to set the female members of the household to buzzing around in curiosity, disapproval, and sundry other states of mind.

To be sure, even though a man rigs up his own outfit, he never gets it quite to suit him. Every season sees the downfall of some cherished scheme, the failure of some fond contrivance. Every winter sees you again fussing over your kit, altering this, substituting that, and flogging your wits with the same old problem of how to save weight and bulk without sacrifice of utility. All thoroughbred campers do this as regularly as the birds come back in spring, and their kind have been doing it since the world began. It is good for us. If some misguided genius should invent a camping equipment that nobody could find fault with, half our pleasure in life would be swept away.

There is something to be said in favor of individual outfits, every man going completely equipped and quite independent of the others. It is one of the delights of single-handed canoeing, whether you go alone or cruise in squadron, that every man is fixed to suit himself. Then if any one carries too much or too little, or cooks badly, or is too lazy to be neat, or lacks forethought in any way, he alone suffers the penalty; and this is but just. On the other hand, if one of the cruisers' outfits comes to grief, the others can help him out, since all the eggs are not in one basket. I like to have a complete camping outfit of my own, just big enough for two men, so that I can dispense a modest hospitality to a chance acquaintance, or take with me a comrade who, through no fault of his own, turns up at the last moment; but I want this outfit to be so light and compact that I can easily handle it myself when I am alone.

Then I am always "fixed," and always independent, come good or ill, blow high or low.

Still, it is the general rule among campers to have "company stores." In so far as this means only those things that all use in common, such as tent, utensils, tools, and provisions, it is well enough; but it should be a point of honor with each and every man to carry for himself a complete kit of personal necessities, down to the least detail. As for company stores, everybody should bear a hand in collecting and packing them. To saddle this hard and thankless job on one man, merely because he is experienced and a willing worker, is selfish. Depend upon it, the fellow who "hasn't time" to do his share of the work before starting will be the very one to shirk in camp.

The question of what to take on a trip resolves itself chiefly into a question of transportation. If the party can travel by wagon, and intends to go into fixed camp, then almost anything can be carried along—trunks, chests, big wall tents and poles, cots, mattresses, pots and pans galore, camp stove, kerosene, mackintoshes and rubber boots, plentiful changes of clothing, arsenals of weapons and ammunition, books, folding bath-tubs —what you will. Anybody can fit up a wagon-load of calamities, and hire a farmer to serve as porter. But does it pay? I think not.

Be plain in the woods. In a far way you are emulating those grim heroes of the past who made the white man's trails across this continent. Fancy Boone reclining on an air mattress, or Carson pottering over a sheet-iron stove! We seek the woods to escape civilization for a time, and all that suggests it. Let us sometimes broil our venison on a sharpened stick and serve it on a sheet of bark. It tastes better. It gets us closer to nature, and closer to those good old times when every American was considered "a man for a' that" if he proved it in a manful way. And there is a pleasure in achieving creditable results by the simplest means. When you win your own way through the wilds with axe and rifle you win at the same time the imperturbability of a mind at ease with itself in any emergency by flood or field. Then you feel that you have red blood in your veins, and that it is good to be free and out of doors. It is one of the blessings of wilderness life that it shows us how few things we need in order to be perfectly happy.

Let me not be misunderstood as counseling anybody to "rough it" by sleeping on the bare ground and eating nothing but hardtack and bacon. Only a tenderfoot will parade a scorn of comfort and a taste for useless hardships. As Nessmuk says: "We do not go to the woods to rough it; we go to smoothe it—we get it rough enough in town. But let us live the simple, natural life in the woods, and leave all frills behind."

An old campaigner is known by the simplicity and fitness of his equipment. He carries few impedimenta, but every article has been well tested and it is the best that his purse can afford. He has learned by hard experience how steep are the mountain trails and how tangled the undergrowth and downwood in the primitive forest. He has learned, too, how to fashion on the spot many substitutes for "boughten" things that we consider necessary at home.

The art of going "light but right" is hard to learn. I never knew a camper who did not burden himself, at first, with a lot of kickshaws that he did not need in the woods; nor one who, if he learned anything, did not soon begin to weed them out; nor even a veteran who ever quite attained his own ideal of lightness and serviceability. Probably Nessmuk came as near to it as any one, after he got that famous ten-pound canoe. He said that his load, including canoe, knapsack, blanket-bag, extra clothing, hatchet, rod, and two days' rations, "never exceeded twenty-six pounds; and I went prepared to camp out any and every night." This, of course, was in summer.

In the days when game was plentiful and there were no closed seasons our frontiersmen thought nothing of making long expeditions into the unknown wilderness with no equipment but what they carried on their own persons, to wit: a blanket, rifle, ammunition, flint and steel, tomahawk, knife, an awl, a spare pair of moccasins, perhaps, a small bag of jerked venison, and another of parched Indian corn, ground to a coarse meal, which they called "rockahominy" or "coal flour." Their tutors in woodcraft often traveled lighter than this. An Indian runner would strip to his G-string and moccasins, roll up in his small blanket a pouch of rockahominy, and, armed only with a bow and arrows, he would perform journeys that no mammal but a wolf could equal. General Clark said that when he and Lewis, with their men, started afoot from the mouth of the Columbia River on their return trip across the continent, their total store of articles for barter with the Indians for horses and food could have been tied up in two handkerchiefs. But they were woodsmen, every inch of them.

Now it is not needful nor advisable for a camper in our time to suffer hardships from stinting his supplies. It is foolish to take insufficient bedding, or to rely upon a diet of pork, beans, and hardtack, in a country where game may be scarce. The knack is in striking a happy medium between too much luggage and too little. A pair of scales are good things to have at hand when one is making up his packs. Scales of another kind will then fall from his eyes. He will note how the little, unconsidered trifles mount up; how every bag and tin adds weight. Now let him imagine himself toiling uphill under an August sun, or forging through thickety woods, over rocks and roots and fallen trees, with all this stuff on his back. Again, let him think of a chill, wet night ahead, and of what he will really need to keep himself warm, dry, and well ballasted amidships. Balancing these two prospects one against the other, he cannot go far wrong in selecting his outfit.

In his charming book *The Forest,* Stewart Edward White has spoken of that amusing foible, common to us all, which compels even an experienced woodsman to lug along some pet trifle that he does not need, but which he would be miserable without. The more absurd this trinket is, the more he loves it. One of my camp-mates for five seasons carried in his "packer" a big chunk of rosin. When asked what it was for, he confessed: "Oh, I'm going to get a fellow to make me a turkey-call, some day, and this is to make it 'turk.'" Jew's-harps, camp-stools, shaving-mugs, alarm-clocks, derringers that nobody could hit anything with, and other such trifles have been known to accompany very practical men who were otherwise in light marching order. If you have some such thing that you know you can't sleep well without, stow it religiously in your kit. It is your "medicine," your amulet against the spooks and bogies of the woods. It will dispel the koosy-oonek. (If you don't know what that means, ask an Eskimo. He may tell you that it means sorcery, witchcraft—and so, no doubt, it does to the children of nature; but to us children of guile it is the spell of that imp who hides our pipes, steals our last match, and brings rain on the just when they want to go fishing.)

No two men have the same "medicine." Mine is a porcelain teacup, minus the handle. It cost me much trouble to find one that would fit snugly inside the metal cup in which I brew my tea. Many's the time it has all but slipped from my fingers and dropped upon a rock; many's the gibe I have suffered for its dear sake. But I do love it. Hot indeed must be the sun, tangled the trail and weary the miles, before I forsake thee, O my frail, cool-lipped, but ardent teacup!

The joys and sorrows of camp life, and the proportion of each to the other, depend very much upon how one chooses his companions—granting that he has any choice in the matter at all. It may be noticed that old-timers are apt to be a bit distant when a novice betrays any eagerness to share in their pilgrimages. There is no churlishness in this; rather it is commendable caution. Not every good fellow in town makes a pleasant comrade in the woods. So it is that experienced campers are chary of admitting new members to their lodges. To be one of them you must be of the right stuff, ready to endure trial and privation without a murmur, and—what is harder for most men—to put up with petty inconveniences without grumbling.

For there is a seamy side to camp life, as to everything else. Even in the best of camps things do happen sometimes that are enough to make a saint swear silently through his teeth. But no one is fit for such life who cannot turn ordinary ill-luck into a joke, and bear downright calamity like a gentleman.

Yet there are other qualities in a good camp-mate that are rarer than fortitude and endurance. Chief of these is a love of nature for her own sake—not the "put on" kind that expresses itself in gushy sentimentalism, but that pure, intense, though ordinarily mute affection which finds pleasure in her companionship and needs none other. As Olive Shreiner says: "It is not he who praises nature, but he who lies continually on her breast *and is satisfied*, who is actually united to her." Donald G. Mitchell once remarked that nobody should go to the country with the expectation of deriving much pleasure from it, as country, who has not a keen eye for the things of the country, for scenery, or for trees, or flowers, or some kind of culture; to which a New York editor replied that "Of this not one city man in a thousand has a particle in his composition." The proportion of city men who do thoroughly enjoy the hardy sports and adventures of the wilderness is certainly much larger than those who could be entertained on a farm; but the elect of these, the ones who can find plenty to interest them in the woods when fishing and hunting fail, are not to be found on every street corner.

If your party is made up of men inexperienced in the woods, hire a guide, and, if there be more than three of you, take along a cook as well. Treat your guide as one of yourselves. A good one deserves such consideration; a poor one is not worth having at all. But if you cannot afford this expense, then leave the real wilderness out of account for the present; go to some pleasant woodland, within hail of civilization, and start an experimental camp, spending a good part of your time in learning how to wield an axe, how to build proper fires, how to cook good meals out of doors, and so forth. Be sure to get the privilege beforehand of cutting what wood you will need. It is worth paying some wood-geld that you may learn how to fell and hew. Here, with fair fishing and some small game hunting, you can have a jolly good time, and will be fitted for something more ambitious the next season.

In any case, be sure to get together a company of good-hearted, manly fellows, who will take things as they come, do their fair share of the camp chores, and agree to have no arguments before breakfast. There are plenty of such men, steel-true and blade-straight. Then will your trip be a lasting pleasure, to be lived over time and again in after years. There are no friendships like those that are made under canvas and in the open field.

CHAPTER II

THE SPORTSMAN'S CLOTHING

FOR ordinary camping trips an old business suit will do; but be sure that the buttons are securely sewn and that the cloth is not worn thin. It is somewhat embarrassing to come back home, as a friend of mine once did, with a staring legend of XXX FAMILY FLOUR emblazoned on the seat of his trousers. It may be well to take along a pair of overalls; they are workmanlike and win the respect of country folk. Men who dwell in the woods the year 'round are practical fellows who despise frills and ostentation. Many a tenderfoot has had to pay double prices for everything, and has been well laughed at in the bargain, because he sported a big bowie knife or a fake cowboy hat-band.

When one is preparing for a long, hard trip, it pays to give some heed to the clothing question. As a rule, the conventional hunting costumes of the shops are as unfit for the wilderness as they are for the gymnasium. They are designed for bird hunters, who carry heavy loads of shotgun shells, and little else, and who can tumble into a civilized bed at night. Canvas and corduroy are the materials most used. These cloths wear well, are generally of fairly good color for the purpose, are not easily soiled, and they do not collect burs; but this is about all the good that can be said of them. Canvas is too stiff for athletic movements, a poor protection against cold, and not so comfortable in any weather as wool. Corduroy wears like iron, but it is too heavy for hot days, not nearly so warm in cold weather as its weight of woolen goods, and it is notoriously heavy and hard to dry when it has been soaked through. Neither canvas nor corduroy are good absorbents of perspiration, nor do they let it evaporate freely. Both of them are too noisy for still-hunting. Even when they are not rasping against grass and underbush, there is a *swish-swash* of the trousers at every step. They are also likely to chafe the wearer.

A sportsman's clothing should be strong, soft, light, warm for its weight, of inconspicuous color, and easy to dry after a wetting. It should be self-ventilating, and of such material as absorbs the moisture from the body. It should fit so as not to chafe, and should be roomy enough to give one's limbs free play, permitting him to be active and agile.

Underwear.

The quality of one's underwear is of more importance than his outer garments. It should be of pure, soft wool throughout, regardless of the season. Cotton or silk are clammy and unhealthful when one perspires freely, as he is sure to do when living an active life out of doors, even in midwinter, and they chill the skin when one is drenched by a shower or when he rests after exertion. The air of the forest is often damp and chilly, especially at night and in the early morning hours. And you must expect to get a ducking now and then, and to be exposed to a keen wind when topping a ridge after a hard climb. At such times you are likely to catch a bad cold, or sow the seeds of rheumatism, if your underclothing is of any other material than wool. Thick underwear is not recommended, even for winter. It is better to have a spare undershirt of a size larger than what one commonly wears, and to double-up in cold weather or on frosty nights. Two thin shirts worn together are warmer than a thick one weighing as much as both. This is because there is a layer of warm air between them. The more air contained in a garment, other things being equal, the warmer it is. One soon realizes this when he spreads a blanket on the hard ground and lies down on it, thus pressing out the confined air. Drawers should be loose around the thighs and knees, but snug in the crotch. Remember that woolen goods will shrink in washing, unless the work is skilfully done; so do not get a snug fit at the start.

It is unwise to carry more changes of underwear,

handkerchiefs, etc., than one can comfortably get along with. They will all have to be washed, anyway, and so long as spare clean ones remain no man is going to bother about washing the others. This means an accumulation of soiled clothes, which is a nuisance of the first magnitude.

Overshirts.

Overshirts should be loose at the neck, a size larger than one ordinarily wears, for they will surely shrink, and a tight collar is not to be tolerated. The collars should be wide, if the shirts are to be used in cold weather, so that they can be turned up and tied around the neck. Gray is the best color, the dark blue of soldiers' or firemen's shirts being too conspicuous for hunters. It is well to sew two small pockets on the shirt just below where the collar-bone comes. These are to receive the watch and compass, which should fit snugly so as not to flop out when one stoops over. If the watch is carried in the fob pocket of the trousers it will be unhandy to get at, on account of the belt, and it is more likely to be injured when one wades out of his depth or gets a spill in shallow water.

Neckerchiefs.

A neckerchief should be worn, preferably of silk, because that is easy to wash and dry out. It protects the neck from sunburn, keeps it warm in cold weather, and is useful to tie over the hat and ears when the wind is high or the frost nips keenly. In case of cramps it is a good thing to tie over the stomach. A bright color, white or red especially, should be avoided if one expects to do any hunting.

Coats and Jerseys.

A heavy coat is a nuisance in the woods. It would only be worn as a "come-and-go" garment when one is traveling to and from the wilderness, and around camp in the chill of the morning and evening. For the latter purpose a heavy jersey or sweater is much better, besides being more comfortable to sleep in, and easier to dry out. It should be of gray or light tan color, and all-wool of course. The objections to a sweater are that it is easily torn or picked out by brush, it attracts burs almost as a magnet does iron filings, and it soaks through in a smart shower. But if a coat of thin, very closely woven khaki, "duxbak," or gabardine, large enough to wear over the sweater, is taken along, the perfection of comfort in all kinds of weather is attained. Such a coat is rain-proof, sheds burs, and keeps out not only the wind but the fine, dust-like snow which, on a windy day in winter, drives through the air, forces itself into every pore of a woolen fabric, and, melting from the heat of the body, soaks the garment through and through. With the above combination one is fixed for any kind of weather. On hot days his overshirt and trousers will be all the outer clothing he will want; if it threatens rain, he will add the coat; mornings and evenings, or on cold, dry days, he will substitute the sweater; and when it is both cold and windy, or cold and wet, all three will be worn. In any case the coat is merely considered as a thin, soft, rain-proof and wind-proof, but self-ventilating, skin, the heat-giving and sweat-absorbing part of the clothing being worn underneath. To combine the two in one garment would defeat the purpose, for it would be clumsy and would not dry out quickly. A free outlet for the moisture from the body, or a thick absorbent of it that can be taken off and dried out quickly, is a prime essential of health and comfort in all climates, and at no time more so than when the mercury stands far below zero.

For those who prefer a single heavy coat, rather than tolerate the "bunchy" feeling of several layers of different materials, I would recommend, for steady cold weather, a Mackinaw coat of the best obtainable quality, such as sheds a light rain; poor ones soak up water like a sponge.

Trousers.

Do not seek to keep your legs dry by wearing waterproofed material. Nothing but rubber or pantasote will shed the water when you forge through wet underbrush, and they would wet you most uncomfortably by giving no vent to perspiration. Take your wetting, and dry out when you get back to camp. Strong, firmly woven woolen trousers or knickers are best for the woods in cold weather, and khaki or duxbak for warm weather.

The color of a woodsman's clothing should be as near invisibility as possible—unless he ranges through a country infested with fools with guns, in which case a flaming red head-dress may be advisable. By the way, it is bad practice when one is calling turkeys to hide in the brush or behind a tree. Sit right out in the open. So long as you are motionless the turkey will not recognize you as a human being, whereas a man attracted by your calling will. The same rule holds good when one is on a deer stand, or "holding down a log" on a runway. As for inconspicuous clothing, take a hint from the deer and the rabbit, from the protective plumage of grouse and woodcock. Most shades of cloth used for men's clothing are darker than they should be for hunting. What seems, near by, to be a light brown, for instance, looks quite dark in the woods. The light browns, greens, and drabs are indistinguishable from each other at a few rods' distance. The color of withered fern is good; so are some of the lighter shades of covert cloth, such as top-coats are made of; also the yellowish-green khaki. White (except amid snow) and red are the most glaring colors in the woods. An ideal combination would be a mottle of alternate splotches of brown or drab and light gray, which, at a short distance in the woods, would blend with the tree trunks and would not look entirely opaque. Many men who think themselves properly dressed for still-hunting, and are so in the main, spoil it all by a flopping hat, a bright neckerchief, a glittering buckle, or rasping covering for their legs.

Color.

Leggings should be of woolen cloth, preferably of loden, which is waterproof. Those of canvas, pantasote, or leather are too noisy. When a man is in the woods to see what is going on in them he should move as quietly and make himself as unnoticeable as possible, whether he carries a gun or not. Leggings should not be fastened with buckles, hooks, or springs, but should lace through large eyelets or fasten with a puttee strap. Buckles and hooks catch in the grass and glitter in the sunlight, besides being

Leggings.

hard to manage when covered with mud or ice; hooks are easily bent out of shape; springs are too stiff for pedestrians. Many recommend cloth puttees instead of leggings. A puttee of the kind I mean is a piece of stout woolen cloth four or five inches wide and fully nine feet long, to be wrapped spirally around the leg, starting from the ankle and winding up to the knee, overlapping an inch or two at a turn, and fastened at the top by tapes sewn on like horse-bandages. It is claimed that nothing else so well supports the veins of the legs in marching, that they are more comfortable and noiseless than ordinary leggings, and that they afford better protection against venomous snakes, as the serpent's fangs are not so likely to penetrate the comparatively loose folds of cloth. Puttees should be specially woven with selvage edges on both sides, for if merely hemmed they will soon fray at the edges. It is not advisable to wear them in a thickety country.

Shoes.

Nothing in a woodsman's clothing is of more importance than his foot dressing. The two unpardonable sins of a soldier are a rusty rifle and sore feet. So they should be regarded by us campers. The shoes and stockings should fit snugly, so as not to chafe from friction, but they should on no account be tight enough to bind. The shoes should be well broken in before starting.

High-topped hunting boots that lace up the leg are well enough for engineers and stockmen, but for hunters or others who travel in the wilderness, either afoot or afloat, they are much too heavy and clumsy. A pair of strong shoes with medium soles and bellows tongues, not over seven inches high, nor weighing an ounce more than two and a half pounds to the pair, will do for ordinary wear. They should be pliable both in soles and uppers. No one can walk well in boots with thick, stiff soles. Hob-nails are recommended only for fishermen and mountaineers. They should be of soft iron, as steel ones slip on the rocks. Their heads should be large and square, not cone-shaped. A few hob-nails along the edges of the soles and heels will suffice, those of most importance being the two on either side of the ball of the foot. If the middle of the sole is studded with them they are likely to hurt the feet. The leather should be well soaked before they are driven in.

It is not a bad plan to drive a few protruding nails in the heels and soles of one's shoes, in a particular pattern, so that one can infallibly recognize his own footprints when back-trailing. This will also assist one's companions if they should have occasion to search for him.

The best shoe-laces are made from rawhide belt-lacing, cut in strips and hardened at the ends by slightly roasting them in the fire.

Waterproofing Leather.

Shoes to be worn in cool weather may well be water-proofed, but for warm weather they should not, for waterproofed leather heats the feet; and so, by the way, do rubber soles. If one has much marching to do he had better take his chances of getting his feet wet now and then than to keep them overheated all the time, and consequently tender.

An excellent Norwegian recipe for waterproofing leather is this:

> Boil together two parts pine tar and three parts cod-liver oil. Soak the leather in the hot mixture, rubbing in while hot. It will make boots waterproof, and will keep them soft for months, in spite of repeated wettings.

Moccasins.

For canoeing, still-hunting, and for long marches in the dry season, as well as for use around camp, wear either thick moccasins or light moccasin-shoes (the latter should not weigh over one and a half pounds to the pair).

The importance of going lightly shod when one is to do much tramping is not always appreciated. Let me show what it means. Suppose that a man in fair training can carry on his back a weight of forty pounds for ten miles on good roads, without excessive fatigue. Now shift that load from his back and fasten half of it on each foot—how far will he go? You see the difference between carrying on your back and lifting with your feet. Very well; a pair of hunting shoes of conventional store pattern weighs about three pounds; a pair of moose-hide moccasins weighs eleven ounces. In ten miles there are 21,120 average paces. It follows that a ten-mile tramp in the big shoes means lifting some eight tons more footgear than if one wore moccasins. Nor is that all. The moccasins are soft and pliable as gloves; the shoes are stiff, clumsy, and likely to blister the feet.

If your feet are too tender, at first, for moccasins, add insoles of birch bark or the dried inner bark of red cedar. After a few days the feet will toughen, the tendons will learn to do their proper work without crutches, and you will be able to travel farther, faster, more noiselessly, and with less exertion, than in any kind of boots or shoes. This, too, in rough country. I have often gone tenderfooted from a year's office work and have traveled in moccasins for weeks, over flinty Ozark hills, through canebrakes, through cypress swamps where the sharp little immature "knees" are hidden under the needles, over unballasted railroad tracks at night, and in other rough places, and enjoyed nothing more than the lightness and ease of my footwear. After one's feet have become accustomed to this most rational of all covering they become almost like hands, feeling their way, and avoiding obstacles as though gifted with a special sense. They can bend freely. One can climb in moccasins as in nothing else. So long as they are dry, he can cross narrow logs like a cat, and pass in safety along treacherous slopes where thick-soled shoes might bring him swiftly to grief. Moccasined feet feel the dry sticks underneath, and glide softly over the telltales without cracking them. They do not stick fast in mud. One can swim with them as if he were barefoot. It is rarely indeed that one hears of a man spraining his ankle when wearing the Indian footgear.

Moccasins should be of moose-hide, or, better still, of caribou. Elk-hide is the next choice. Deerskin is too thin, hard on the feet for that reason, and soon wears out. The hide should be Indian-tanned, and "honest Injun" at that—that is to say, not tanned with bark or chemicals, in which case (unless of caribou-hide) they would shrink and dry hard after a wetting, but made of the raw hide, its fibers thoroughly broken up by a plentiful expenditure of elbow-grease, the skin softened by rubbing into it the brains of the animal, and then smoked, so that it will dry without shrinking and can be made as pliable as before by a little rubbing in the hands. Moccasins to be used in a prickly-pear or cactus country must be soled with rawhide.

Ordinary moccasins, tanned by the above process (which properly is not tanning at all), are only pleasant to wear in dry weather. But they are always a great comfort in a canoe or around camp, and are almost indispensable for still-hunting or snow-shoeing. They weigh so little, take up so little room in the pack, and are so delightfully easy on the feet, that a pair should be in every camper's outfit. At night they are the best foot-warmers that one could wish, and they will be appreciated when one must get up and move about outside the tent.

In a mountainous region that is heavily timbered, moccasins are too slippery for use after the leaves fall.

"Packs" and "Shanks."

Oil-tanned shoe-packs are better than moccasins for wet weather. When kept well greased with tallow (oil softens them too much) they are waterproof, and much more comfortable than rubber shoes. "Shanks" made by stripping the hide from the hind legs of moose, caribou, or elk, without splitting it, using the bend of the hock for the heel of the boot, and sewing up the toe part, when properly tanned are impervious to water and snow, and are beyond comparison the warmest and driest of footwear for high latitudes. Caribou or reindeer skin makes the best. It is remarkably tough, moderately elastic, warmer for its weight than any other material, more impervious to wind, drier than any other kind of leather, and it has the singular property of tightening when wet, or at least not stretching like all other skins. Shanks are sometimes made of green hide, but only for temporary purposes, as they soon wear out; when tanned they are very durable. The hide should be tanned with bark, as alum destroys its good qualities. The hair should be left on and worn outside, the shanks being carefully dried away from the fire, after using, or the hair will drop out.

Never hang your moccasins before the fire to dry; they would shrink too small for your feet, and become almost as stiff and hard as horn. Scrape off as much moisture as you can, stuff them full of dry grass or some other elastic, absorbent substance, and hang them in a current of air where they can dry slowly. Then rub them soft.

Wading Boots.

Rubber boots I never wear, save when working in the marshes, or for a short time in muddy, sloppy weather around a cabin or fixed camp. I would rather get wet from water than from perspiration. Canvas wading shoes, with eyelets at the toes to let the water run out, or old shoes with slits cut in them (not wide enough to let in gravel), are good to use when fishing.

Waterproof Clothing.

A mackintosh or other long-tailed coat is as out of place in the woods as an umbrella on shipboard. An oilskin slicker, topped off by a sou'wester, may be all right in a boat or over decoys, on horseback, or when driving; but anything of this sort is too heavy, too draggling, too hot, too awkward to shoot from, when one is afoot; and the brush soon tears it. For a woodsman an army poncho is better, either of rubber or (much more durable) of pantasote. It makes a good ground-sheet at night. The infantry size is 45x72 inches, the cavalry 72x84, the latter being large enough to serve as a shelter, but heavy to tote around. A waterproof poncho weighing only one pound can be made from thin enameled cloth, at a cost of about forty cents; but it is easily torn.

Hats.

The best head-gear for general wear is a Stetson hat of army pattern. It stands rain, and keeps its shape under a good deal of abuse. The natural smoke-color of the felt is best. The brim should be wide enough to keep rain and snow from falling down the back of one's neck. Remove the leather sweat-band and substitute one of flannel, which is far more comfortable in all weathers, and sticks well to one's head, so that the hat is not easily knocked off by wind or boughs.

In the fall or winter take also a knitted wool cap

In Still Waters

that can be drawn down over the ears. It makes a good nightcap, which you will need on cold nights when sleeping in the open or under canvas.

For very hot weather a pith helmet with yellow lining is better than a hat.

Head-Nets.

If a head-net is taken, get one long enough to button under the coat, and dye the bobbinet *black*, for black is easier to see through than white or colored stuff. A head-net is somewhat of a nuisance, particularly when you want to smoke or spit; but in some localities, especially in the far north, it is almost indispensable at times on account of the thick clouds of mosquitoes. It is also useful in hunting wild bees.

Gloves.

A pair of buckskin gloves or gauntlets, pliable and not too thick, should be carried by any man who goes fresh from the office to the woods. Rowing and chopping will quickly blister tender hands. Woolen gloves, as a protection from cold, are too easily wet through, and then are little better than none. But in very cold weather it is best to wear woolen ones under loose fur mittens, the latter being hung from the neck by strings.

Belts.

The belt, if one is worn, should be loose. A belt drawn tightly enough to hold up much weight may cause rupture. Suspenders should be worn if the trousers are heavy. A cartridge belt should be worn cowboy fashion, sagging well down on the hips. Woven ones are more comfortable than leather, and do not cause verdigris to form on the cartridges as any leather belt will do, no matter how well it may be greased. Loops closed at the bottom collect dirt and grit. A leather belt with loops long enough to cover the bullets is best for a sandy region. If there is a big, shiny buckle, wear it to the rear; for sunlight glittering on it will scare away game.

When traveling in foreign lands, where the climate is different from our own, dress after the custom of the country. In nearly all wild regions there are civilized residents who can give the desired pointers.

CHAPTER III

PERSONAL KITS

IT is hard to generalize on outfits, because men's requirements vary, according to the country traversed, the season of the year, and personal tastes. Let no one imagine that he must lay in everything mentioned here, for any one trip.

One's health and comfort in camp depend very much upon what kind of bed he has. In nothing does a tenderfoot show off more discreditably than in his disregard of the essentials of a good night's rest. He comes into camp after a hard day's tramp, sweating and tired, eats heartily, and then throws himself down in his blanket on the bare ground. For a time he rests in supreme ease, drowsily satisfied that this is the proper way to show that he can "rough it," and that no hardships of the field can daunt his spirit. Presently, as his eyes grow heavy and he cuddles up for the night, he discovers that a sharp stone is boring into his flesh. He shifts about, and rolls upon a sharper stub or projecting root. Cursing a little, he arises and clears the ground of his tormentors. Lying down again, he drops off peacefully and is soon snoring. An hour passes, and he rolls over on the other side; a half hour, and he rolls back again into his former position; ten minutes, and he rolls again; then he tosses, fidgets, groans, wakes up, and finds that his hips and shoulders ache from serving as piers for the arches of his back and sides.

The Prime Necessity.

He gets up, muttering, scoops out hollows to receive the projecting portions of his frame, and again lies down. An hour later he reawakens, this time with shivering flesh and teeth a-chatter. How cold the ground is! The blanket over him is sufficient cover, but the same thickness beneath, compacted by his weight and in contact with the cold earth, is not half enough to keep out the bone-searching chill that comes up from the damp ground. This will never do. Pneumonia or rheumatism will follow. He arises, this time for good, passes a wretched night before the fire, and dawn finds him a haggard, worn-out type of misery, disgusted with camp life and eager to hit the back trail for home.

The moral is plain. This sort of roughing it is bad enough when one is compelled to submit to it. It kills twice as many soldiers as bullets do. When it is endured merely to show off one's fancied toughness and hardihood it is rank folly. Even the dumb beasts know better, and they are particular about making their beds.

This matter of a good portable bed is the most serious problem in outfitting. A man can stand almost any hardship by day, and be none the worse for it, provided he gets a comfortable night's rest; but without sound sleep he will soon go to pieces, no matter how gritty he may be.

Cots.

For camping in summer or in early autumn, when means of transportation permit it, the best camp bed is a compactly folding cot, such as is specially made for military and sportsmen's use; it weighs but sixteen pounds, and folds into a package 3 ft. x 4 in. x 5 in. A thin mattress of cotton or curled hair, or a doubled comforter as a substitute, is of even more importance on such a cot than the blanket that one covers himself with; for to sleep on taut canvas with nothing but a blanket under you is little more restful than lying on a board floor, and, if the nights are chilly, you will suffer from cold underneath. A cot and mattress, when you can carry them, save much time and work in bed-making and tent-trenching, and they keep the bedding clean, besides affording a comfortable lounge by day. A cot, however, is not at all comfortable in real cold weather, because, no matter how much bedding you have, you cannot keep it tucked in snugly around you, owing to the narrowness of the cot.

But suppose you are traveling light, perforce—what then? Cot or no cot, the first requisite is a mattress of

Mattresses.

some sort, either ready-made or extemporized on the spot. An air mattress is luxurious, but expensive, unreliable and cold in zero weather, and useless if punctured; but for summer camping, especially by us middle-aged or older fellows, who may have grown a trifle stiff and rheumatic from many a night on the bare, damp ground, it is a perquisite fairly won. Cork mattresses are favored by such canoeists as are not obliged to make long portages, being easily dried, and making good life-preservers. But they are rather bulky, and none too soft nor warm. Down quilts, though the warmest covering for their weight, are not warm underneath one's body, as the pressure squeezes out their confined air. A canvas stretcher swung on long poles makes a good spring bed for hot weather; but if the nights are chilly there will be a cold draught along the floor (always the coldest part of a tent) which will soon chill one to the bone. If it be made double, forming a bag open at both ends that can be stuffed with grass or browse, it is improved; but any such contrivance takes considerable time to rig up properly, and the tent may not be long enough for the poles and their supports.

Nearly every book and magazine article on camping that I have read extols a bed of balsam browse shingled

Browse Beds.

in between a pair of logs. Balsam is good; but, unfortunately, throughout the greater part of our country there is no balsam, nor even hemlock, nor spruce, nor any other kind of tree that affords even passable browse, in the fall, for this sort of bed.

For all-round service, in all sorts of countries, I prefer to carry with me a narrow bag of 10-cent bed ticking, $2\frac{1}{2}$ feet wide and $6\frac{1}{4}$ feet long, to be filled with grass, leaves, or such other soft stuff as one may find on the camping ground. Such a bag weighs but $1\frac{1}{3}$ pounds, takes up little room when empty, is useful in packing, and a man can make a good mattress with it —one that will not spread out nor pack hard—in less than half the time it would take to shingle browse or rig up a stretcher. If wet stuff must be used for filling, spread the rubber blanket or poncho on top of the bag, and all will be well.

Bedding.

Blankets should be all-wool, and firmly woven, so as to shed dirt. California blankets are best, then Hudson Bay or Mackinaw. The quality of our regular army blanket is excellent for the purpose, but do not get one that is narrow and folds at the end—you cannot roll up in it so snugly as if it were almost square. For extremely cold climates nothing equals a robe (not bag) of caribou-hide with the hair on, as it is warmer and drier for its bulk and weight than any other material.

A separate pillow-bag, to be filled in camp like the bed-tick, is another soft thing that no experienced woodsman despises. For horsemen a saddle is supposed to be all the pillow needed; but it is nothing of the sort—a mound of earth is better.

Sleeping-Bags.

Sleeping-bags have their good and bad qualities. Those which open only part way down are abominations, hard to get into and out of, and hard to air properly and to dry. No matter how waterproof the outside cover may be, the blanket or fur lining will surely get damp, both from the air and from the exudations of the sleeper. The only sleeping-bags worth considering are those that can easily be opened and spread wide in the sunlight or before the fire, which should be done every morning. Even so, they cannot so quickly be aired and dried as blankets, unless the lining is entirely removable from the cover.

An explorer of wide experience both in the arctic and antarctic regions gives his opinion of sleeping-bags as follows:

> For the first two or three days the sleeping-bag is a thing of comfort and a joy, and then it gradually gets worse and worse. The perspiration that collects in the bag during the night freezes immediately we leave it in the morning, and there is not sufficient heat from the sun to dry the bag when it is packed on the sledge. The bag, therefore, has to be thawed

out by our bodies each night, so that it gradually becomes heavy with moisture, and more and more uninviting.—LIEUT. ARMITAGE, *Two Years in the Antarctic*.

It is snug, for a while, to be laced up in a bag, but not so snug when you roll over and find that some aperture at the top is letting a stream of cold air run down your spine, and that your weight and cooped-upness prevent you from readjusting the bag to your comfort. Likewise a sleeping-bag may be an unpleasant trap to be in when a squall springs up suddenly at night, or the tent catches fire.

I think that one is more likely to catch cold when emerging from a stuffy sleeping-bag into the cold air than if he had slept between loose blankets. A waterproof cover without any opening except where your nose sticks out is no more wholesome to sleep in than a rubber boot is wholesome for one's foot. Nor is such a cover of much practical advantage, except underneath. The notion that it is any substitute for a roof overhead, on a rainy night, is a delusion.

Blankets can be wrapped around one more snugly, they do not condense moisture inside, and they can be thrown open instantly in case of alarm. In blankets you can sleep double in cold weather. Taking it all in all, I choose the separate bed-tick, pillow-bag, poncho, and blanket, rather than the same bulk and weight of any kind of sleeping-bag that I have so far experimented with. There may be better bags that I have not tried.

The "Carry-All."

There is a form of camp bed known as a "carry-all" that deserves mention. It may be described as a bag open at both ends, with a flap on each side to cover the sleeper, and shorter flaps for feet and head, the whole being made of stout waterproofed canvas, and fitted with straps and buckles. Two large pockets at the head end contain spare clothing, and thus form a pillow for the night. The blankets, and other articles, can be rolled up within this cover, and the whole affair is then quickly buckled up, making a convenient pack, rainproof all around. The bag part of the affair can be stuffed full of browse, grass, or such other bedding as the country affords; and poles can be run through it at either side, and across the ends, so as to form either a spring-bed or a hammock. The chief objection to this contrivance, as now made, is its weight, which is 10 pounds. A cotton bed-tick, pillow-bag, silk shelter-cloth, and poncho of pantasote sheeting, together weigh only 6½ pounds, and each of them is good for something by itself when you are on the trail. The addition of a good, heavy blanket brings the weight up to about 15 pounds, for one man's bedding, pack-cloth, *and shelter*—and these are plenty for anybody until frosts set in.

Shelter-Cloth.

The shelter-cloth here referred to is of waterproofed balloon silk, 7x8 feet, with eyelets (small steel rings sewed on by hand, not mere metal eyelets) around the edges at intervals of about a foot, the contrivance weighing from 2 to 2½ pounds. This makes a small roll on top of one's knapsack, or serves as a pack-cloth. It makes a good shelter or windbreak when one takes a side trip of a day or two from camp. Such side trips are generally the pleasantest and most profitable days in my experience. One sees more, learns more, and gets closer to nature when he is far off in the woods by himself than when he is around camp or hunting with companions.

Individual Cooking Kits.

To the same end it is well to take with you an individual cooking kit. This is not formidable. A frying-pan and a large tin cup, with the sheath-knife, are sufficient; though a quart pail is a useful addition. Instead of a frying-pan, for such trips, I like a U. S. Army mess kit, procured from a dealer in second-hand military equipments for twenty cents. It consists of two oval dishes of tinned steel which fit together and form a meat can 8 inches long, 6½ inches wide, and 1½ inches deep, weighing ¾ of a pound. In this a ration of meat is carried on the march. When the dishes are separated the lower one serves as a plate, and is deep enough for soup. The upper dish has a folding handle which locks the two together, and it makes a fair frying-pan.

The Preston individual cooking kit, made of aluminum, is commendable for those who care to spend more money on such a thing. It can be procured from army outfitters.

Sheath-Knives.

On the subject of hunting knives I am tempted to be diffuse. In my green and callow days (perhaps not yet over) I tried nearly everything in the knife line from a shoemaker's skiver to a machete, and I had knives made to order. The conventional hunting knife is, or was until quite recently, of the familiar dime-novel pattern invented by Colonel Bowie. Such a knife is too thick and clumsy to whittle with, much too thick for a good skinning knife, and too sharply pointed to cook and eat with. It is always tempered too hard. When put to the rough service for which it is supposed to be intended, as in cutting through the ossified false ribs of an old buck, it is an even bet that out will come a nick as big as a saw-tooth—and Sheridan forty miles from a grindstone! Such a knife is shaped expressly for stabbing, which is about the very last thing that a woodsman ever has occasion to do, our lamented grandmothers to the contrary notwithstanding.

A camper has use for a common-sense sheath-knife, sometimes for dressing big game, but oftener for such homely work as cutting sticks, slicing bacon, and frying "spuds." For such purposes a rather thin, broad-pointed blade is required, and it need not be over four or five inches long. Nothing is gained by a longer blade, and it would be in one's way every time he sat down. Such a knife, bearing the marks of hard usage, lies before me. Its blade and handle are each $4\frac{1}{4}$ inches long, the blade being 1 inch wide, $\frac{1}{8}$ inch thick on the back, broad pointed, and continued through the handle as a hasp and riveted to it. It is tempered hard enough to cut green hardwood sticks, but soft enough so that when it strikes a knot or bone it will, if anything, turn rather than nick; then a whetstone soon puts it in order. The Abyssinians have a saying, "If a sword bends, we can straighten it; but if it breaks, who can mend it?" So with a knife or hatchet. The handle of this knife is of oval cross-section, long enough to give a good grip for the whole hand, and with no sharp edges to blister one's hand. It has a $\frac{1}{4}$ inch knob behind the cutting edge as a guard, but there is no guard on the back, for it would be useless and in the way. The handle is of light but hard wood, $\frac{3}{4}$ inch thick at the butt and tapering to $\frac{1}{2}$ inch forward, so as to enter the sheath easily and grip it tightly. If it were heavy it would make the knife drop out when I stooped over. The sheath has a slit frog binding tightly on the belt, and keeping the knife well up on my side. This knife weighs only 4 ounces. It was made by a country blacksmith, and is one of the homeliest things I ever saw; but it has outlived in my affections the score of other knives that I have used in competition with it, and has done more work than all of them put together.

Jackknives.

For ordinary whittling a good jackknife is needed. It should have one heavy blade $2\frac{3}{4}$ or 3 inches long, tempered hard enough for seasoned hickory, but thick enough not to nick or snap off; also a small, thin blade that will take a keen edge and keep it. The best pattern is an "easy-opener," which has part of the handle cut away so that one can open it without using his thumb-nail, which may be wet and soft, or brittle from cold. There should be no sharp edges on the handle, which is preferably of ebony.

Hatchets.

A woodsman should carry a hatchet, and he should be as critical in selecting it as in buying a gun. The notion that a heavy hunting knife can do the work of a hatchet is a delusion. When it comes to cleaving carcasses, chopping kindling, blazing thick-barked trees, driving tent pegs or trap stakes, and keeping up a bivouac fire, the knife never was made that will compare with a good tomahawk. The common hatchets of the hardware stores are unfit for a woodsman's use. They have broad, thin blades with beveled edge, and they are generally made of poor, brittle stuff. A camper's hatchet should have the edge and temper of a good axe. It must be light enough to carry in one's belt or knapsack, yet it should bite deep in timber. There is but one way to get this seemingly contradictory result, and that is to make the blade long and narrow, like an Indian tomahawk, or like a Nessmuk double-blade, thus putting the weight where it will do the most good. When there is a full-grown axe in camp I carry a tomahawk of 12-ounce head. The handle is just a foot long. Its grip is wound with waxed twine to give a good hold when one's hand is wet. This little tool has been my mainstay on several bitter nights when I was lost in the forest, or in a canebrake, and without it I would have fared badly.

For a canoeing trip, or any journey on which a full-sized axe cannot be taken with the camping equipment, a half-axe with 2-pound head and 18-inch handle is about right. With it one can fell trees big enough for an all-night fire made Indian fashion. If such a tool is carried from the belt (seldom advisable) its muzzle should be attached by a frog that works on a loose rivet, thus forming a hinged joint, then the handle will swing free from brush and will not be in the way when you sit down.

Whetstone.

For a light and quick-cutting hone, to keep knives and hatchet in order, take a piece of cigar box about two by six inches and glue to each side a strip of emery cloth, coarse on one side, fine on the other. Or, if you don't mind the weight, get a quite small double whetstone, coarse and fine on opposite sides. This may be carried in a light leather wallet, along with the following articles:

Emergency Kit.

Small coil of copper snare wire. Needle and thread. Safety pins. One or two short fishing lines, rigged. Spare hooks. Minnow hooks (with half the barb filed off) for catching bait.

These things with your gun, a dozen rounds of ammunition, hatchet, knives, matches, compass, map, money, pipe and tobacco, should always be with you, or where they can be snatched up at a grab in case of emergency. Then you are always "fixed."

If a needle compass is chosen, try to get one with a pearl point on the north end of the needle; it is easier to see in dark weather, and easily remembered. If you must put up with a common one in which the north end of the needle is merely blackened, scratch B=N (Black equals North) on the case. This seems like an absurd precaution, does it not? Well, it will not seem so if you get lost. The first time that a man loses his bearings in the wilderness his wits refuse to work. He cannot, to save his life, remember whether the black end of the needle is north or south. A card compass is better than one with a needle, if the case is deep enough for the card to traverse freely when inclined, but it is more bulky.

Compass.

An expensive watch should be left at home. A dollar watch is good enough where there are no trains to catch. Take with you the sheets of an almanac for the months in which you will be out. They are useful to regulate the watch, show the moon's changes, and, by them, to determine the day of the month and week, which one is apt to forget when he is away from civilization.

Timepiece.

Do not on any account omit a *waterproof* matchbox, preferably of such pattern as has a cover that cannot drop off. A bit of candle is a good thing to carry in one's pouch to start fire in a driving rain.

Matchbox.

Procure, if possible, a good map of the region to be visited. The best maps for any part of the United States for which they have been published are the topographical sheets issued by the U. S. Geological Survey, and sold at five cents each. A list of those published up to date can be had by applying to the Director, U. S. Geological Survey, Washington, D. C. Most of these sheets are on a scale of two miles to the inch. They are printed in three colors, and show every watercourse, big or little, every road and important trail, bridges, ferries, fords, mines, settlements, and, what is of high importance to a traveler, they give contour lines (usually for

Maps.

every 100 feet in mountainous regions, and at lesser intervals for more level country).*

Maps should be cut up into sections about 4 by 6 inches, numbered, and carried (together with a key-map that one makes himself) in an envelope made of tracing cloth. The required sheet is placed on top, and can be made out through the envelope without removing it, thus protecting the map from tearing, soiling, wet, and from blowing away.

Stationery.

Note-books should be of such paper as is ruled in squares, which are useful in rough mapping and sketching. Take along some postal cards, and a timetable of the road by which you expect to return.

Wear a money belt. Gold coin is more trusty than banknotes, as one is liable to get a ducking at any time. Quarter eagles are best, being more easily changed by country folks than higher denominations.

Medicines.

In the matter of medicines, every man must take into account his personal equation and the ills to which he is most subject; but there are certain risks that we all run in common when we venture far from civilization, such as wounds, fractures, snake-bites, attacks of venomous insects, malaria, footsoreness, ivy poisoning, and others that will be mentioned in the chapter on *Accidents*.

As for myself, no matter how light I travel, I always carry either in a pocket or in my hunting pouch a soldier's first-aid packet. This can be procured from a dealer in surgical instruments or from a camp outfitter. It contains two antiseptic compresses of sublimated gauze, an antiseptic bandage, an Esmarch triangular bandage with cuts printed on it showing how to bandage any part of the body, and two safety pins, inclosed in a waterproof cover, the whole being very light and compact.

In snake time I also keep by me at all times a hypo-

* I regret to say that these sheets are of uneven merit. Some of them are accurate, while others, particularly of the wilder mountainous districts, are filled with details that exist only in the draughtsman's imagination. Thorough revision of many sheets is urgently needed.

A Proud Moment

dermic syringe with tubes of potassium permanganate and strychnin, the use of which will be explained hereafter. A permanganate solution will precipitate a sediment in a week or two. It is better to carry separately the crystals and a little vial of distilled water. A small bottle of unguentine and some cathartic pills generally complete the list for a short trip.

When going far from medical or surgical aid, I might pack along a box containing the following kit:

3-in. artery forceps and needle-holder combined.
Tooth forceps.
Surgeon's needles: 2 straight medium,
1 curved medium,
1 curved small.
Surgeon's silk, coarse and fine.
Catgut ligatures.
3 2-in. rolled bandages.
1 yd. sublimated gauze, in bottle.
Absorbent cotton.
Mustard plasters.
Belladonna plasters.
Hypodermic syringe.
Bernays' antiseptic tablets.
*Potassium permanganate, ½-grain tablets.
*Cocain and morphin tablets (cocain 1-5 gr., morphin 1-40 gr., sod. chlor. 1-5 gr.)—*local anæsthetic*.
*Morphin (¼ gr.) and atropin (1-150 gr.) tablets—*intense pain*.
*Strychnin sulphate, 1-30 gr. tablets—*surgical shock, etc.*
Quinin, 3 gr. capsules—*malaria, etc.*
Sun cholera tablets—*dysentery, etc.*
Senega compound, tablets—*coughs, colds.*
Compound cathartic pills.
Soda mint tablets—*sour stomach, heartburn, ivy poisoning.*
Trional—*sleeplessness.*
Unguentine—*burns, sunburn, insect bites, bruises.*
McClintock's germicidal soap—*cleansing wounds.*
Vaselin.
8 oz. brandy, in two small bottles.

One such kit is enough for a large party. It will be used mostly on the natives.

An ulcerated tooth is a bad thing to fight in the wilderness—grizzly bears are nothing to it. Some natives have an unpleasant way of extracting an aching

* The tablets starred are carried in the hypodermic case.

molar, a bit at a time, by prying it out with an awl. Paul Kruger used to cut his out with a knife. A word to the wise is sufficient: Forceps.

Fly Dopes.

When traveling in the South or Southwest (anywhere from Missouri down), I add a 4-ounce bottle of chloroform, which, after exhaustive experiments, I have found to be the only thing that can be depended upon to put chiggers (redbugs) to sleep in the cuticle of H. Kephart. I will pay my respects to these microscopic fiends, and to other torments of the woods and swamps, in the chapter on *Pests*, wherein will also be found various formulas for fly dopes, to which the reader is referred.

In spring and autumn I usually carry a tiny vial of oil of anise, which is very attractive to various animals whose acquaintance I wish to cultivate—from bees to bears. One drop of anise will lure for half a mile radius.

Acids.

In hot weather it is well to carry, each for himself, a little citric acid, if there are no lemons in the outfit. The crystals added to water make a refreshing lemonade, and they are valuable to neutralize alkaline water and make it potable. Wyeth's lemonade tablets are still better. When much water is to be corrected, as when making a long trip through an alkaline country, it is preferable to use hydrochloric (muriatic) acid, one teaspoonful to the gallon of water.

Clothes Bag.

Spare clothing should be packed in a bag by itself. It is well to make this in saddle-bag shape, one side to be used for clean clothes and the other for soiled ones, the whole serving as a pillow if you have no regular pillow-bag. For an ordinary trip the following will suffice:

Jersey or sweater, two undershirts, two pairs drawers, three pairs socks, spare overshirt, moccasins, gloves, three handkerchiefs, woolen pyjamas (not linen), if you have room. In summer add a head-net; in winter, German socks, lumberman's rubbers (if you cannot get shanks), knit cap, and a pair of mitts.

Toilet Bag.

In a sponge-bag carry:

Towel (old and soft), soap, comb, toothbrush, pocket mirror; the soap in a soft rubber tobacco-pouch. The razor and strop, if you carry them, go elsewhere.

If you smoke, stow a spare pipe in your kit—the koosy-oonek will get one, sure. If you wear glasses, take along an extra pair.

In one's camp kit it is advisable to have a holdall, or a japanned box, in which are kept such things as these (contents varying, of course, according to personal requirements):

Repair Kit.

Rifle-rod and brush, gun grease, cut wipers, oiled rags, screw driver (T-shaped, folding, with 3 blades), 6-in. half-round bastard file, a few assorted nails and tacks, two sizes soft wire, side-cutting parallel pliers, pocket tape-measure, pocket scales, scissors, awl, waxed-ends (get a shoemaker to make them for you if you don't know how), sewing and darning needles, linen thread, beeswax, strong twine, darning cotton, spare buttons, safety pins, split rivets, small pieces of mending cloth and leather, a rawhide belt-lace, 1 doz. large rubber bands.

In fitting up such a repair kit, be sparing of bulk and weight. Of nails, wire, rivets, include only enough for a few small jobs.

In winter it pays to carry a pair of smoke-colored goggles, to prevent snow-blindness—likewise in summer if you are much on the water. These are better than green or blue ones, because they are less opaque and there is less loss of color in objects seen through them. They should fit well. The glasses should be surrounded by fine wire gauze, the edges covered with velvet, and the part crossing the bridge of the nose similarly covered. The Eskimo kind of eye-shades are better for high latitudes than glasses. They consist of two wooden disks, each with a T-shaped slit cut in it to see through, with a narrow strap to go over the bridge of the nose and another to go around the head. Such shades give perfect vision, do not collect moisture, and, when removed, do not give the sensation of darkness that is experienced after removing colored glasses.

Goggles.

A pantasote pouch, 10x12 inches, is a convenient

receptacle for small stores, and makes a good carrier for one's necessities when he is traveling without a coat. For a knapsack, the pattern used by our regular infantry is as good as any.

Pouch.

A canteen should not be a cheap affair merely covered with flimsy flannel, but one of service pattern, incased in felt and this covered with duck. If the outside is immersed when the canteen is filled it will keep three pints of water cool for several hours. Filled with hot water at night, it makes a comfortable addition to one's blanket on a cold night.

Canteen.

Every camper is supposed to have his own ideas about guns, fishing tackle, boats and cameras. I will offer no advice here about any of these things beyond saying that a fisherman, or any one else who takes his vacation in the woods at a time when most game is out of season, may do well to carry a .22 caliber rifle, or a pocket rifle, for such "small deer" as may be available for the pot, not overlooking the comestible frog. A pocket rifle with 15-inch barrel and skeleton stock is almost as easily carried as a pistol, and can be shot with much greater precision. If a telescope sight of three or four diameters (not more) is mounted on it, you can drive tacks with the tiny bullet at 40 feet, and hit squirrels in the head nearly every time at 30 yards—if you are a marksman. The best .22 cartridges are the Long Rifle (not to be confounded with the inferior .22 Long), the .22-7 and the .22 Automatic. See that the rifle is specially chambered and rifled for one or other of these. They are very accurate up to 100 yards or more.*

Pocket Rifle.

*For a detailed discussion of rifles for big game hunting I may refer to my chapter on The Hunting Rifle in the book entitled *Guns, Ammunition, and Tackle* (American Sportsman's Library; edited by Caspar Whitney. New York, Macmillan).

CHAPTER IV

TENTS AND TOOLS

TENTS were invented long before the dawn of history, and they are still used as portable dwellings by men of all races and in all climes—and still the perfect tent has not been invented. Every year sees countless campers busy with new contrivances in canvas or other material—and still the prehistoric patterns hold their own. There is a fascination about tent life that may be partly due to its uncertainties. The utmost pinnacle of comfort is reached when one lies at night under taut canvas, with a storm roaring toward him through the forest, and chortles over the blissful certainty that no wind can blow *his* tent down. And it takes just one second of parting guys and ripping cloth to tumble him off his perch and cast him headlong into the very depths of woe.

A tent should be easy to set up. It should shed heavy rains, and should stand securely in a gale. It should keep out insects and cold draughts, but let in the rays of the camp-fire and plenty of pure air. It should be cool and air yon summer days, but warm and dry at night. All of which is easily said.

For a fixed camp, or any camp that can be reached by wagon, a wall tent is generally preferred. It is easy to set up, and has plenty of head-room. With the addition of a fly, a ground-cloth, and a tent stove, it can be made cosy in any kind of weather. But a wall tent, with its necessary poles, is too heavy and bulky for anything but a wagon trip. Men who travel in untracked forests, deserts, or mountains, usually require a more portable shelter.

Wall Tent.

A 10x12-foot wall tent is large enough for a party of four. It should be used only for sleeping quarters, and as a shelter for personal kits and other perishables. A separate fly should be taken along, to be used as a roof for the dining space, and to cover the box or other contrivance that is used for an outdoor cupboard. If there are more than four in the party, take another tent. Two small tents are easier to transport and to pitch than one large one, and they have the supreme advantage that the snorers can then be segregated in a limbo of their own. Guides usually furnish their own shelters, but this should be understood beforehand. It is well to have the tents made to open at both ends, so that they can have a complete circulation of air on hot days. In this case, two tents may be joined together whenever desirable.

Tent Cloth.

As for tent materials, the choice depends upon whether it is the intention to go light or not. For fixed camps, 10-ounce double-filling army duck is the thing. The cheap single-filling duck is neither strong nor rain-proof. Second-hand army tents that are in good, serviceable condition, having been condemned only for stains or other trifling defects, may be bought very cheaply from dealers who get them at government auctions. These army tents are always well designed and well made.

Waterproof Tents.

Where expense is not considered, and extra weight is not objectionable, no material equals pantasote. It is perfectly waterproof, embers from the camp-fire will not burn holes in it, it is not sticky in hot weather nor brittle in cold, and its wearing qualities are excellent. For a light tent, sail drilling, and for a very light one, unbleached sheeting or silk, should be used, the material in either case being waterproofed by one or other of the processes mentioned hereafter. Tents of waterproofed balloon silk of excellent quality and strongly made can now be bought ready-made in all shapes and sizes. A tent of this kind big enough for one man to bivouac in is made that weighs only 2½ pounds; a 7½x 7½ miner's tent weighs but 6 pounds, and an *A* tent of the same size only 7½ pounds. The strength of a tent depends more upon the reinforcement of the grommets and seams than upon the kind of cloth used. The lines of greatest strain should be reinforced, in light tents, by linen tape.

Thin, closely woven cotton goods, such as sheeting or muslin, will shed ordinary rains if pitched at a higher angle than 45°, but if set up at a lower angle than this, the water will penetrate. A long, hard rain will soak such cloth through and through, and even heavy canvas, if not waterproofed or protected by a fly, will absorb so much water that if the inside of the cloth be touched by so much as one's finger a steady drip of water will come through at that spot so long as the rain lasts.

A fly not only makes the roof watertight, but keeps the tent much cooler on a hot day.

When traveling light, a fly cannot be carried, and the tent itself must be light and thin; consequently it should be waterproofed. If such treatment is properly applied it not only renders the tent dry throughout the worst storm, but prevents it from absorbing water, whereas a common tent will take up so much water that its weight is greatly increased. Waterproofing also prevents mildew, and allows one to roll up his tent when it is wet on the outside, if he is in a hurry. It is only within a few years that ready-made waterproof tents have been supplied by outfitters.

Waterproofing Canvas. If a common tent is purchased, or the camper makes one for himself, he can waterproof it by either of the following processes:

Dissolve ½ pound of alum in 4 gallons of boiling rain-water. It is essential that soft water be used. Similarly, in a separate vessel, dissolve ½ pound of sugar of lead (lead acetate) in 4 gallons of water. This is double the proportion of alum usually recommended, and better results will follow from it, because it insures the precipitation of all the lead in the form of sulphate. Let the solutions stand until clear; then pour the alum liquor into a clean vessel, and add the sugar of lead solution. Let stand a few hours. Then pour off the clear liquor, thoroughly work the fabric in it, so that every part is quite penetrated, squeeze out, stretch and dry. Remember that sugar of lead is poisonous if taken internally.

This treatment fixes acetate of alumina in the fibers of the cloth. The final washing is to cleanse the cloth from the useless white powder of sulphate of lead that is deposited on it. Cloth treated in this manner sheds rain, and makes a tent proof against sparks and embers from the camp-fire. Clothing may also be made rain-proof in this way, though still porous, so as to allow perspiration to pass through and evaporate. Rain-water will penetrate it wherever the cloth binds tightly.

To waterproof cloth with paraffin, proceed as follows:

> Cut the paraffin into thin shavings, so as to dissolve readily. Dissolve it in turpentine or benzin, using as much wax as the liquid will take up. Apply with a varnish brush to the tightly stretched goods. To hasten the solution of the paraffin, place the mixture in a warm room, or where the hot sun will strike it (but not, of course, near the fire) and stir it now and then.
>
> Or, get a cake of paraffin, lay the cloth on a table, and rub the outer side with the wax until it has a good coating, evenly distributed. Then iron the cloth with a medium-hot flatiron, which melts the wax and runs it into every pore of the cloth.

Do not oil a tent. Linseed oil rots the fiber, and cloth so treated will be sticky in hot weather.

Tents to be used in very cold weather should not be waterproofed, because, if they are, they will become brittle at low temperatures and may break in folding. Moreover, it should be borne in mind that a traveler's greatest discomfort in cold weather is from moisture generated from within and condensing on the inner surface of clothing or tent cloth that is not sufficiently porous to let it escape. Dr. Frederick A. Cook, the antarctic explorer, says:

> "A scientifically ideal tent wall would be a double sheeting of some gauzy material, the two thicknesses being separated from each other about one inch. This would freely permit the escape of the internal humidity, which is always the curse of polar workers, while it would sufficiently prevent the penetration of the wind. It would, perhaps, be an excellent idea to have window spaces, spread with gauzy or porous material, made in the front of this tent near the peak—mosquito netting is by no means out of place on the polar ice-fields, for it is an excellent wind guard, retaining the internal heat, while easily allowing the escape of moisture."

The tent to which he refers is one of his own design, a very light affair to be used in arctic work.

Dyeing Canvas.

It is an advantage to have a tent dyed to a light green or tan color. This moderates the glare of the sun, makes the tent less attractive to flies, and renders it less conspicuous in the woods, which latter is worth considering in some localities where undesirable visitors may drop in. A few packages of dye may be used before waterproofing. Two pounds of ground white oak bark in $3\frac{1}{2}$ gallons of boiling water will dye canvas a tan color.

Sod-Cloth.

Every tent should have a sod-cloth, which is a strip about nine inches wide joined to the bottom of the tent on the inside, to be held down by small logs, stones, or earth. This keeps out draughts, insects, and other pests. If the lower edges of the tent are left loose, cold air will be sucked in along the floor and will chill the sleepers.

Ground-Cloth.

A waterproof ground-cloth, covering most of the floor of the tent and lapping over the sod-cloth, is a good thing if it can be carried along. In small tents intended for mountaineering and similar work, this ground-cloth is sometimes sewed fast to the bottom of the tent, sod-cloths being dispensed with. Such a tent cannot blow away when the weight of the occupants is inside, and it has the minor advantage that small articles dropped on the floor will not be lost. But a fixed floor-cloth is objectionable in cold weather, especially if water be boiled within the tent, because the steam condenses and runs down the inside of the tent, and it should be allowed to run off into the snow along the edges.

Mosquito Bar.

In fly time a netting to keep out insects is a prime necessity. The mesh of ordinary mosquito netting is too open, and the material is too easily torn, and bobbinet is likewise too weak. The best insect discourager is cheese-cloth. In summer it is a good plan to have a duplicate tent of cheese-cloth hung inside from the ridge or peak; then the canvas may be left wide open on sultry nights.

If a stove is to be used in the tent, the pipe-hole should be guarded by an asbestos ring or collar, which rolls up with the tent. A tin guard is a squeaky thing when the wind blows.

Tent Fittings.

Metal tent slides are better than wooden ones, being lighter and not given to swelling, shrinking, and splitting. Steel tent pins, twisted somewhat like a lariat pin, are better than wooden pegs, as they are more easily driven in rocky ground, hold better, and are not so bulky. They should be carried in a bag of their own, or some of them will probably be misplaced or lost. In a wooded region one can depend upon cutting pegs where he camps, but it is better to carry them unless one is going particularly light. Pegs should be at least a foot long. If made of green wood, select hard wood that has no pithy core, and harden the points by slightly charring them in the fire.

All tents that are made to close up tightly at night should have ventilators, covered with cheese-cloth, and with flaps on the outside to tie down in bad weather. It is more unhealthful to sleep in a tightly closed tent than in an ordinary bedroom with all the windows closed, for the cubic contents of an average tent are less, the air in it is soon poisoned, and the interior is damp besides. Napoleon declared that his troops kept in better health when bivouacking under the stars than when sleeping in tents. It is far better to leave the front of the tent wide open, even in cold weather, than to close it up and sleep in a damp, stuffy atmosphere.

The most healthful form of tent, and the one favored by guides, lumbermen, and others who live in the woods, is a lean-to or shed-roof affair with open front, before which a big log fire is kept going all through the night. The heat from the fire is reflected by the tent roof upon the ground below, drying it out, and keeping the sleepers warm through the coldest night. This, however, takes a lot of wood, a good-sized hardwood tree being consumed in a single night, and the labor of chopping is rather severe to any one but a good axeman; but the work is well repaid by the exquisite comfort of lying

Lean-to Tent.

before the blazing backlogs on a cold night, warm as toast, and breathing deeply the fresh air of the forest. Such a tent is never damp and cheerless, as all closed tents are apt to be. Tent-makers always make these shed-roof or "baker" tents with a door-flap sewed to the top, to be stretched out forward like an awning when the tent is open. A better plan is to have the door-flap separate from the tent, and so fitted with grommets or eyelets that it can be attached either to the top or to one side of the tent, as preferred. In warm weather, when no all-night fire is needed, it may be hung from the top as an awning, and the tent may be closed up by it when the occupants are away; but on nights when a fire is kept going the flap should be stretched forward vertically from the windward side of the tent front, so as to check the draught from that direction, and the fire should be built close to the tent, the front of which is left wide open. For a camp that is not shifted every day or two, the shed-roof tent is the most comfortable kind of shelter, for a timbered region, in all kinds of weather.

A Tent.

For extreme portability, lightness, and ease of pitching, the *A* tent is recommended. Nothing is better, in the long run, for a trip in summer, where portages must be made and camp shifted at frequent intervals. In this case no poles are used. A strong tape is sewed along the ridge of the tent, ending in a loop at each end, from which a light rope is extended and stretched between two trees, the rope being made taut by two forked poles bracing it up at each end of the tent, and outside of it. Such an arrangement is secure against heavy gales. For a small tent the ridge rope should be about twenty-five feet long. It should be of braided cotton, treated to a bath of hot linseed oil, and stretched until dry; then it will neither shrink, stretch, nor kink. A metal slide or tightener near each end of the rope will keep it taut without crotched poles.

The Hudson Bay form of *A* or wedge tent economizes cloth and weight by making the ends round and the ridge short. A waterproof silk tent of this pattern,

6x9x7 feet, weighs only 6 pounds. A so-called "canoe tent" is made that combines some of the advantages of the shed-roof tent with an arrangement whereby it can be set up with only one pole. The "protean" tent is of similar pattern.

Miner's and Sibley Tents.

The pyramidal miner's tent, and the conical Sibley, require only one pole, and this may be jointed, so as to pack easily on an animal or in a canoe. Both of these patterns have so steep a pitch that they shed rain very well, and on this account may be made of thin material. They also stand well in heavy winds, when properly pitched, the Sibley especially. The miner's tent, which covers a square ground space, affords more room for beds than a conical tent of equal cubic capacity. Both of these forms are suitable for travel in a treeless region where a tent pole must be carried. The claim that a Sibley tent can be heated by an open fire inside is not well borne out, because the opening at the top is too small to let out the smoke when green wood is burned, as must often be the case. If the tent is to be heated, a regular Sibley tent stove should be carried along.

Teepee.

There is only one kind of tent that can be heated by an open fire, inside, without smoking the occupants out, and that is the Indian lodge or teepee (pronounced *tee*-pee), and even it is likely at times to resemble the inside of a chimney-flue unless its owners know just how to manage it. However, taking it all around, the teepee is the most comfortable portable home for all regions, and for all kinds of weather, that human ingenuity has devised. It is more secure in a gale than any other form of tent that does not depend upon neighboring trees to hold it up. It sheds rain well, because its pitch is steep. It can be thrown wide open in a moment, or it can be closed tightly all around and still kept well ventilated by the hole at the top. A fire can be kept going within the tent, directly under the smoke-hole, and right in the middle of the inclosed space, where it will do the most good. Meals can be cooked over this open fire, and the steam and smells will be wafted out through the smoke-hole. By manipulating the smoke-flaps or wind-guards the "chimney" may be made to draw, in almost any kind of weather. With the tent closed, and a trifling smudge of dried fungus going in the center, mosquitoes can be kept at a respectful distance. There is no center-pole to stumble against, nor guy to trip over. The tent is easily set up, and it can quickly be taken down and rolled up into a small parcel. To set up a teepee properly, ten or a dozen straight, slender poles are needed, and these are often hard to find, even in a dense forest. But one can make shift with three poles set up as a tripod, or even with one, the latter being braced against a tree, and its lower end jabbed into the ground. Teepees are not to be had of tentmakers, except to order.

Canoeist's Tent.

An excellent form of tent for all-round service, being warm, well-ventilated, rain-proof, easy to set up, secure in a gale, and affording plenty of head-room for its size, is the one here illustrated. It is the favorite tent of that veteran canoeist, Mr. Perry D. Frazer, whose book on *Canoe Cruising and Camping* is the most practical manual of its kind that has been published. The cuts and details here given are supplied by Mr. Frazer, partly in a personal letter, and partly from an article by him in *Shooting and Fishing*. (Figs. 1 and 2.)

The material is dark brown 10-ounce duck. The tent is octagon in form, 8½ feet in diameter and 8½ feet high. Each width of duck measures 38 inches. The length of each breadth, inclusive of the end left below hem for sod-cloth, is 10 feet 2 inches. The door is 5 feet 6 inches (actual length along goods). The awning is 5 feet 8 inches long; it fastens down with large brass hooks and eyes, at sides and bottom. The door is about 14 inches wide at top and about 20 inches at bottom. The awning is usually left up, and a flap of mosquito-bar closes the opening. The awning has two thin jointed poles and cord guys.

In the rear of the tent is a window, 8 inches square, filled with bobbinet, giving a good circulation of air. Its flap is 13x14x18 inches, with grommets in outer

FIG. 1.

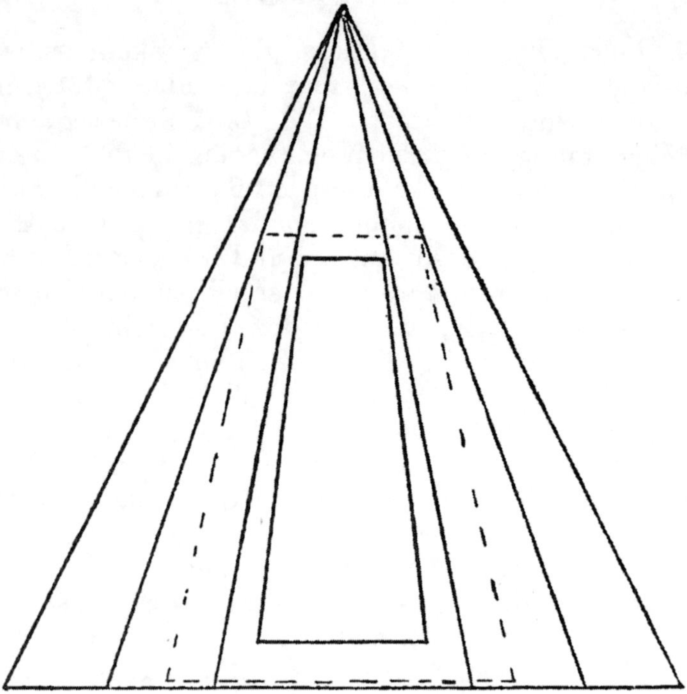

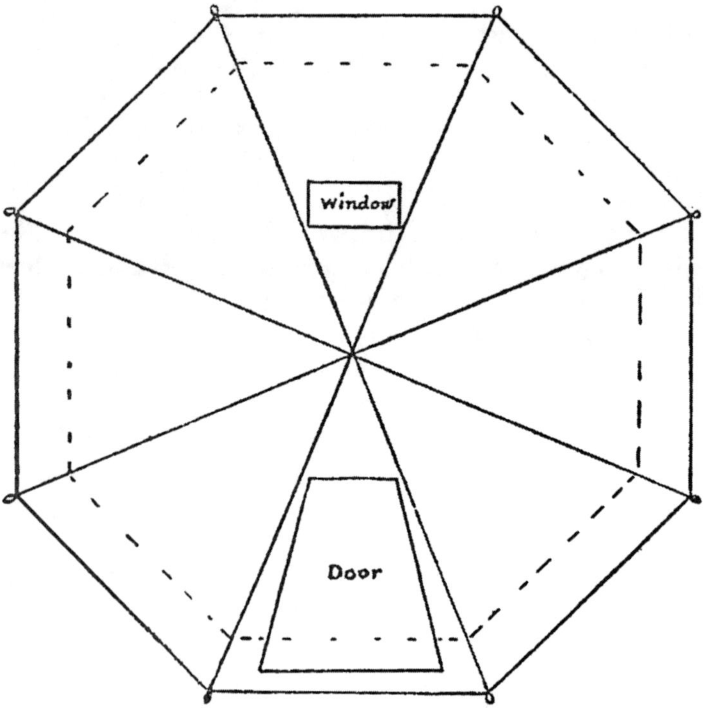

FIG. 2.

Real Comfort in the Open

corners to hold stick, so that it can be stretched for air, and to keep out rain. The sod-cloth is 6 inches wide. (Fig. 3.)

The floor-cloth lies over the sod-cloth, making the tent impervious to cold draughts, dampness, and insects. The octagonal floor-cloth fastens to the sides of the tent with grommets and small wooden buttons, so that it can be left with tent when folded, or taken out at will. It is slit from front to pole, so that the forward edges can be turned back, as shown by the dotted line, when one comes into the tent with muddy feet. The "sill" under the door is 5 inches high. Its rationale is this: It keeps the bottom of the tent in what is practically one piece, so that when the latter is stretched taut every peg finds its proper place, without any measuring, and the tent sets true; besides, in conjunction with the sod-cloth and floor-cloth, it makes the bottom of the tent proof against cold and insects at the very point where other tents are weak, namely, at the door. Twelve-inch meat skewers are used for pegs, and it will be noticed that the tent only requires eight of them.

FIG. 3.

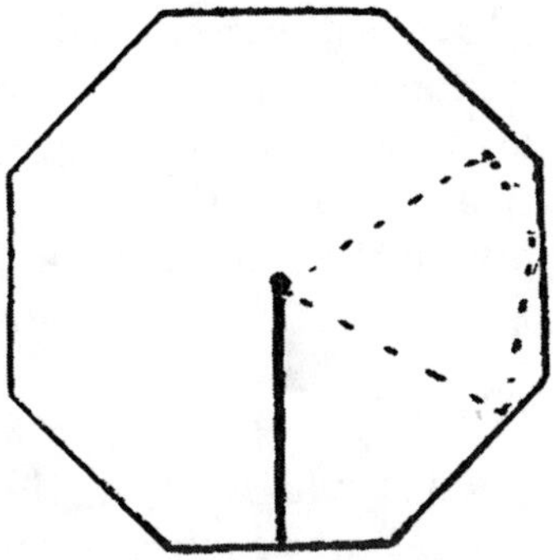

Floor-cloth

This tent folds into a parcel about 24 x 12 x 3 inches, and weighs about 32 pounds, with poles and pegs. Mr. Frazer says: "This is my favorite tent for canoeing trips early in the spring and late in the fall, when a snug water and wind-proof tent is desirable. It would be too heavy for inland trips, where it would have to be carried; but if made of waterproofed muslin or 6-ounce duck, it would be ideal for light trips. I had the second one of this type that was made. It was designed by J. E. G. Yalden of New York, but his tent was too small, and I had mine made wider. A number of tents of this type are now used by canoeists, and for all-round use they are grand tents. S. Hemmenway and Son, 54 South St., New York, have the working drawings. I think the price, without poles or pegs, is twelve dollars, but it may be less. . . . I have timed the owner of one of these tents while in the act of setting it. Three minutes were consumed in driving the eight steel pegs and hoisting the pole into position. Once set, let the wind blow as hard as it may, the owner need never fret, for it would be hard to trip this style of tent. Its sides being so steep, it will turn water as readily as if it were greased. One may stand upright in it, and there is room for one cot or for two beds on the ground."

Tent Hangers.

In any tent with a ridge-pole two screw-eyes should be put in it at opposite ends from which to suspend by cords a straight stick to hang clothes on. Wire clothes hangers and candle holders, and metal lantern hangers and gun-racks, which fit on the upright poles of tents, and wall pockets, which are very convenient receptacles for odds and ends, are supplied by camp outfitters. The hangers are particularly useful in Sibley, miner's, or other one-pole tents. It pays to take such things.

Tent Furniture.

Folding tables, stools, and chairs, and even folding bath-tubs, are made in large quantities for military and campers' use. They save time and trouble in fixing up a camp, but it is better to make one's own simple furniture on the spot, if anything like a hard trip is contemplated. There are two articles of ready-made furniture, however, that are well worth packing along if the party is not traveling very light indeed, and these are a rolling table-top and a set of folding shelves. The table is made of pantasote, with pockets on the under side which are stiffened by thin wooden slats. The table is set up by driving a stake into the ground at each corner, connected by cross-pieces on which the top rests, the latter being 2x3 feet when opened, and weighing only 3 pounds. The shelves are made of canvas, similarly stiffened by slats, forming, when set up on four poles, a cupboard of three shelves 2 feet long, weighing 3 pounds. As boards are seldom obtainable in the wilderness, the tables and shelves may be worth the trouble of carrying them.

Axe.

A full-sized axe should be taken along whenever it is practicable to carry one. Its head need not weigh more than $3\frac{1}{2}$ or 4 pounds. With this one tool a good axeman can build anything that is required in the wilderness, and he can quickly fell and log-up a tree large enough to keep a hot fire before his lean-to throughout the night.

If an axe is bought ready handled, see that the helve is of young growth hickory, straight grained, and free from knots. Sight along the back of the helve to see if it is straight in line with the eye of the axe, then turn it over and see if the edge of the axe ranges exactly in line with the center of the hilt (rear end of handle), as it should, and that the hilt is at right angles to the center of the eye. A good chopper is as critical about the heft and hang of his axe as a shooter is about the balance of his gun. If the handle is straight, score a $2\frac{1}{2}$-foot rule on it, in inches. Get the axe ground by a careful workman. The store edge is not thin enough or keen enough.

An axe lying around camp has a fatal attraction for men who do not know how to use it. Not that they will do much chopping with it; but somebody will pick it up, make a few bungling whacks at a projecting root, or at a stick lying flat on the ground, drive the blade through into the earth and pebbles, and leave the edge nicked so that it will take an hour's hard work to put it in decent order again. And the fellow who does this is the one who could not sharpen an axe to save his life. It never seems to occur to him that an axe is of no use unless its edge is kept keen, or that the best way to ruin it is to strike it into the ground, or that a chopping block will prevent that. You may loan your last dollar to a friend; but never loan him your axe, unless you are certain that he knows how to use it.

Camp Tools.

A file should be taken along, its chief use being to sharpen the axe when you are far from grindstones.

When going into fixed camp it is well to take along a small hand-saw, which is very useful in making camp furniture. Make up your mind that it will have to be thrown away when you leave for home, because some one will surely use it in sawing meat bones. It may be well to take a crosscut saw for the special benefit of those who are rather proud of the fact that they do not know how to chop firewood. A spade may be taken for trenching, and for excavating the oven, camp refrigerator, refuse pit, cache, and so forth. A wooden spade, however, or a sapling chopped to a wedge at one end and hardened in hot ashes, will generally suffice.

A few small tools in a rolled holdall may be handy at times, and an inch auger is often useful around a permanent camp. Nails will be needed in such a camp; and, if the ground is reached by wagon, take with you some boards for making a table, benches, etc.

When traveling with horses, take a hammer, a few spare horseshoes and their nails, some copper rivets, washers, and a set, awls, saddler's thread, rawhide thongs, and a good length of rope. Never venture into an arid region without one or two *large* canteens for carrying water.

Lanterns.

An acetylene lantern is a good thing. An ordinary bicycle lamp, from which the clamp has been removed, and a wire bail attached to the top, is especially good for coon hunting, night fishing and picking up frogs at night. Carbide is much easier to carry than kerosene, which, if so much as a drop escapes anywhere near your provisions, will taint them. If oil is preferred, though, a good way to carry it is in quart cans such as are made for heavy oils, leather dressings, etc. These have a stopper which unscrews and exposes the opening of a small spout within. A folding pocket lantern for candles is best when one is in light marching order; but let it be of brass; those made of tin or aluminum are much too frail. Candles, for the amount of light they give, are much bulkier than carbide.

A coil of fifteen or twenty yards of half-inch rope is

a good thing to have around a permanent camp. It will be useful should you find a bee-tree and elect to rob the bees, or as an aid in reaching the nests of hawks, etc. If you have a dog with you, take along a few yards of strong wire, this to be strung between two trees as a "trolley wire," to which to chain him.

Rope.

When camping in a canebrake country have a huntsman's horn in the outfit. Leave it with the camp-keeper, who will blow it every evening about an hour before supper. The sound of a horn carries far, and its message is unmistakable. It is a dulcet note to one who is bewildered in a thick wood or brake.

Horn.

CHAPTER V

UTENSILS AND FOOD

"Old horse! old horse! what brought you here?"

"From Sacarap to Portland Pier
I've carted stone this many a year;
Till, killed by blows and sore abuse,
They salted me down for sailors' use.

"The sailors they do me despise;
They turn me over and damn my eyes;
Cut off my meat, and scrape my bones,
And pitch me over to Davy Jones."

—*Old chanty.*

A COLLAPSIBLE camp stove, or other sheet-iron affair, may be convenient in a fixed camp, if one has a darky to look after it. When you shift camp every day or so, such a thing is an intolerable nuisance to clean up and pack around. Either it or its pipe is forever getting jammed "out of whack." Besides, it compels you to cut all your cooking wood into short lengths.

Fire-Irons.

Meals as good as any that ever came out of stove can be cooked over an open fire. Even when it rains, a bonfire can be built to one side and hard coals shoveled from it to a spot sheltered by bark or canvas where the cooking is done. If they can easily be carried, it is a good scheme to take along a pair of fire-irons. These are simply two pieces of flat steel (iron would bend too easily when heated) about 2 feet long, $1\frac{1}{2}$ inches wide, and $\frac{1}{8}$ inch thick, which are used to support the frying-pan and coffee-pot over the fire.

Ovens.

A Dutch oven of cast-iron is very serviceable on any trip that permits carrying so heavy a utensil. Why are none made of cast aluminum?

When a Dutch oven cannot be carried, a folding

reflector of sheet-iron or aluminum (the latter lighter, but not nearly so strong) should be substituted. The reflector here mentioned is such as our great-grandmothers used to bake biscuit in, before a hearth fire. The top slants like a shed roof, and the bottom like another shed roof turned upside down, the bread pan being in the middle. The slanting top and bottom reflect heat downward upon the top of the baking and upward against its bottom, so that bread, for instance, bakes evenly all around. A prime advantage of this cunning utensil is that baking can proceed immediately when the fire is kindled, without waiting for the wood to burn down to coals, and without danger of burning the dough. Fish, flesh and fowl can be roasted to a turn in this contrivance. It has several better points than an oven, chief of which is its portability, as it folds flat; but it is inferior for corn bread, army bread, etc., and impossible for pot-roasts or braising—a Dutch oven being the thing for such purposes.

The best size of reflector for two men is 12x12x8 inches, the pan of which holds just a dozen biscuits. For four men, a good size is 16x18x10. A wire broiler packs inside the reflector; it is not necessary for broiling meat, but it is handy for the purpose, and especially for broiling fish.

Frying-Pan.

When there are more than three men in the party, take two frying-pans, one of the ordinary shallow-pattern, and the other deeper, like the pan of a chafing-dish, with a tight cover. The latter is for frying in deep fat, and also for use as a sauce-pan. Frying-pans with folding handles are convenient for tramping trips; but the common ones with solid handles are more satisfactory when you are cooking. There is no need of adding a long wooden handle if you build the right kind of a cooking-fire.

Coffee-Pot.

The best coffee or tea this side of Elysium is brewed, not in a spouted vessel, but in a little tightly lidded pail, from which the volatile aromas that are the quintessence of goodness in these delectable fluids cannot escape as they would from an open spout. If, however, you must be conventional, then get a miner's coffee-pot, in which the spout is an integral part of the pot. A soldered spout, the moment your back is turned, begins to melt at the joint from the fierce heat of an open fire, and then—*potztausend himmel donnerwetter*, off goes the nozzle!

A Kit For Four.

A party of four men, traveling in moderately light order, should have a cup, plate, knife, fork and a full-sized dessert spoon apiece; and, for company kit, two frying-pans, a pan or folding wash-basin to mix dough in, and four small covered kettles or pails, nesting. The smallest pail is for coffee or tea; the next size for cereals; the next for hot water, boiling vegetables, and as a double boiler in combination with No. 2; the largest kettle (which should be of stout metal and with a wire ring *riveted* on the cover) being for stews, soups and baked beans, and for any other baking in a hole under the camp-fire. Make a rule of using them in this order; then you will never have more than one greasy pot to clean, which is an item deserving forethought. Kettles do all the work of saucepans, and they are more useful all 'round, because they can either be set on the coals or hung above the fire, or be buried under it; besides, you can carry water in them, and they have covers to keep the heat in and the ashes out. Aluminum is the best material, especially for the larger kettle. All such vessels should be *low and broad;* then they will boil quickly and will pack well. If their bottom edges are rounded they will be easier to clean and less abrasive to one's back when making portages.

Plates should be deep enough to eat soup out of; pie pans are about right. They, too, are preferably of aluminum, because this metal holds heat better than tin, iron or crockery. This is well worth considering when you are to eat in the frosty air, for, if your plate be not hot, your gravy will turn to tallow and your flapjack be a clammy thing that your hungriest dog will not eat. Venison fat, like that of mutton, cools quickly to tallow; and I believe it was Colonel Carter of Cartersville who declared that "there is no crime equal to putting a hot duck on a cold plate." By the same token, aluminum is not so good for coffee cups and for the handles of such vessels as are to be used over the fire.

Copper utensils are dangerous, unless thoroughly tinned on the inside; and tin is very easily melted off from utensils placed over an open fire. Fruits should be cooked in granite or other enameled ware; but if you must use tinware remove the fruit as soon as it is done. Tin plates are hard to wash. Enameled ware is nice so long as it remains smooth, but its surface flakes off easily, particularly in cold weather.

The handles of tablespoons used in cooking should be bent over at the end so as to form hooks. Then if the spoon should slip from your fingers when you are stirring the kettle it is not so apt to fall into the soup. This kink deserves special mention by the Young Men's Guild of Good Life. To make ordinary cups nest, cut through the lower part of the handles and bend them outward a little.

The following utensils are also desirable if they can be carried without too much trouble: A folding canvas water bucket, an oven, or a folding reflector to bake in, a wire broiler that fits in the reflector when packing up, an extra tablespoon or two, a tea-ball or coffee-strainer, and salt and pepper shakers *capped.* A combined can-opener and corkscrew may be needed.

A party going into fixed camp can add to the above equipment at its discretion; but it is unwise to add much unless a hired cook goes along, for every utensil must be washed frequently, and there is no chore that the human male so cordially despises and so brazenly shirks as dish-washing. Take as few dishes as you can well get along with and keep *them* clean. Dirty dishes lying around are even worse nuisances in camp than they would be at home, for the woods have four-and-twenty kinds of flies and doodle-bugs to the city's one. So, I repeat, go light in pots and tableware. Plates, trenchers, wash-basins, baskets, even cups, buckets and barrels, can be made out of bark and withes, so as to be very neat and clean. Directions how to select materials for the purpose and how to rig them up will be given in another chapter.

When transportation is easy it pays to pack the bread, bags of flour, etc., in a tin wash-boiler or two, which are wrapped in burlaps and crated. These make capital grub boxes in camp, securing their contents from wet, insects and rodents. Ants in summer and mice at all times are downright pests of the woods, to say nothing of the wily coon, the predatory mink, the inquisitive skunk, and the fretful porcupine. The boilers are useful, too, on many occasions, to catch rain-water, boil clothes, waterproof and dye tents, and so forth. After all these things have been done in them they are properly seasoned for cooking a burgoo.

Tin Grub Boxes.

In a summer camp of the glorified picnic order, wooden plates are always useful, saving much washing and being convenient for side dishes. But in a paper birch country they are superfluous.

No matter how lightly one travels he should carry several yards of cheese-cloth. There is nothing so good to bar out mosquitoes and other pests, to hang game and fish in, to keep flies out of things, and it is useful for strainers, pudding-bags, table-cloth. There may come warm days, even late in the fall, when the flies will come out and blow your venison, if it be unprotected. A smudge is not to be relied upon, for if the smoke be dense enough to keep flies at a distance it will dry up the meat and make it taste like very bad dried beef.

Cheese-Cloth.

Plain dishes well cooked, of such food as "sticks to the ribs," are what men want who are taking hearty exercise in the open air. When weight and bulk must be cut down as far as practicable, and hard travel is ahead, there is nothing so good as pork, flour, beans, tea (or coffee) and salt. These are the mainstays of lumbermen, trappers, prospectors, miners and soldiers, who certainly know, if any men do, what kind of food the human machine needs to keep it up to the highest physical efficiency, and what will keep best in all

Substantial Foods.

weathers and stow most compactly. Anything added to these staples is a luxury, to be carried or not, according to one's means of transportation.

Many things that we crave in town would rank as "baby foods" in the woods, and rightly so, for they will not do to climb hills with, chop trees, paddle canoes, tote burdens, nor will they sustain the wilderness hunter from dawn to dusk. "After a hearty breakfast of oatmeal," says an experienced mountaineer, speaking of one of his craft, "he will be ravenously hungry in two hours, of cornmeal, after three hours, of bacon and bread, after four or five hours, while pork and beans will sustain him from six to ten hours and give the utmost physical buoyancy and strength."*

Variety.

As a rule, however, one can add to the variety of this bill of fare by substituting, for some of the pork and flour and beans, some butter, concentrated soups, dried milk, cereals, evaporated vegetables, dried fruits, and he may add sugar, vinegar and a few other condiments, which, with game and fish, will enable him to dine sumptuously every day. Variety of food is quite as welcome in camp as it is anywhere else. Canned goods, however, and fresh vegetables, add enormously to the weights to be carried, owing chiefly to the water that is in them. This will be noticed in the "heavy" ration lists that follow.

Standard Rations.

The United States Army ration is often taken as the standard of what men require in camp and field. But it is more liberal than most campers need, the soldiers getting a rebate for food not used by them, and much being allowed for accidental waste. I am speaking now of the garrison ration. The army travel ration, which consists only of bread, canned beef, canned baked beans, roasted coffee and sugar, amounts to 2 68-100 pounds of solid food for one person one day. I will give in the next chapter four ration lists for four men two weeks, graded according as they travel, light or heavy, in warm weather or in cold. The quantities are sufficient without counting on game or fish. These

* F. Marion Wilcox, *The Rockies of Canada.*

lists are based upon my own experience. It has been my practice for years to weigh personally, and note down at the time, the amount of provisions taken on my lone camping tours, as well as those taken by the various parties that I have accompanied, and similarly to record the quantities left over at the end of the trip. I have also collected many ration lists compiled by practical woodsmen, and have spent considerable time in studying and comparing them. They vary remarkably, not so much in aggregate weights as in the proportions of this and that. On the whole, my own records have been of most assistance.

Cold-Weather Food.

It will be noticed that the cold-weather ration that I give is about one-third more liberal than that for warm weather, and that the addition is mostly in fatty and oily foods. A man who eats little fat meat when living in the city will find that when he travels hard in cold weather and sleeps in the open air his system will demand more fatty food. The experience of travelers in the far North bears out the results of scientific analysis, that foods containing fats and oils are more nutritious and heat-producing than any others. But a steady diet of bread and bacon is likely to breed scurvy; so a supply of dried vegetables and fruits should be added. Men living in the open also develop a craving for sweets that is out of all proportion to what they experience in town. This is a normal demand, for sugar is stored-up energy. I have allowed liberally for this, and also for the increased consumption of coffee and tea that is the rule (owing somewhat to the fact that they lose strength from exposure to the air).

Tobacco.

For those addicted to it, tobacco should be considered a necessity; and an extra supply should be carried for presents, for it is always appreciated. A good brand of cut plug is best for outdoor smoking, as it holds fire well, burns "cool," keeps well and does not blow out of one's pipe with every puff of wind. About six ounces a week per man is a fair allowance for steady smokers.

If butter is not taken, its weight in my ration lists

should be substituted in pork. Similarly other substitutions may be made in the other components. Condiments will not be despised when the game and fish supply is low; they make a new dish out of yesterday's leavings.

Substitutions.

A steady diet of baking-powder bread or biscuits will ruin the stomach if persisted in. Bread can be raised with yeast powder or lungwort, or by the sour-dough process; otherwise one should vary his diet with unleavened bread of corn-meal or flour. Self-raising flour is more likely to spoil than plain flour, and it will not do for thickening, gravies, dredging, etc. Flour and cornmeal should be sifted before packing.

Packing Meat.

Ham will keep, even in warm weather, if packed in a paper bag so as to keep out flies. It will keep indefinitely if sliced, fried or boiled, and put up in tins with melted lard poured over it to keep out the air. Meat of any kind will quickly mold if packed in tins from which air is not excluded.

Preserving Butter.

Butter will keep well in a hot climate, with flavor little impaired, if thoroughly boiled, skimming off the scum as it rises till the melted butter is clear as oil, and then soldering it up in canisters. Another method, borrowed from the Indians, is to melt it with slippery-elm bark, in the proportion of a drachm of the latter to a pound of butter, keeping them heated together a few minutes, and then straining off the fat.

A Good Friture.

A frying fat superior to lard is made by melting together over a slow fire equal parts of lard and beef suet, and packing in a covered pail or pry-up tin. It has a higher melting point than lard, and tastes better than plain lard or bacon grease.

Beverages.

Ground coffee should be put up in small tins. If in large canisters, it will lose strength rapidly from repeated exposure to air. On trips of more than three weeks it is better to carry the green berries, roast them in the frying-pan and pulverize by pounding in a bag. Tea is more bracing than coffee. Cocoa and chocolate have high nutritive value.

Canned Meats.

Canned meats do well enough for a quick luncheon now and then, but are unwholesome and unappetizing for steady diet. Canned corned beef, however, makes passable hash. Some smoked herring and dried codfish might be substituted for some of the meat. Ordinary canned soups are mostly water; get condensed soups. Soup from the raw materials can only be made in fixed camps as it takes at least half a day to prepare.

Soup-Stock.

I have added canned consommé to the "heavy" ration-list because it is an ideal soup-stock for campers. Without good stock it is impossible to make a good soup, and it is seldom that men in the wilderness have both the material from which to make it and the time to spare. Many campers carry beef extract in the fatuous hope of using it in soup-stock or for beef tea, but it has neither the flavor of soup-stock nor any nourishment whatever.

Eggs.

Don't depend upon buying fresh eggs, potatoes, etc., where you leave the railroad, unless you have been there before and are sure of the place's resources. Eggs can be carried anywhere if packed in pasteboard boxes with compartments, and stowed in wooden boxes. To preserve eggs, varnish them with vaselin, being careful not to leave the smallest particle of shell unprotected with it. This is a much more reliable preservative than salt, bran, paper, paraffin, or other common methods.

Milk.

Milk or cream is now put up in soluble powdered form, which is better flavored and lighter to carry than condensed milk or evaporated cream, and not so mussy. It can be dissolved even in ice-cold water, and its keeping qualities are all that can be desired. Desiccated eggs can also be procured from camp outfitters. Their chief value is for use in mixing flapjacks, etc.

Traveling Rations.

In a small box or basket carry separately enough food for the meals to be eaten while traveling from the railroad to the first camping ground; it will save unpacking *en route*.

Soap.

Tar soap is best for campers' use, since it makes a good lather in any kind of water, hard or soft, hot or cold. A light coat of its lather helps to keep off mosquitoes. Take along a bar of naphtha soap for washing woolens; it can be used with cold water, and will save the flannels from shrinking.

Directions for preparing emergency rations, such as jerked venison, pemmican and rockahominy or pinole, will be given in another chapter.

CHAPTER VI

A CHECK-LIST—PACKING UP

ON the following list, such articles as should be dispensed with when traveling light are *starred;* those used only on special trips are *queried.* This is intended as a check-list, to be modified according to circumstances. No one expedition will require everything that is listed here. Take only what you know you will need. The things that "might come in handy" should be left at home:

OUTFIT FOR FOUR MEN IN THE WILDERNESS.

EACH MAN.

WEAR:

Coat (duxbak or khaki; Mackinaw, if preferred, in winter).
Knickers or trousers (firm, closely woven gray kersey, tweed, or homespun).
Undershirt, drawers, stockings, or socks (woolen).
Overshirt (gray flannel).
Money belt.
Shoes (light leather hunting; heavier, with hobnails, for mountaineering).
Leggings (loden, or cloth puttees).
Hat (smoke-colored felt, flannel sweat-band, ventilators).
Neckerchief (gray silk).
Belt and sheath-knife.

IN POCKETS:

Purse.
Jackknife.
Waterproof matchbox.
Loose matches.
Pipe.
Tobacco.
Compass.
Watch.
Map.
Note-book.
Pencil.
Handkerchief.
Pocket lens (?)

POUCH:

Tomahawk (muzzled).
Quart pail (containing cup, spoon, and small oiled silk bag each of salt, sugar, tea).
Bouillon capsules.
Sweet chocolate.
Wallet, with fish lines, etc. (*See* page 30.)
First-aid packet.
10 cartridges.
Field cleaner for rifle.
Broken shell extractor.
Almanac sheets.
Timetable.
Postal cards.
Trapping scent (?).

In summer:

Hypodermic, etc.
Fly-dope.
Head-net (black) (?)
Chloroform (?)
Citric acid (?)

In winter:

Snow goggles.

CARRY:

Rifle, gun, or rod, in case.
Camera (?).
Field glass (?).

PACK UP:

Spare clothing, in double bag. (*See* page 34.)
Poncho.
Waders (?).
Knapsack, or pack-strap.
Canteen (?).
Ammunition.
Fishing tackle.
*Landing net.
Individual mess kit.
Shelter-cloth (?).
*Cot.
Mattress or bed-tick.
Blankets.
Pillow-bag.
Toilet bag. (*See* page 34.)
*Razor and strop.
Toilet paper.
Repair kit (only part of it on a hard march). (*See* page 35.)
Medicines. (*See* page 32.)

Matches (tin box).
*Spare pipe.
Tobacco.
Spare glasses (?).
Stationery (?).
Shoe grease.
*Camp chair.

COMPANY STORES.

Tent, and ridge-rope, if any.
*Poles and pins (the latter in a bag).
*Fly for dining roof.
*Ground-cloth.
*Tent hangers.
*Roll-up table top.
*Roll-up shelves.
Axe.
File.
*Nails and tacks.
Screw eyes (?).
Lantern.
Carbide, candles, or oil.
*Spade.
*Panel saw (tied between thin boards).
Prospecting pick (?).
Cold chisel (?).
Small tools in roll-up case.
*Rope.
Heavy twine.
Cheese-cloth.
Boards (?).
Huntsman's horn (?).
4 kettles with covers, nested.
2 frying-pans.
Reflector.
*Dutch oven.
*Wire broiler.
4 each, knives, forks, spoons, plates, cups.
2 tablespoons.
*Butcher knife, long.
Salt and pepper shakers.
Pantasote bucket, folding.
Pantasote wash basin, folding (on tramping trip used only for mixing dough).
*Dish pan, small.
*Coffee strainer.
Can opener.
*Corkscrew.
*Fire irons.
Dish towels (2), dish clouts (3).

Soap.
*Cook book.
*Thermometer.
*Sulphuric acid, or alum and saltpeter, for curing skins.
Insect powder and "gun," if you camp in summer, or intend to occupy an old camp.

If traveling in boat or canoe, add a large sponge for bailing, and a pound or two of beeswax for stopping leaks.

If going by pack-train, add, besides horse trappings, a shoeing and pack-mending kit.

If it is the intention to build a cabin, add:

Crosscut saw.
Froe. (Even if roofing paper is carried, this will be useful.)
1½ in. framing chisel.
Window (glazed), or some oiled paper, or translucent parchment.
Hinges.
Nails, including wrought nails for battening door.
Miner's shovel, instead of spade.
And perhaps a broadaxe, mattock, jack plane, and auger.
If convenient, take some tin and a soldering set for making a vermin-proof closet or chest, and some wire netting for cages of wild animals you may capture.

RATION LISTS, FOUR MEN, TWO WEEKS. (56 RATIONS.)

	LIGHT.		*HEAVY.*	
Meats, etc.	*Summer.*	*Winter.*	*Summer.*	*Winter.*
Salt pork	..	10 lbs.	..	10 lbs.
Bacon	12 lbs.	12	10 lbs.	10
Ham	5	5	5	5
Corned Beef (canned)	4	4	4	4
Concentrated soups	2½	2½	1½	1½
Canned consommé	..	..	2	2
Fresh eggs	..	..	5 (4 doz.)	5
Butter	..	..	6	6
Cheese	1	1	1	1
Lard	3	3	3	3
Dried milk (*or* evaporated cream, 6 cans)	2½	2½	2½	2½
	30	40	40	50
Bread, etc.				
Fresh bread	..	..	5	5
Hard biscuit	5	5	..	..
Flour	25	25	25	25
Corn-meal (yellow)	3	10	3	10
Buckwheat flour	..	3	..	3
Rolled oats	3	3	3	3
Rice	3	3	3	3
Macaroni	1	1	1	1
Baking powder (Royal)	1	1	1	1
Baking soda	1	1	1	1
	42	52	42	52

Vegetables.				
Potatoes (fresh)	..		30 (½ bu.)	30
" (evaporated)	4	4	..	..
Onions (fresh)	4	6	4	6
Beans	4	6	4	6
Split peas	4	4	4	4
Tomatoes (canned)	..	..	5 (2 cans)	5
Sweet corn (canned)	..	..	2½ (1 can)	2½
	16	20	49½	53½
Beverages.				
Coffee (roasted, whole, *or* 5 lbs. ground)	3	3	3	3
Tea	½	½	½	½
Whitman's cocoa	½	½	½	½
	4	4	4	4
Sugar, etc.				
Sugar (granulated)	5	5	5	5
Maple sugar	5	5	..	..
Maple syrup	..	..	3 (1 qt.)	6 (½ gal.)
Preserves, jam, marmalade	..	..	5	5
	10	10	13	16
Acids.				
Vinegar	..	1 (1 pint)	..	1
Pickles	..	..	2	2
Lemons	..	..	4 (2 doz.)	..
Citric acid	¼	..	..	..
	¼	1	6	3
Fruits, etc.				
Evaporated apples, peaches, apricots	2	4	2	2
Prunes (stoned)	1	1	2	2
Raisins (seeded)	1	1	1	1
Canned peaches, plums, cherries, pears, cranberries	..	..	10 (4 cans)	10
Shelled nuts	1	1	1	1
	5	7	16	16
Condiments.				
Salt (if allowing for curing skins, etc., take 10 lbs.)	2	2	2	2
Pepper (white)	1 oz.	1 oz.	1 oz.	1 oz.
Cayenne or Chili	1 oz.	1 oz.	1 oz.	1 oz.
Worcestershire sauce	..	..	1 bot.	1 bot.
Olive oil	..	..	1 bot.	1 bot.
Mustard	..	..	x	x
Sage	..	..	x	x
Parsley	..	..	x	x
Mixed herbs	..	..	x	x
Nutmeg	..	..	x	x
Curry powder	..	..	x	x
Ginger	..	..	x	x
	2⅛	2⅛	5	5
Total	109⅜ lbs.	136⅛ lbs.	176 lbs.	200 lbs.

Add Soap, Matches.

Packing Supplies.

Pack the pork, cheese and bread in parchment paper; the flour, meal, cereals, vegetables and dried fruits in bags; the butter, frying fat, coffee, tea, sugar and salt in pry-up tin cans. Some camp outfitters supply these small bags and tins of proper size to stow in waterproof provision bags of their own make, and it saves much trouble to buy them ready made. Label everything plainly, and especially the sugar and salt, so that one may not be taken for the other. Bottles should be packed in corrugated paper or in excelsior. Mason jars are nice to pack butter, jam, etc., in, but they are heavy.

Camp chests are very convenient when it is practicable to carry them; but they should be small, weighing not over fifty or sixty pounds each when packed, so that one man can easily handle them unassisted. If they are specially made, cottonwood is the best material (if thoroughly seasoned boards can be had—otherwise it warps abominably). It is the strongest and toughest wood for its weight that we have, and will not splinter. For the ends and lids of small chests, $\frac{5}{8}$-inch stuff is thick enough, and $\frac{3}{8}$-inch for the sides, bottoms and trays. The bottom should have a pair of $\frac{5}{8}$-inch cleats for risers and the top a similar pair to keep it from warping, unless the chests are to go on pack animals. Strap-hinges and hasp, a brass padlock and broad leather end-straps (not drop-handles) should be provided, and the chest painted. The best size is 24x18x 12 inches, this being convenient for canoes and pack-saddles. A pine grocery box of this size, with $\frac{3}{4}$-inch ends and $\frac{3}{8}$-inch sides, top and bottom, weighs only 12 pounds, and will answer the purpose very well. Screw a wooden handle on each end, say 5x2 inches, with a hand-hold gouged out of the under side. A tin bread-box is convenient in a canoe for carrying the utensils and food used while traveling.

Check off every article in the outfit as it is stowed and keep the inventory for future reference.

I append here a list of things taken on a three-days' side trip from camp in the fall of the year, when the nights are frosty. It is assumed that the tramper goes alone; also, that he proposes to have plenty to eat on the trip, with good shelter and a warm bed at night. With this equipment, should he have fair luck in hunting, he can keep to the woods for a week, without stocking up:

A Knapsack Trip.

COLD-WEATHER TRAMPING KIT.

CARRIED.

Clothes worn, sheath-knife, articles in pockets, as hitherto specified.	
Rifle, with sling	8 lbs.
PACKED ON BACK.	
Shelter-cloth	2 "
Blanket	8 "
Bed-tick	1¼ "
Jersey	2¼ "
Half-axe, in muzzle	2⅛ "
20 cartridges	1 "
Mess can, quart pail, tin cup, spoon	1 "
Pillow-bag, spare socks, toilet-bag, first-aid pkt., twine, matches, wallet, field cleaner, wipers, vaselin	⅝ "
Pack harness	1¼ "
	19½ "
Three days' provisions, namely:	
Bacon	2½ "
Bread (previously baked in camp)	3½ "
Tea	⅛ "
Sugar	⅝ "
Salt, pepper	¼ "
Sweet chocolate	½ "
	7½ "
Total	35 lbs.

There are several things to be looked after in good season before starting on a camping trip. If your shoes are new, oil them and break them in. If your rifle is new, do not dream of carrying it into the wilderness until you have "sighted it up," testing the elevations at various ranges, and making sure that the sights are accurately aligned. If your fishing tackle

The Last Look Around.

is old, overhaul and test it thoroughly. If you have a hollow tooth, get it filled. Pare your nails closely, or they will soon be badly broken. Get your hair cropped short. See that you have a good supply of small change when you start. Don't carry off your bunch of keys. Be on hand early at the station and see to it personally that your humble but precious duffel all gets aboard.

And now, *bon voyage!*

CHAPTER VII

THE CAMP

"And they shall dwell safely in the wilderness and sleep in the woods."—*Ezekiel.*

GOOD camping grounds are seldom far to seek in a hilly country that is well wooded. There are exceptions, as in the Ozarks, where the rock is a porous limestone, the drainage mostly underground, and there are no brooks, nor are springs as common as one would expect, though when you do strike one it is a big one. Here a traveler must depend for water chiefly on the creeks and rivers, which may be miles apart. In a level region, whether it be open plain or timbered bottom land, good water and a high and dry site may be hard to find. In any case, when men are journeying through a wild country that is strange to them, they should begin at least two hours before sunset to keep a bright lookout for a good place on which to spend the night, and when such is found they had better accept it at once than run the risk of "murdering a night" farther on, wherever the powers of darkness may force them to stop.

Camp Sites. The essentials of a good camp site are these:

1. Pure water.

2. Wood that burns well. In cold weather there should be either an abundance of sound downwood or some standing hardwood trees that are not too big for easy felling.

3. An open spot, level enough for the tent and campfire, but elevated above its surroundings so as to have good natural drainage. It must be well above any chance of overflow from the sudden rise of a neighboring stream. Observe the previous flood marks.

4. Grass or browse for the horses (if there are any) and bedding for the men.

5. Straight poles for the tent, or trees convenient for attaching the ridge rope.

6. Security against the spread of fire.

7. Exposure to direct sunlight during a part of the day, especially during the early morning hours.

8. In summer, exposure to whatever breezes may blow; in cold weather, protection against the prevailing wind.

It is well to avoid an old camping ground. Its previous occupants will have stripped it of good kindling and downwood, and they and their dogs may have left behind them a legacy of rubbish and fleas.

Precautions as to elevation and drainage are especially needful in those parts of our country that are subject to cloudbursts. I have seen a ravine that had been stone-dry for months fill fifteen feet deep, in a few minutes, with a torrent that swept trees and bowlders along with it; and it is quite common in many parts of the West for wide bottoms to be flooded in a night. When I was a boy in Iowa, a "mover" camped for the night on an island in Coon River, near our place. He had a bag of gold coin, but was out of rations. A sudden flood left him marooned the next morning on a knoll scarce big enough for his team and wagon. He subsisted for a week, like his horses, on the inner bark of cottonwood, and when a rescue party found him he was kicking his bag of gold over the few yards of dry ground that were left of his domain.

Bottom lands, and deep woods where the sun rarely penetrates, should be avoided, when practicable, for they are damp lairs at best, and in warm weather they are infested with mosquitoes. A ravine or narrow valley between steep hills is a trap for fog, and the cold, heavy air from the head of the hollow pours down it at night, while an undertow of warmer air drawing upward now and then makes the smoke from one's camp-fire shift most annoyingly.

New clearings in the forest are unhealthy, for the sun gets in on plants that are intolerant of strong light, they rot, and poisonous gases arise from their decay, as well as from the recently disturbed soil. If one is obliged to camp in a malarial region he should not leave the camp-fire until the sun is up and the fog dispelled.

Sandy beaches, and low, gravelly points, are likely to swarm in summer with midges.

Granting that one has much choice in the matter, he should select, in summer, an open knoll, a low ridge, or, better still, a bold, rocky point jutting out into a river or lake. A low promontory catches the cool breezes, which disperse fog and insects, and it is soon dried whenever the sun shines. If one can be found that has a clump of trees on it, pitch the tent in such position that it will get the direct rays of the morning and the evening sun, but will be shaded during the heat of the day. This is the ideal site for a summer camp.

In cold weather seek an open, park-like spot in the forest, where surrounding trees will break the wind; or a "bench" (natural terrace backed by a cliff) on the leeward side of a hill. In the latter case, build your fire against the cliff, and shield the tent with a wind-break. The rock will reflect heat upon the tent, and will serve as a smoke-conductor as well.

On a hillside that is mostly bare, if there be a thicket or a cluster of evergreen trees, get on the downhill side of it. The stream of cold air from above will jump this obstacle and will leave an eddy of comparatively warm, still air immediately below it.

The tent should not be set under a tree where it would catch the drip of dew and rain or of snow-laden boughs, nor near a dead tree, nor amid trees that are shallow-rooted (such as basswood and hemlock), for these are liable to be overthrown by a storm. Avoid, if practicable, the neighborhood of large trees that have brittle limbs (the aspens, poplars, willows, cottonwood, butternut, catalpa, yellow locust, silver maple). Trees that are "poor in fat" (the oaks, poplars, willows, maples, elms, ashes) are much more likely to be struck by lightning than are those "rich in fat" (beech, birch, chestnut, basswood).

Starting a Lean-to Shelter

The Fixed Camp

Having selected a site for the camp, clear it of brush, stubs, dead leaves, and rotten wood. Decayed down-wood and loose, flat stones are likely, in a southern country, to harbor tarantulas and scorpions, which abound as far north as Missouri. If dry leaves and grass are so thick on the ground as to be dangerous, be careful in burning them off to light them at only one spot at a time, and stand by it with a green bough to whip the fire into subjection if it burns too fast.

Making Camp.

The celerity with which a camp is made depends upon the training and willingness of the men, and the system by which their duties are parceled. Let us suppose that there are four in the party, besides the teamster or packer. Then let No. 1, who is cook, get out the provisions and utensils, rig up the fireplace, build a fire, and prepare the food for cooking, while No. 2 is rustling wood and water. Meantime Nos. 3 and 4 clear the ground and smooth it off, cut tent pegs and poles, unpack the tent, and summon all hands for a minute to assist in raising the tent and pegging it "square." Then the cook goes on with his proper duties, the axeman cuts and beds a chopping-block and gets in night-wood, and the canvas-men turn bed-makers. Thus, by the time supper is ready, which will be within an hour, or less, the camp will be properly made, and every one's work is done save the unfortunate scullion's.

Pitching an *A* Tent.

To set up an *A* tent, draw the ridge rope tight between two trees, and fasten each end with a clove hitch, unless the line has stretchers. Then stake out the four corners in a true rectangle (that is, make each corner a right angle, instead of having them askew). Then drive the other pegs. If the soil is thin, drive each peg at a sharp angle and lay a flat rock over the slant of it. If the ground is so sopping wet, or so sandy, that pegs will not hold, dig a rather deep hole where each peg should stand, and in it bury a rock or a fagot of brush that has a bit of rope tied to it which is left sticking out a few inches above the ground; stamp the earth down, and tie the projecting ends of rope into the grommets. Now stretch the ridge line taut with your rope-slides, or by bracing it up with a forked sapling near each end. Do not neglect to trench the tent. It is miserable business to crawl out into a driving storm at night and dig a ditch by lantern-light—worse still to awake to a realization that trenching is too late to save your soaking possessions. "Make yourself ready in your cabin for the mischance of the hour, if so it hap."

Setting up a Wall Tent. To pitch a wall tent, four men proceed as follows:

Nos. 1 and 2 procure canvas, and Nos. 3 and 4 the poles.

Nos. 3 and 4 lay the ridge-pole on the ground, in the direction that the tent is to stand; then lay the uprights at each end of ridge-pole and at right angles to it, on the side opposite that from which the wind blows. They then drop the tent pins and hammers at their respective ends of the tent; then drive a pin at each end of the ridge to mark front and rear. Meanwhile, Nos. 1 and 2 unroll the tent and spread it out over the ridge-pole and on both sides of it.

Nos. 1 and 3 now go to the rear, and Nos. 2 and 4 in front, and slip the pins of the uprights through the ridge-pole and tent. If a fly is used, it is placed in position over tent, and the loops of the long guys over the front and rear pole pins. No. 4 secures center (door) loops over center pin in front, and No. 1 in rear. Each goes to his corner, No. 1 right rear, No. 2 right front, No. 3 left rear, No. 4 left front.

All draw bottom of tent taut and square, the front and rear at right angles to the ridge, and fasten it with pins through the corner loops, then stepping outward two paces from the corner, and a pace to the front (Nos. 2 and 4) or rear (Nos. 1 and 3), each securely sets a long pin, over which is passed the extended corner guy rope. Care must be taken that the tent is properly squared and pinned to the ground at the door and four corners before raising it.

Nos. 1 and 3 now go to the rear, Nos. 2 and 4 to the front pole, and raise the tent to a convenient height from the ground, when Nos. 2 and 3 enter and seize their respective poles, and all together raise the tent until the upright poles are vertical. While Nos. 2 and 3 support the poles, Nos. 1 and 4 tighten the corner guys, beginning on the windward side. The tent being thus temporarily secured, all set the guy pins and fasten the guy ropes, Nos. 1 and 2 to the right, Nos. 3 and 4 left, and then the wall pins.

This is the army method, and it is the best.

Erecting Sibley Tent.

For a Sibley tent, make a loop in one end of its lash rope, and another at such distance from this as will mark the radius of the tent when set up taut; also another loop farther out marking the radius of the guys, if the tent has a wall. Drive a peg in the center of the space that the tent is to cover, loop the end of the line over it, and, with another peg used alternately in the other loops, draw two concentric circles on the ground. Drive the pegs and guy stakes on these circles, respectively, loop on the grommet lines to the former, raise the tent, and then make all taut.

The Teepee.

To erect a teepee: The site must be level, or very nearly so. Cut the requisite number of straight, slim lodge-poles (ten or twelve), and two longer poles for the smoke-flaps. Trim them carefully, for if stubs are left on them they will make the canvas leak. Tie three of them together with the lash rope about eighteen inches from the top, and about the same distance above where the top of the teepee cover will come. Set these up as a tripod, the butts equidistant on a circle described on the ground as above. For a teepee of 12 feet diameter they will be 10 feet 5 inches apart, measuring straight from one to the other. Carry the rope around them a few times where they are tied together, and let it trail. Lean all the other poles, save one, against the top of the tripod, spacing their butts equidistant around the circle. Tie the top of the teepee cover, at the point between the flaps, to the remaining lodge-pole, and lift it into place. Insert the smoke-poles in the pockets of the flaps, carry the cover around the outside of the framework, and pin or lace it together in front. Peg the cover down, and anchor the tent by drawing the lash rope tight to a crotch driven into the ground inside the tent and on the windward side. Pitch the tent with its door to leeward of the prevailing winds. When there is no wind, keep both smoke-flaps open. When it blows, raise the flap to windward and lower the other. When the wind blows directly against the entrance, close both flaps, and raise the bottom of the door cover a little to

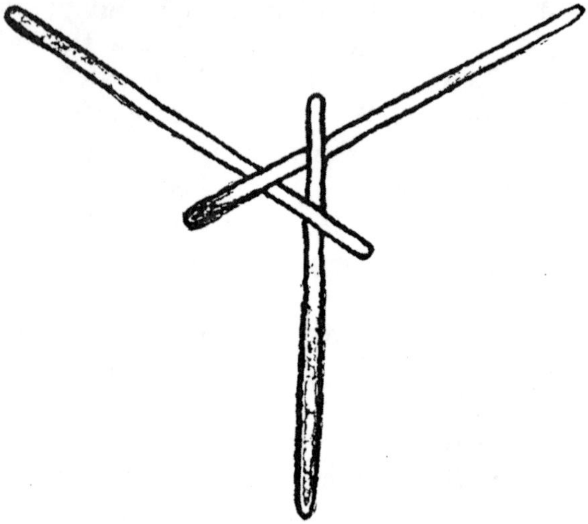

FIG. 4.

create a draught. By the way, do not call the teepee a wigwam; the latter is a fixed residence, the former portable.

Tents on Rocky Ground.

Some time it may be necessary to set up a tent or other camp on ground which is so rocky that stakes cannot be driven into it. In such case, two tripods can be erected at a convenient distance apart for the ridge-pole or rope, the tops of the tripods interlocking as shown in the illustration. A self-supporting framework for a shed-roof camp is also shown. (Figs. 4 and 5.)

Browse Bed.

To make a bed of browse, first smooth the ground, leaving no stubs, stones, or hummocks. Then cut head- and foot-logs a foot thick, and side-logs, which may be somewhat smaller, and pin them down with inverted crotches, making a rectangular framework on the ground to keep the browse in place. Next fell a thrifty balsam or hemlock (spruce, pine, or even cedar will do in a pinch) and strip off the fans, using none that cannot be broken off by one's fingers. Now lay a course of boughs a foot long against the head-log, butts down and to the front, then shingle another layer in front of these, and so on down to the foot of the bed, leaving only the tips of the boughs showing. Such a bed is luxurious in proportion to its depth and freshness. It should be

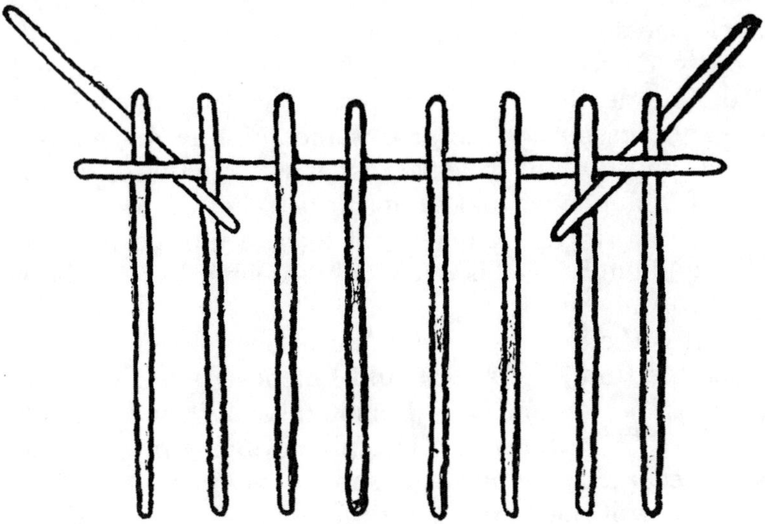

Fig. 5.

renewed every day. It takes considerable time and labor to make. I prefer the individual bed-tick, filled by each man to suit himself.

Hang the salt pork or bacon to a tree beside the fireplace, where it is handy; it will not spoil in the weather.

Precautions. If mice, wood rats, porcupines, skunks, or other thieving varmints annoy you, hang the edibles by wires or cords from branches, or from a stout wire run from one tree to another, and shelter them from sun and rain. Put matches and candles where they can quickly be found in the dark.

When camping with a pack-train, pile the packs

neatly together and cover them with canvas, and similarly pile and protect the saddles, making especially sure that the lash ropes cannot get wet, and that nothing will be buried out of sight, off somewhere by itself, if snow falls during the night. Soldierly system in all such matters pays a big dividend in time and good temper. A tenderfoot's camp looks like a hurrah's nest.

Wild hogs are literally the *bêtes noires* of southern campers. Your thin-flanked, long-legged, sharp-nosed razorback, with tusks gleaming from his jaws—he or she of the third or further removed generation of feral lawlessness—is the most perverse, fearless, and maliciously destructive brute in America, wolverines and "Indian devils" not excepted. Shooting his tail off does not discourage him, rocks and clubs are his amusement, and no hint to leave that is weaker than a handful of red pepper baked inside a pone o' bread will drive him away. A hog-proof fence around camp, unsightly though it be, is one's only safeguard in southern wildwoods.

Fixed Camps.

If it is the intention to remain in one place for a considerable time, the site should be chosen with particular care. It should have a good outlook but not a free inlook, being picturesque and secluded. The tent should be floored, otherwise it will be unpleasant in wet weather and its contents will get musty or mildewed. Mildew attacks leather first, then woolens, and cotton goods last of all.

A separate dining space and kitchen should be built, if for no other reason than to keep insects and vermin out of the sleeping tent. Make a dining-table by driving four stakes into the ground for legs, nailing cleats across the ends, and covering the top with straight sticks or boards, On each side of it build a bench on the same principle. Over these erect a framework, on which stretch a tarpaulin or tent fly. Near the fireplace build a kitchen table, with a shelf underneath for utensils, condiments, baking powder, lard, etc., and with space below for a box or other bin for potatoes and onions.

Make some rustic chairs, stools, and benches. As Thoreau says, "None is so poor that he need sit on a pumpkin—that is shiftlessness."

Dig a sink or rubbish hole near the kitchen table, for dishwater, tin cans, and such other refuse as will not burn, and into this throw every day a layer of ashes or earth. Then you will not be bothered so much by flies. Have a definite place for the latrine, and build it as soldiers do, leaving a paddle in the excavated earth behind it. Whoever wrote "Deuteronomy" was a good camper.

Sink.

For a refrigerator, dig a hole in the ground, stone it up or line it with bark, and cover the top; or, if you have ice, bore a few holes for drainage in the bottom of a box or barrel, sink it in the ground to its top, and cover with burlaps or a blanket. If fresh venison is put in a spring the outside of the meat will get white and stringy but the inside will keep sweet for several weeks. Tie a white rag to a branch or bush directly over this water-cache, to scare away animals. In winter, cut a hole in the ice, fasten the meat to a stick by a rope or thong, let the meat down into the water, just below the ice, with the stick resting across the orifice. If it is desired to cache meat in this way, put blocks of ice over the hole and throw water on the mass until it freezes together. No land animal can disturb such a store, and the venison will keep fresh and palatable for a couple of months at least.

Cold Storage.

Butter and milk should not be stored near anything that has a pronounced odor, for they would be tainted. As soon as the camp ground is reached the butter tin or jar should be placed in a net or bag and sunk in the spring or cold brook, the string being tied to the bank so that a freshet may not carry the food away or bury it out of sight. Later, if you stay in that place, a little rock-lined well can be dug near the spring, and covered securely so that coons and porcupines cannot plunder it. There are camps so situated that the following note may be of service: Milk can be kept sweet for several days by adding a spoonful of grated horseradish to one or two gallons of milk.

Caches.

To cache provisions in trees, fasten a pole from one tree to another at a height of 15 to 20 feet from the ground, and peel the bark from the tree trunks to hinder animals from climbing them; wrap the provisions in canvas and then in oilskin (if you have it), and wire or tie them to the pole. The odor of oilskin is said to be offensive to wolverines and other predatory beasts. A further precaution is to make a St. Andrew's cross (X-shaped), hang it from the pole, and suspend the parcel from the end of one arm of the cross, so that every puff of wind will set it swinging.

A cache or secret storehouse for heavy tools, bedding, utensils, etc., that you may want to leave at the camp until the next season, may be dug in a dry bank and roofed over with logs and earth, the interior being lined with dry grass and poles or bark. The old Indian method of digging a jug-shaped hole in a knoll, casting the excavated earth into a stream, lining the cache with hay and hides, and sealing it with the same piece of sod (about twenty inches in diameter) that was removed when beginning to dig the neck of the hole is an excess of precaution nowadays.

Wood Yard.

A chopping-block is the first thing needed about a camp. The axe, when not in use, should always be stuck in that particular block, where any one can find it when wanted, and where it will not injure men or dogs.

Do not let the axe lie outdoors on a very cold night; the frost would make it brittle, so that the steel might shiver on the first knot you struck the next morning.

Stretch a stout line between two trees where the sunlight will strike, and air your blankets on it every day or two when the weather is pleasant. Against a straight tree near the tent make a rack, somewhat like a billiard-cue rack, in which fishing rods can be stood, full rigged, without danger of being blown down.

Of course, it takes time and hard work to make everything snug and trim around camp; but it pays, just the same, to spend a couple of days at the start in rigging up such conveniences as I have described, and getting in a good supply of wood and kindling. To rush right off hunting or fishing, and leave the camp in disorder, is to eat your dough before it is baked.

CHAPTER VIII

THE CAMP-FIRE

"I am a woodland fellow, sir, that always loved a great fire."—*All's Well that Ends Well.*

Cold night weighs down the forest bough,
  Strange shapes go flitting through the gloom.
But see—a spark, a flame, and now
  The wilderness is home!

—*Edwin L. Sabin.*

THE forest floor is always littered with old leaves, dead sticks, and fallen trees. During a drought this rubbish is so tinder-dry that a spark falling in it may start a conflagration; but through a great part of the year the leaves and sticks that lie flat on the ground are too moist, at least on their under side, to ignite readily. If we rake together a pile of leaves, cover it higgledy-piggledy with dead twigs and branches picked up at random, and set a match to it, the odds are that it will result in nothing but a quick blaze that soon dies down to a smudge. Yet that is the way most of us tried to make our first outdoor fires.

One glance at a camper's fire tells what kind of a woodsman he is. If one would have good meals cooked out of doors, and would save much time and vexation —in other words, if he wants to be comfortable in the woods, he must learn how to produce at will either (1) a quick, hot little fire that will boil water in a jiffy, and will soon burn down to embers that are not too ardent for frying; or (2) a solid bed of long-lived coals that will keep up a steady, glowing, smokeless heat for baking, roasting, or slow boiling; or (3) a big log fire that will throw its heat forward on the ground, and into a tent or lean-to, and will last several hours without replenishing.

These arts are not so simple as they look. To practice them successfully in all sorts of wild regions we must know the different species of trees one from another, and their relative fuel values, which, as we shall see, vary a great deal. We must know how well, or ill, each of them burns in a green state, as well as when seasoned. It is important to discriminate between wood that makes lasting coals and such as soon dies down to ashes. Some kinds of wood pop violently when burning and cast out embers that may burn holes in tents and bedding or set the neighborhood afire; others burn quietly, with clear, steady flame. Some are stubborn to split, others almost fall apart under the axe. In wet weather it takes a practiced woodsman to find tinder and dry wood, and to select a natural shelter where fire can be kept going during a storm of rain or snow, when a fire is most needed.

Choosing Fuel.

There are several handy little manuals by which one who has no botanical knowledge can soon learn how to identify the different species of trees by merely examining their leaves; or, late in the season, by their bark, buds, and habit of growth.*

But no book gives the other information that I have referred to; so I shall offer, in the present chapter, a little rudimentary instruction in this important branch of woodcraft.

It is convenient for our purpose to divide the trees into two great groups, hardwoods and softwoods, using these terms not so loosely as lumbermen do, but drawing the line between sycamore, yellow birch, yellow

*A complete manual of the trees of the United States and Canada is C. S. Sargent's *Manual of Trees* (Houghton, Boston). A handsomely illustrated work of general scope is Julia Roger's *The Tree Book* (Doubleday, N. Y.). Less expensive works which suffice to identify the trees of northeastern America are H. L. Keeler's *Our Native Trees* (Scribner, N. Y.); F. S. Mathews' *Familiar Trees and Their Leaves* (Appleton, N. Y.); Alice Lounsberry's *Guide to the Trees* (Stokes, N. Y.); C. S. Newhall's *Trees of Northeastern America* (Putnam, N. Y.); H. E. Parkhurst's *Trees, Shrubs and Vines of the Northeastern United States* (Scribner, N. Y.). On southern trees, Alice Lounsberry's *Southern Wild Flowers and Trees* (Stokes, N. Y.) is a convenient field-book. Simple methods for identifying trees after the fall of leaves are given in A. O. Huntington's *Studies of Trees in Winter* (Caldwell, Boston).

pine, and slippery elm, on the one side, and red cedar, sassafras, pitch pine and white birch, on the other.

As a general rule, hardwoods make good, slow-burning fuel that yields lasting coals, and softwoods make a quick, hot fire that is soon spent. But each species has peculiarities that deserve close attention. The knack of finding what we want in the woods lies a good deal in knowing what we *don't* want, and passing it by at a glance.

Uninflammable Woods.

The following woods will scarcely burn at all when they are green: aspen (large-toothed), black ash, balsam, box elder, buckeye, pitch pine, sassafras, sourwood, sycamore, tamarack, tupelo (sour gum), water oak, poplar (tulip), service berry. Butternut, chestnut, red oak, red maple, and persimmon burn very slowly in a green state. Such woods are good for backlogs, hand-junks or andirons, and for side-logs in a cooking-fire that is to be used continuously. Yellow birch and white ash, on the contrary, are better for a camp-fire when green than when they are seasoned. It may be said, in general, that green wood burns best in winter, when the sap is down. Trees that grow on high, dry ground burn better than those of the same species that stand in moist soil. Chestnut cut on the summits of the southern Appalachians burns freely, even when green, and the mountain beech burns as ardently as birch.

Spitfire Woods.

Arbor-vitæ (northern "white cedar") and chestnut burn to dead coals that do not communicate flame. They, as well as box elder, red cedar, hemlock, sassafras, tulip, balsam, tamarack, and spruce, make a great crackling and snapping in the fire. All of the soft pines, too, are prone to pop. Certain hardwoods, such as sugar maple, beech, white oak, and sometimes hickory, must be watched for a time after the fire is started, because the embers that they shoot out are long-lived, and hence more dangerous than those of softwoods; but they are splendid fuel for all that. Split logs are more likely to snap from the outside than from the inside, and should be laid with the heart-side out.

Woods that are hard to split are enumerated in the chapter on *Axemanship.* It should be noted, however, that some woods which are very stubborn when seasoned are easily split while green, such as hickory, beech, dogwood, sugar maple, birch, slippery elm.

Stubborn Woods.

Best of all firewoods is hickory, green or dry. It makes a hot fire, but lasts a long time, burning down to a bed of hard coals that keep up an even, generous heat for hours. Hickory, by the way, is distinctly an American tree; no other region on earth produces it. Following the hickory, in fuel value, are the chestnut oak, overcup, post, and basket oaks, pecan, the hornbeams (ironwoods), and dogwood. The latter burns finally to a beautiful white ash that is characteristic; apple wood does the same. Black birch also ranks here; it has the advantage of "doing its own blowing," as a Carolina mountaineer said to me the other day, meaning that the oil in the birch assists its combustion so that the wood needs no coaxing. All of the birches are good fuel, ranking in about this order: black, yellow, red, paper, and white. Sugar maple was the favorite fuel of our old-time hunters and surveyors, because it ignites easily, burns with a clear, steady flame, and leaves good coals; but it is too valuable a tree, nowadays, to be cast into the fire, save where a hopelessly defective one is found.

The Best Fuel.

Locust is a good, lasting fuel; it is easy to cut, and, when green, splits fairly well; the thick bark takes fire readily, and the wood then burns slowly, with little flame, leaving pretty good coals; hence it is good for night-wood. Mulberry has similar qualities. The best of the oaks for fuel, especially when green, is white oak; it also splits very readily. The scarlet and willow oaks are among the poorest of the hardwoods for fuel. Cherry makes only fair fuel. White elm is poor stuff, but slippery elm is better.

In some respects white ash is the best of green woods

for campers' fuel. It is easily cut and split, is lighter to tote than most other hardwoods, and is of so dry a nature that even the green wood catches fire readily. It burns with clear flame, and lasts longer than any other free-burning wood of its weight.

Softwoods Inferior.

Most of the softwoods are good only for kindling, or for quick cooking-fires. Liquidambar, magnolia, poplar (tulip), catalpa, red cedar, and willow are poor fuel. Seasoned chestnut and tulip split easily and make a hot fire, but crackle and leave no coals. Balsam fir, basswood, and the white and loblolly pines make quick fires but are soon spent. The gray (Labrador) pine is considered good fuel in the far North, where hardwoods are scarce. Seasoned tamarack is fairly good. Spruce is poor fuel, although, being resinous, it kindles easily and makes a good blaze for "branding up" a fire. Sycamore and buckeye, when thoroughly seasoned, are good fuel, but hard to split. Alder burns readily and gives out considerable heat, but is not lasting. The wood of the large-toothed aspen will not burn in a green state, but when dry it burns freely, does not crackle, lasts well, and leaves good coals. The best green softwoods for fuel are white birch, paper birch, soft maple, cottonwood, and quaking aspen. For a cooking-fire that will burn quickly to coals, without smoke, the bark of dead hemlock, hickory, pine, or sugar maple cannot be excelled.

Driftwood.

As a rule, the timber growing along the margins of large streams is softwood. Hence driftwood is generally a poor mainstay for an all-night fire, unless there is plenty of it on the spot.

Kindling.

Besides kindling and the firewood proper, one often needs some kind of tinder to start a fire. The bark of all species of birch is excellent for this purpose, as well as for torches. It is full of resinous oil, blazes up at once, will burn in any wind, and wet sticks can be kindled with it. The shredded inner bark of dead cedar or cottonwood burns like paper.

Tinder will not be needed if pine knots, or splits of dry pine, or cedar, can be procured. Pine knots are the heavy, resinous stubs of limbs that are found on dead pine trees They are almost imperishable, and those sticking out from old rotten logs are as good as any. Pitch pine affords the best knots. The knots of balsam fir are similarly used; but hemlock knots are worthless. A good way to start a fire is to take three such knots, whittle some shavings from their less resinous small ends, without detaching the shavings, set the knots up as a tripod, butts together, small ends down, and shavings touching—then light the latter. Splits from a pine stump that has been burned on the outside are fat with resin. A stump may often be found that has rotted nearly to the ground but has a sound, dry core from which good kindling can be split.

In a hardwood forest the best kindling, sure to be dry underneath the bark in all weathers, is procured by snapping off the small dead branches, or stubs of branches, that are left on the trunks of medium-sized trees. Do not pick up twigs from the ground, but choose those, among the downwood, that are held up free from the ground. Where a tree is found that has been shivered by lightning, or one that has broken off without uprooting, good splinters of dry wood will be found. In every laurel thicket there is plenty of dead laurel, and, since it is of sprangling growth, most of the branches will be free from the ground and snap-dry. They ignite readily and give out intense heat.

It is a good test of one's resourcefulness to make a fire out of doors in rainy weather. The best way to go about it depends upon local conditions. Dry fuel, and a place to build the fire, can often be found under big uptilted logs, shelving rocks, and similar natural shelters, or in the core of an old stump. In default of these, look for a dead softwood tree that leans to the south. The wood and bark on the under side will be dry—chop some off, split it fine, and build your fire under the shelter of the trunk, if you want to

Making Fire in Wet Weather.

use it for only a short time. If it is necessary to camp in the rain without artificial shelter, and no rocky ledge can be found, pick out a big green tree the larger the better—that leans a good deal. Be sure that it is big enough not to be weakened by an all-night fire. If the rain is driving, and you have a blanket, lean a couple of saplings against the tree and spread your blanket over them to shelter the fire until it is well started, or lean large sticks or splits against the tree, in the shape of half a cone, leaving a cavity at the base in which you can insert kindling.

To Light a Match in the Wind.

Face the wind. Cup your hands, backs toward wind, match held with its head pointing toward rear of cup —*i.e.*, toward the wind. Remove right hand just long enough to strike match on something very close by; then instantly resume former position. Flame of match will run up the stick, instead of blowing away from it.

Making Fire without Matches.

Fire may be made without matches by drawing the bullet or shot from a cartridge, pouring out all but about one-fourth of the charge, putting the cartridge in the gun (muzzle up), and loosely ramming down a piece of dry cotton cloth upon it. Fire the gun either toward the ground or straight up into the air; it will ignite the rag. One should have some punk or tinder by him at the time.

Tinder.

Punk is of two kinds: (1) dry fungus, such as the shelf-like toadstools (*polyphori*) that grow on the boles of trees (oak, maple, birch, beech, locust, especially), not the hard, woody fungi, but those that are soft and leathery; also dried puff-balls; (2) wood that has decayed from a fungus growth ("conkesy," "dozed" or "dotey" wood, it is called by timbermen), such as is often found in dead trees or stumps, or under the excrescences of growing maples, birches, and other trees. Green toadstools can soon be dried out before the fire. The inner part of such a fungus, as well as dozed wood, will ignite readily from a spark, but does not flame, and will carry fire for hours. It makes a very good smudge to drive away mosquitoes.

Extemporized tinder is quickly made by tearing (not cutting) a strip of cotton cloth, leaving the edges fluffy, and rolling it up like a roller bandage, leaving one end projecting a little; into this end rub crushed gunpowder, leaving a few grains uncrushed, or the ashes of a cigar will do. The ashes of tobacco, Indian corn, sunflower, and some other plants, contain enough saltpeter to make good touch-paper by rubbing them into cloth or soft paper. Dry dung, especially horse-dung, when broken up, takes a spark readily, and so do dried moss and dried willow catkins.

Sparks may be struck from flint, quartz, or pyrites, by striking them a glancing blow with the back of a knife, or other piece of hard steel. It takes more skill to catch the spark than to produce it. When the sun shines, the lens of a camera, field-glass, or telescope sight may be used as a burning-glass. Even a watch crystal, removed, and three-fourths filled with water, forms a lens that, if held very steadily, will ignite punk or tinder.

How to Build a Fire.

To make a fire burn well there is one thing even more necessary than kindling or firewood, and that is *air.* It is from neglecting this invisible factor that most novices fail. The fuel must not be tumbled together; it must be built systematically, so that air can draw under it and upward through it, even after the tinder and small kindling have burned up. The latter should never be used to support the larger sticks.

The best way to make a fire quickly, and one that is sure to keep on burning as long as it is fed, is, first, to lay two good-sized sticks on the ground as a foundation, then across them at right angles lay a course of dry twigs or splinters, not quite touching each other; on these, at one side, place your tinder, of paper, bark, or whatever it may be; then on top of this put two other cross-sticks, smaller than the bed-sticks; over this a cross-layer of larger twigs, and so on, building the pile cob-house style, and gradually increasing the size of the sticks. Such a pile will roar within half a minute after a match is touched to it, and if the upper courses are of split hickory, or other good hardwood, it will all burn down to live coals together.

In cold weather, when the camp-fire is depended upon to keep the men warm all night, it should be built higher than the general level of the camp, first, because you will get more heat from a fire built somewhat higher than your bed, and, second, because, unless it is built upon a rock, or hard, naked earth, it will eat its way down in the forest refuse.

There are forty-eleven ways of building a camp-fire; but only three of them are basic and orthodox. The others are mere variants, or schisms, from the true faith. The three are: (1) the hunter's fire; (2) the trapper's fire; (3) the Indian's fire. This is how to build them:

The Hunter's Fire.—Best for a shifting camp, because it affords, first, a quick cooking-fire with proper supports for the utensils, and afterward a good camp-fire for the night when the weather is not severe. Select a tree not less than a foot thick at the butt (ash or softwood if you have not a full-sized axe). Fell it, and cut from the butt end two logs about six feet long. Lay these side by side, about fifteen inches apart at one end and six or eight inches at the other. Lay a course of small, dry sticks across the middle of them, and on this place your tinder. At each end of this course lay a green hand-junk, about eight inches thick, to support the larger wood. Across them, parallel with the bed-logs, lay dry sticks, and on them build a cob-house of short split wood that will make coals. Fill in with small kindling around the tinder, and touch it off. The upper courses of wood will soon burn to coals, which will drop between the logs and set them to blazing on the inner side. After supper, night-wood is piled on top of the junks. In the morning there will be fine coals with which to cook breakfast.

The Trapper's Fire.—Best for a fixed camp in cold weather, before a lean-to or shanty tent. If there is no big bowlder or ledge of rocks on the camp site, build a wall of rocks about six feet in front of the lean-to, with two stone "andirons" at right angles to them; or, drive two big stakes in the ground, slanting backward, against them pile on top of each other three logs at least a foot thick, and place two thick, short hand-junks in front of them to support the fore-stick. Select for this purpose green wood that is hard to burn. Plaster mud in the crevices between the logs, around the bottom of stakes, and around the rear end of hand-junks, for otherwise the fire will quickly attack these places. Such a fireplace is meant to reflect the heat forward, conduct the smoke upward, and serve as a windbreak in front of camp. Build the fire between the hand-junks, and cut plenty of six-foot logs for night-wood. Have a separate cooking-fire off to one side.

The Indian's Fire.—Best where fuel is scarce, or when one has only a small hatchet with which to cut night-wood. Fell and trim a lot of hardwood saplings. Lay three or four of them on the ground, butts on top of each other, tips radiating from this center like the spokes of a wheel. On and around this center build a small, hot fire. Place butts of other saplings on this, radiating like the others. As the wood burns away, shove the sticks in toward the center, butts on top of each other, as before. This saves much chopping, and economizes fuel. Build a little windbreak behind you, and lie close to the fire. Doubtless you have heard the Indian's dictum (southern Indians express it just as the northern and western ones do): "White man heap fool; make um big fire—can't git near; Injun make um little fire—git close. Uh, good!"

Fires built especially for purposes of cookery will be described hereafter.

CHAPTER IX

MARKSMANSHIP IN THE WOODS

OUT of the thousands of men who go out every fall to hunt with the rifle, only a few have any opportunities, during the close season, for rifle practice under conditions similar to those they will meet in the wilderness. By far the larger number must be content with such facilities as they can find on a rifle range, where the shooting is done at known distances, over a clear field, at stationary targets, and with no time limit.

The fortunate few who live all the year 'round in thinly settled regions, where they can try their rifles in the woods whenever they feel like it, are prone to think lightly of the city man's rifle clubs. I will never forget the remark that a backwoodsman once made when I was trying to entertain him at a rifle match near St. Louis. I had shown him the shooting-house, the target-house, and their appurtenances; had explained our system of scoring and our code of rules; had told him the reasons for using such heavy rifles, sensitive triggers, pronged butt-plates, cheek-pieces, palm-rests, vernier and wind-gauge sights—all that; and then I bade him watch some of our experts as they made bull's-eye after bull's-eye, seldom missing a space the size of a man's head, shooting offhand, at 200 measured yards. I thought that my friend would be impressed. He was; but not quite as I had anticipated. After watching the firing for a long time in silence, he turned to me and remarked: "If it weren't for the noise and the powder smoke, this would be a very ladylike game."

Of course, I was piqued at this, and felt like giving the honest fellow a peppery reply. And yet, many a time since, as I have sat, chilled to the bone, on some crossing in the high Smokies, straining my ears for the bear-dogs far below; or, tired beyond speech and faint from hunger, as I lay down beside a log in the great forest, all alone; or, blown by hard climbing till my heart seemed bursting, as I wiped the mist from my eyes, and got down on all fours to follow a fresh spoor into the hideous laurel fastness of Godforsaken—aye, many a time I have looked backward and thought, "You were right, partner; it was a very ladylike game."

But let us not be too hard on the city man's rifle range. It is all he has, to burn powder on, and it is far better than no range at all. The pity is that he does not make better use of it. (I speak now of civilian, not military, ranges.) It was a blunder when we abandoned the old Standard American rules, which did at least recognize the rifle as a weapon instead of a toy, and were led astray by a foreign system for which we have not yet found so much as an English name. The "schuetzen" system does teach a man to hold steadily and to let off delicately, and this is the A B C of marksmanship. But it stops there. It teaches the A B C forward and backward till the pupil becomes, perhaps, wonderfully expert in such exercise; but it never gets beyond A B C and Z Y X. It weds a man to a toy, so that any practical weapon seems awkward to him. It teaches him to drive a nail with a bullet; but it makes him too slow—altogether too slow for the man's game of hunting or war. The most hopeful sign of our time, from a rifleman's viewpoint, is the move to establish, near all of our large cities, military rifle ranges, to which civilians will be admitted for target practice. Offhand shooting at the shorter ranges with regular hunting rifles, or with military rifles, together with skirmish drill, is excellent training for hunters of big game.

But in any case, practice! Use a .22 in a city basement, if you can do no better. It is practice, intelligently varied practice, that makes the marksman.

As for a hunting rifle, get the best that you can, of course; but do not worship it. Bear in mind that, whatever its trajectory and killing power, it is only a gun, and can kill nothing that you miss with it. When you get into the real wilderness, far away from rich men's preserves and summer hotels, you will find there some mighty hunters who make mighty kills with guns of the vintage of 1866, or earlier—guns that would bring only the price of scrap-iron in New York.

Get sights that you can *see*, and such as you are not likely to overshoot with when taking quick aim. Take pains to get what suits your eyes, and spare no time in the adjustment. Never take an untried gun into the woods. That is no place to align sights and test elevations. Never trust the sights as they are placed on the gun at the factory. Test them not only from rest, but offhand, too; for a light rifle charged with high-power ammunition is likely to shoot several inches higher (or in some other direction) when fired from muzzle-and-elbow rest, at 50 yards, than it does when shot offhand, albeit it may be an accurate weapon when rightly used.

Now, as for adjusting the elevation—a most important matter—first, by all means, find the "point-blank" of your weapon by actual test. Take nobody's say-so for it. If your dealer assures you that a certain rifle shoots practically point-blank up to 200 or 300 yards, "trust him not; he's fooling thee." Never lose sight of the fact that, in a timbered country, nine-tenths of big game is shot inside of 75 yards. Now it is a prime essential that your rifle should be so sighted that its bullet will not rise or fall outside a one-inch circle at 25 yards, a two-inch circle at 50 yards, a three-inch circle at 75 yards. If it has been sighted to strike center at 200 yards, it will shoot far above these limits at the short distances here mentioned, no matter how powerful may be the charge. Let me give an example, to show how easily one can be fooled in such matters:

Here is a high-power rifle. The initial velocity of its bullet is 2,000 feet a second; trajectory $5\frac{1}{2}$ inches at 100 yards, when shot 200 yards. At the factory the sights have been set for the latter distance, by aiming with top of bead just touching bottom of an eight-inch bull's-eye. In other words, the gun shoots four inches above the point actually aimed at. Now, at 100 yards this gun will shoot two inches too high, plus the trajectory ($5\frac{1}{2}$ inches), minus sight allowance (angle of line of aim to line of fire depending upon height of front sight above axis of bore—say one-half-inch allowance midway of range)—that is to say, this rifle shoots seven inches too high at 100 yards! Is that "practically point-blank"? How would you like it?

As a general rule, a high-power rifle for hunting big game should have its sights adjusted, with precision, for two distances, namely, to strike *the point actually aimed at*, when shooting offhand, first at 80 yards, and (second adjustment) at 160 yards. Then fix the rear sight so that it cannot work down below the 80-yard point, and notch the 160-yard point so you can feel it with your thumb-nail, without looking. With the 80-yard elevation your rifle will shoot on a line practically level up to 100 yards; with the 160-yard elevation it is "good" for a deer's vitals at any distance up to 200 yards, under all conditions that make such long shots justifiable. It will not shoot over nor under an eight-inch circle at any distance up to 200 yards, when aimed for the center. But carry the rifle habitually with sight set for 80 yards; then you can decapitate a grouse or squirrel, strike a bear through the eye at close quarters, and kill a deer 100 yards away when only his head is visible, without making any allowance for distance in either case—always provided, my brother, that your own part of the performance is up to scratch. A rifle using black powder should be sighted for 50 and 100 yards, respectively.

As for trigger-pull, suit yourself; but never tolerate a trigger that will easily jar off. Remember, too, that your trigger finger will soon get calloused in the woods, and that it will often be numb with cold.

Have a sling-strap on your gun, particularly if you are to hunt in the mountains.

Take only one kind of ammunition when you go after big game. On such a trip one seldom shoots at small fry, unless the large animals fail to show themselves; even then, one shoots no more than he needs, and if he does occasionally blow a grouse to pieces it doesn't matter. If he should take along both full-power and reduced charges, he would always be fussing over his elevations, and he might some day find himself with a squirrel load in his gun, confronting a moose. Be sparing in your load of ammunition. When one hunts large game, even where it is plentiful and unprotected, he will not average two shots a day, allowing liberally for misses and for pot-boilers on small game.

Fifty rounds are ample for a two-months' trip into farthest no-man's land, and twenty are enough for a month wherever the number of heads allowed is limited. Remember what a weight of lead you carried around last year, and how much of it you lugged back home, or gave away.

The targets offered by large animals in the woods are about as different as anything could be from the targets used on rifle ranges. If you are still-hunting, the odds are long that you will not see the game until it is sneaking stealthily but swiftly away. Then there are trees in the way, and brush; your footing may not be secure; the light may be shining in your eyes; and, with it all, you must shoot quick, or lose the opportunity. Yet, if you shoot so quickly that you merely aim at the animal as a whole, instead of at some one particular spot, the chances are that you will miss altogether—yes, miss a full-grown deer at twenty paces. The points to be observed are: To be as alert at all times as though you were hunting grouse without a dog; to get your gun in position the instant that you see the game; to pick out, as quick as lightning, a clear space through which to fire; but, *above all things*, not to shoot until you are absolutely certain that it is game you are shooting at; and then to dwell on the aim just long enough to see your bead clearly and to hold for a vital spot. Beyond that, do not hesitate the fraction of a second. To give a novice an idea, I would say that three or four seconds is a fair average interval between raising the rifle and firing, when a deer has been jumped in the forest. It is not so much the hands, but the eyes and brain, that must be quick, very quick.

Of course, this is only a general proposition. Many times one has a chance for deliberate aim (though not often when he is still-hunting). Yet I think it is best to spend most of one's target ammunition in snap-shooting. By snap-shooting with the rifle I do not mean merely glancing along the barrel and disregarding the sights. You must see your bead, and, in casc of open sights, you must see that the bead is well down in the notch; but it is snap-shooting to press the trigger instantly when it first touches, or rather when it swings close to, the object that you want to hit, instead of waiting to swing back and steady down, as one would do when aiming deliberately. To snap-shoot at the right instant, without pulling off to one side, is a fine art.

The main trouble, in such cases, is to select the right spot to shoot at, and then to find it over the sights. With a deer, for example, the color is so neutral and the outlines are so indistinct, even in good light, that a man's eyes can seldom distinguish the exact spot that he wants to hit. He judges where it must be, from the general bulk of the animal and the position in which it is presented.

For a broadside shot, the best point to shoot for is immediately behind the shoulder and only one-third of the way up from breast to withers—that is, where the heart lies. When the body is presented in any other position, shoot, as a rule, at such a point that the bullet, in ranging forward, will pass through or close to the heart. When an animal stands looking at me as a deer often will when it comes in on a runway and one bleats or whistles at it, my favorite shot is the neck. A bullet passing through any animal's neck is almost sure to strike a paralyzing, knock-out blow, because it can scarcely miss a vital part.

In shooting at a running animal, when you are in the timber, do not hold first on the beast and then swing ahead; but pick out an open space that the game will cross, and shoot an instant before it crosses. Then you will, at least, not send your bullet *whack* into an intervening tree.

Aim low when shooting downhill, because then you see more of the upper side of the animal than you ordinarily would. A shot high up is seldom fatal, unless you hit the spine. In making long shots downhill, do not forget that the only distance to be allowed for is that from the mark to a point directly *under* you and *level with the mark.*

Aim dead-on when shooting uphill, unless the range is greater than your rifle is sighted for on a level. The extra allowance for "lift" is so trifling at ordinary ranges that you had better disregard it than overdo the matter.

Deliberate shooting, as distinguished from snap-shooting, can often be practiced at game in an open country, such as many parts of the West. In the East and South, nearly all shooting is in thick timber, although one sometimes gets a shot over the water. Long shots at game standing clearly outlined against the sky or water call for no comment, as they are comparatively easy for one who has had considerable experience on the rifle range, if he does not misjudge the distance and sighting allowance—and if he does not get buck-ague.

This latter affliction is more likely to seize upon the novice when he is sitting on a stand and hears the dogs baying toward him. It is hard on a fellow's nerves to sit there, praying with all his soul that the bear may not run some other way, and yet half doubtful of his own ability to head it off if it does come his way. The chances are that it will by no means run over him, but that it will come crashing through the brush at some point on one side, toward which he will have to run with all his might and main before firing. Now if he does let that bear go through, after all the hard work of dogs and drivers, his shirt-tail will be amputated that night by his comrades and hung from a high pole in the midst of the camp—a flag of distress indeed! Who wouldn't get buck-ague in the face of such alternative?

It is hard on a fellow's nerves, I say, to hear those dogs coming toward him, and to know from the racket

A Good Day's Shoot

An Ideal Camp Fire

that a bear is certainly ahead of them, but *not* to know where or when the brute may emerge, nor what infernal trees and thicket and downwood may be in the way. Can you hit him? That is the question. The honor of the camp is on your shoulders. Ah, me! it is easy to follow the pack on horseback—to chase after something that is running away. But to sit here chewing your mustache while at any moment a hard-pressed and angry bear may burst out of the thicket and find you in his way—nothing but you between him and near-by freedom—gentlemen, it tests nerve! Ask any old soldier whether he would rather charge or *be* charged.

Buck-ague is not the effect of fear. In fact, fear has nothing to do with it. It is a tremor and a galloping of the heart that comes from over-anxiety lest you should fail to score. Precisely the same seizure may come upon you on the target range. That is the only place that I ever experienced it. There is no telling when it may strike. I have known seasoned sportsmen to be victimized by it. Yet, when the critical moment does come, it often turns out that the man who has been shaking like a leaf from pent-up anxiety suddenly grows cold and steady as a rock. Especially is this apt to be the case when a fighting beast comes suddenly in view. Instantly the man's primeval instincts are aroused; his fighting blood comes to the surface; the spirit of some warrior ancestor (dead, maybe, these thousand years) possesses and sways your mild-eyed modern man, and he who trembled but a moment ago now leaps into the combat with a wild joy playing on his heart strings.

CHAPTER X

DRESSING AND KEEPING GAME AND FISH

BUTCHERING is the most distasteful part of a hunter's work—a job to be sublet when you can; but sometimes you can't.

When an animal is shot, the first thing to do is to bleed it. Even birds and fish should be bled as soon as secured. The meat keeps better, and, in the case of a bird, the feathers are more easily plucked. Speaking, now, of large game, do not drop your gun and rush in on a dying beast to stick it, for it might prove an ugly customer in its death struggle. First put a bullet through its heart or spine.

To cut a deer's throat would ruin the head for mounting. Twist its head to one side, with the throat downhill, if possible, so that blood will not flow over the hide; then stick your knife in at the point of the breast, just in front of the sternum or breastbone, and work the point of the knife two or three inches back and forth, close up to the backbone, so as to sever the great blood-vessels. Then if you must hurry on, perhaps after another animal, toss some brush over the carcass, or hang a handkerchief over it, to suggest a trap, and make a brush blaze here and there as you go along, to guide you back to the spot.

If practicable, remove the entrails at once. To do this, it is not necessary to hang the animal up. If you are in a hurry, or if the camp is not far away, it will do merely to take out the paunch and intestines; but if this is neglected putrefaction will soon set in. A bear, especially, will soon spoil, because the fur keeps in the vital heat, so that the body will smoke when opened, even after it has lain a long time in hard-freezing weather.

If the ground is not too rough, nor the distance too

great, a deer may be dragged to camp over the snow or leaves; but drag it head-foremost; if pulled the other way every hair will act as a barb against the ground. Before starting, tie the front legs to the lower jaw. The carcass will slide easier, and the hide will not be so disfigured, if you first drop a bush or small tree by cutting through the roots, leaving a stub of a root projecting for a handle, then tie the animal on the upper side of the bush, and drag away.

Dragging a Deer.

To pack a deer on horseback: first, if your horse is green in the business, let him smell the deer, pet him, and, if necessary, blindfold him until you get the carcass lashed in place. Even then you may have trouble. I have seen a mule get such a conniption fit at the smell of blood that he bucked himself, deer, and saddle, off a cut-bank into a swift river; the girth broke, and that saddle is going yet.

Packing Deer on a Saddle.

Re-cinch your saddle, and, if the deer is too heavy to lift upon the horse's back, fasten your picket-rope to the deer's hind legs, throw the line over the saddle, get on the other side, and haul away until the deer's hocks are up even with the saddle; then quickly snub the rope around the saddle-horn, go around, swing the burden over the saddle, balancing it evenly, and lash it fast. Or, if you wish to ride, move the deer behind the saddle and lash it there, bringing the legs forward on either side and tying them to the rings of the cinch. For thongs, cut strips from the skin of the deer's fore legs. Be sure to fasten the load securely, so that it cannot slip, or you will have a badly frightened horse. By skinning the legs from hoofs to ankles, partly disarticulating the latter, and then tying the legs snugly, they will not dangle and scare the horse, nor catch in underbrush.

Two men can carry a deer on a pole by tying its legs together in pairs, slipping the pole through, and tying the head to the pole. Unless the carcass is tied snugly to the pole, such a burden will swing like a pendulum as you trudge along, especially if the pole is at all springy.

Carrying on a Litter.

A more comfortable way is to make a litter of two poles by laying them parallel, about two and one-half feet apart, and nailing or tying cross-pieces athwart the poles. Whittle the ends of the poles to a size con-

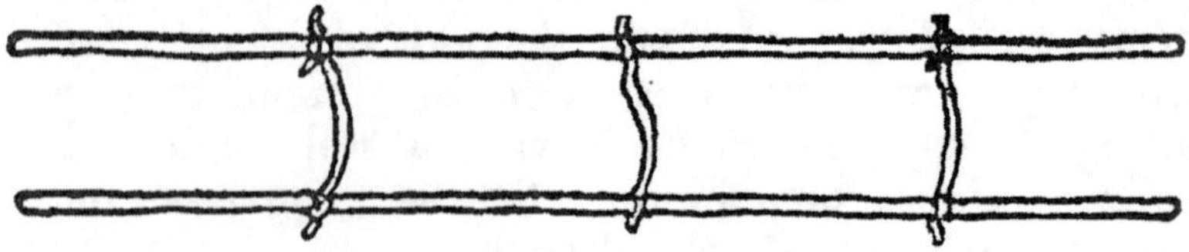

Diagram of an Improvised Litter for Carrying a Deer.

venient for your hands, and fasten to each end of the litter a broad strap, in such a way that it may pass over the shoulders of the carrier and thus take up much of the weight. Then lash the animal securely to the top of the litter.

One man can carry a small deer entire by dragging it to a fallen tree, boosting it up on the log, lengthwise and back down, then grasping the hind legs with one hand and the fore legs with the other, and carrying the load so that its weight is on the back of his neck and shoulders.

Carrying Single-handed.

A better scheme is to cut a slit through the lower jaw and up through the mouth, and another slit through each of the legs between the tendons, just above the hoof; tie the head and legs together, but not too close, and then, by the loop thus formed, swing the burden over your shoulder.

To carry a larger animal pickaback: gut it, cut off the head and hang it up to be called for later, skin the legs down to the knees and hocks, cut off the shin-bones, tie the skin of each fore leg to the hind leg on the same side, put the arms through the loops thus formed, and "git ep!" Or, remove the bones from the fore legs from knee to foot, leaving the feet on, tie the hind legs together and the fore legs to them, thrust your head and one arm through, and carry the burden as a soldier does a blanket-roll.

When one has a long way to go, and can only carry

the hide and the choicer parts of the meat, the best way is to make up an Indian pack, as shown in the illustration. Skin the deer, place a stick athwart the inside of the skin, pack the saddles, hams, and tid-bits in the latter, and roll up and tie in a convenient bundle.

The Indian Pack.

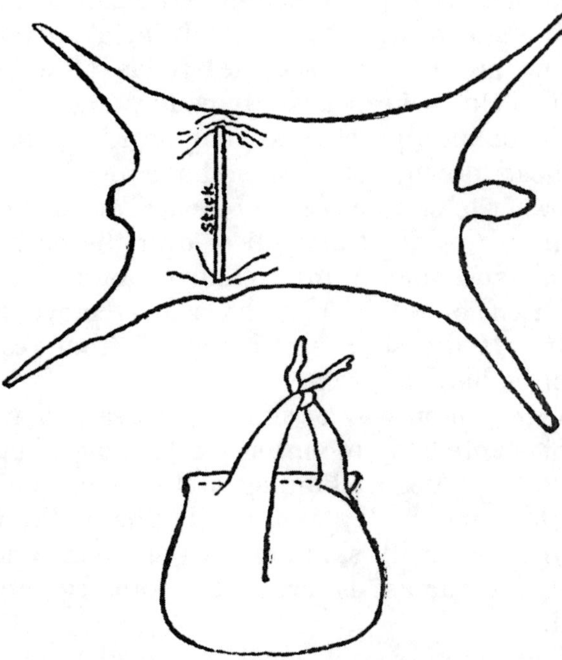

FIG. 6. The Indian Pack.

It is not necessary to hang a deer up to skin and butcher it; but that is the more cleanly way. One man, unassisted, can hang a pretty heavy animal in the following way: Drag it headforemost to a sapling that is just limber enough to bend near the ground when you climb it. Cut three poles, ten or twelve feet long, with crotches near the ends. Climb the sapling and trim off the top, leaving the stub of one stout branch near the top. Tie your belt into a loop around the deer's antlers or throat. Bend the sapling down until you can slip the loop over the end of the sapling. The latter, acting as a spring-pole, will lift part of the deer's

Hanging to Butcher.

weight. Then place the crotches of the poles under the fork of the sapling, the butts of the poles radiating outward, thus forming a tripod. Push first on one pole, then on another, and so raise the carcass free from the ground. If you do not intend to butcher it immediately, raise it up out of reach of roving dogs and "varmints," and put a smudge under it of rotten wood, well banked with stones and earth so that it cannot blow around and set the woods afire. The smudge will help to keep away blow-flies and birds of prey. It is common practice to hang deer by gambrels with the head down; but, when hung head up, the animal is easier to skin, easier to butcher, drains better, and does not drip blood and juices over the neck and head, which you may want to have mounted for a trophy. Dried blood is very hard to remove from hair or fur. If the skin is stripped off from rear to head it will be hard to grain.

The more common way of skinning a deer, when the head is not wanted for mounting, is to hang it up by one hind leg and begin skinning at the hock, peeling the legs, then the body, and finally the neck, then removing the head with skin on (for baking in a hole), after which the carcass is swung by both legs and is eviscerated.

Butchering Deer.

Now let us suppose that you have killed a deer far away from camp, and that you wish to skin and butcher it on the spot, saving all parts of it that are good for anything. You are alone. You wish to make a workmanlike job of it. You can carry only the choicer parts with you that evening, and must fix the rest so that it will not be molested over night.

Of course, you have a jackknife, and either a pocket hatchet or a big bowie-knife—probably the latter, if this is your first trip. First hang the deer, as described above. By the time you are through cutting those poles with your knife your hand will ache between thumb and forefinger; a tomahawk would have been better.

Skinning.—This is your first buck, and you wish to

save the head for mounting. For this, the skin of the whole neck must be preserved, clear back to the shoulders. Cleanse away any blood that may have issued from the nose and mouth, and stuff some dry moss, or other absorbent, in the beast's mouth. Stick your big knife into a log alongside: it is only to look at, for the present. Open your jackknife, insert the point, edge up, where the neck joins the back, and cut the skin in a circle around the base of the neck, running from the withers down over the front of the shoulder-blade to the brisket or point of the breast on each side. Do not skin the head at present—you may not have time for that. Insert the point of the knife through the skin over the paunch, and, following the middle line of the chest, slit upward to meet the cut around the neck. Then reverse, and continue the slit backward to the end of the tail, being careful not to perforate the walls of the belly. Then slit along the inside of each leg from the hoof to the belly slit. If you wish to save the feet for mounting, be particular to rip the skin in a straight line up the *under* side of the leg, starting by inserting the point of the knife between the heel-pads.

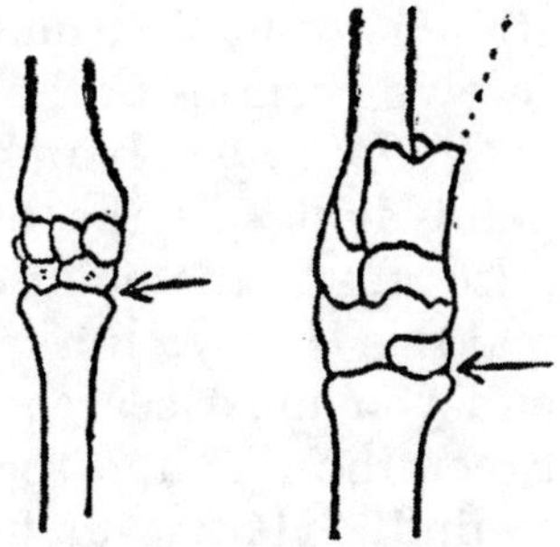

FIG. 7. —→ The Place to Use Your Knife.
From *Forest and Stream.*

Now comes a nice trick, that of severing the shanks. Nearly every inexperienced person starts too high. Study the accompanying illustrations of these joints, noting where the arrow points, which is the place to use your knife. In a deer the joint is about an inch and a half below the hock on the hind leg, and an inch below the knee on the fore leg. Cut square across through skin and muscles, in front, and similarly behind; then, with a quick pull backward against your knee, snap the shank off. The joint of the fore leg is broken in a similar manner, excepting that it is snapped forward.

Having stripped the vertebræ from the tail, now peel

the skin off the whole animal, from the shoulders downward, assisting with your closed fist, and, where necessary, with the knife; but wherever the knife is used be careful to scrape the skin as clean as you can, without cutting it, for every adhering bit of fat, flesh, or membrane must be thoroughly removed before the skin is ready for tanning, and that is easier to do now than after it dries. The whole operation of skinning is much easier while the animal is still warm than after the body has become cold. To skin a frozen animal is a desperately mean job. I have known four old hunters to work nearly a whole afternoon in skinning a frozen bear.

The skin of the body and limbs having been removed, stretch it out flat, hair side down, alongside of you to receive portions of the meat as it is butchered.

Gralloching.—Now take up your big knife, insert its point alongside the breastbone, and cut through the false ribs to the point of the sternum. In a young animal this is easy; but in an old one the ribs have ossified, and you must search for the soft points of union between the ribs and the sternum, which are rather hard to find. Here your knife's temper, and perhaps your own, will be put to the test. The most trifling-looking pocket hatchet would do the trick in a jiffy.

Open the abdominal cavity, taking care not to rupture anything, and prop the chest open a few inches with a stick, or by merely pulling the ribs away from each other. Cut the diaphragm free at both sides and at the back. (It is the membrane that separates the organs of the chest from those of the abdomen.) Everything now is free from the body except at the throat and anus. Reach in and take in your grasp all the vessels that run up into the neck. With knife in the other hand, cut them across from above downward, taking care that you do not cut yourself. Now pull away gradually, helping a little here and there with the knife until all the contents of the visceral cavity lie at your feet, save the lower end of the rectum, which is still attached. With a hatchet, if you had one, you would now split the pelvis. The thing can be done with a large knife, if the animal is not too old, by finding the soft suture at the highest part of the bone and rocking the knife-edge on it. But you may not be able to accomplish this just now. So reach in with the jack-knife, cut carefully around the rectum and urinary organs, keeping as close to the bone as possible, and free everything from the cavity. If water is near, wash out the abdominal cavity and let it drain.

To remove the head: flay back the skin for several inches at base of neck, cut through flesh, etc., to the backbone. Search along this till you find the flat joint between the faces of two vertebræ, separate these as far as you can; then twist the attached part of the body round and round, until it breaks off. Directions how to skin a head for mounting are given in the chapter on *Trophies, etc.*

In butchering, save the liver, heart, brain, milt (spleen), kidneys, and the caul fat. The caul is the fold of membrane loaded with fat that covers most of the intestines. In removing the liver you need not bother about a gall-bladder, for a deer has none. Many a tenderfoot has been tricked into looking for it. In the final cutting up, save the marrow-bones (especially of elk) for eating; the ligaments that lie on either side of the backbone, from the head backward, for sinew thread; the hoofs for glue (if you are far from supply-stores and expect to remain a good while); and perhaps the bladder, paunch, large intestine, and pericardium (outer skin) of the heart, for pouches and receptacles of various kinds, and to make catgut. The scrotum of a buck, tanned with the hair on, makes a good tobacco-pouch.

Butchering on the Ground.

If one is in a hurry, and is not particular about the hide, he can do his butchering on the ground. In that case, lay the animal on sloping ground, with its head uphill; or bend its back over a log or rock; or turn it on its back with its head twisted around and wedged under one side. The old-time way of butchering a buffalo was to turn the carcass on its belly, stretching out the legs on either side to support it. A transverse cut was made at the nape of the neck; then the work man, gathering the long hair of the hump in one hand, separated the skin from the shoulder, laid it open to the tail, along the spine, freed it from the sides, and pulled it down to the brisket. While the skin was thus still attached to the belly it was stretched upon the ground to receive the dissected meat. Then the shoulder was severed, and the fleece, which is the mixed fat and lean that lies along the loin and ribs, was removed from along the backbone, and the hump ribs were cut off with a tomahawk. These portions were placed on the skin, together with the *boudins* from the stomach, and the tongue. The rest of the meat was left to feed the wolves.

Elk and Moose.

In butchering an elk or moose that has antlers, first remove the head. Then turn the body on its back and prop it in position with a couple of three-foot stakes sharpened at both ends, a hole being dug for a moose's withers. Sometimes only the haunches, sirloins and tongue are saved, these being cut away without skinning or gutting the carcass. If a complete job of butchering is to be done, there must be a horse, or several men with a rope, to elevate the body. In this case the lower legs are skinned, the shanks removed, the hide split from throat to tail, the sides skinned free, the windpipe and gullet raised, the pleura and diaphragm cut loose, and the carcass then raised high enough so that the hide can be removed from the rump and back. The rectum, small intestines, and paunch are then loosened and allowed to roll out on the ground. The gullet is cut, the liver taken out, and the diaphragm, lungs and heart removed. Then the skinning is finished over the shoulders and arms. It is best not to cut up the meat until it is quite cold and firm. Then split the carcass in halves along the backbone, and quarter it, leaving one rib on each hind quarter.

Bears are butchered in a similar manner, but without removing the head, of course.

If a hide is to be preserved for some time in a green state, use nothing on it but salt. Spread it out flat, hair side down, stretch the legs, flanks, etc., and rub all parts thoroughly with salt, particular pains being taken to leave no little fold untreated. A moose-hide will take ten or even fifteen pounds of salt. As soon as the salting is done, fold in the legs and roll the hide up.

When a deer has merely been eviscerated and is hung up to be skinned and cut up at a more convenient season, prop open the abdominal cavity with a stick, so that it may dry out quickly. If the weather is warm enough at any hour of the day for flies to come out, keep a smudge going under the carcass. It takes flies but a few minutes to raise Ned with venison. If blows are discovered on the meat, remove them, looking especially at all folds and nicks in the meat, and around the bones, for the blows work into such places very quickly. So long as they have not bored into the flesh they do it no harm.

Care of a Carcass.

It may be said here that even smoked bacon is not immune from blows, and it should not be hung up without a cheese-cloth cover. The fly that blows smoked meats is the same that starts "skippers" in cheese.

Hornaday gives the following rule, in his *Natural History*, for computing the live weight of deer from the dressed weight: Add four ciphers to the dressed weight in pounds, and divide by 78,612; the quotient will be the live weight in pounds.

Computing Weight.

Now for what Shakespeare calls "small deer":

I must take issue with Nessmuk on the art of skinning a squirrel. He says: "Chop off head, tail, and feet with the hatchet; cut the skin on the back crosswise, and, inserting the two middle fingers, pull the skin off in two parts (head and tail). Clean and cut the squirrel in halves, leaving two ribs on the hind quarters." The objection is that, in this case, you throw away the best part of the squirrel, the cheek meat and brain being its special tid-bits. A better way is this: Sever the tail

Dressing Squirrels.

from below, holding your left forefinger close in behind it, and cutting through the vertebræ close up to the body, leaving only the hide on the top side. Then turn the squirrel over and cut a slit down along each ham. Put your foot on the tail, hold the rear end of the squirrel in your hand, and pull, stripping the skin off to the fore legs. Peel the skin from the hind legs, and cut off the feet. Then cut off the fore feet. Skin to the neck; assist here a little with the knife; then skin to the ears; cut off the butts of the ears; then skin till the blue of the eyeballs shows, and cut; then to the nose till the teeth show, and cut it off. Thus you get no hair on the meat, and the whole thing is done in less than a minute.

Dressing Birds.

Turkeys, geese, ducks, and grouse are usually dry picked. If this could be done while the bodies were still warm, it would be no job at all; but after they are cold it generally results in a good deal of laceration of the skin—so much so that sometimes the disgusted operator gives up and skins the whole bird. It would be better to scald them first, like chickens. In dry picking, hang the bird up by one leg, pluck first the pinions and tail feathers; then the small feathers from shanks and inside of thighs; then the others. Grasp only a few feathers at a time between finger and thumb, as close to the skin as possible, and pull quickly toward the head. Then pick out all pin-feathers and quills. Singe the down off quickly, so as not to give an oily appearance to the skin. Ordinarily the down can be removed from a duck's breast by grasping the bird by the neck and giving one sweep of the open hand down one side of the body and then one down the other. In plucking geese or ducks some use finely powdered resin to remove the pin-feathers. The bird is plucked dry, then rubbed all over with the resin, dipped in and out of boiling water seven or eight times, and then the pin-feathers and down are easily rubbed off. To draw a bird: cut off the head, and the legs at the first joint. Make a lengthwise slit on back at base of neck and sever neck bone close to body, also the membrane which holds the windpipe. Make a lengthwise incision from breastbone to (and around) the vent, so you can easily draw the insides, which must be done carefully, so as not to rupture the gall-bladder. The idea that ducks and other game birds should hang until they smell badly is monstrous. If you want to know where such tastes originated, read the annals of mediæval sieges.

Cleaning Fish.

A small trout is easily cleaned without washing by tearing out the gills and drawing the inside out with them. In a large trout the gills should be cut free from the lower jaw and back of head, and a slit cut along the under side from head to fin; the inside is then drawn out by the gills, leaving the fish clean within.

To scale a fish: grasp it by the head, and, using a knife that is not over-keen, scale first one side and then the other, with swift, steady sweeps. The scales below the gills, and those near the fins, are removed by moving the point of the knife crosswise to the fish's length. Next place the knife just below the belly fin and with a slant stroke cut off this, the side fins, and the head, all in one piece. Then remove the back fin, and the spines beneath it, by making a deep incision on each side of the fin and pulling the latter out. The ventral part is removed in the same way. Open the fish, wash it in cold water, scrape off the slime, and then wipe it *dry* with a clean cloth or towel. Large fish, for broiling, should be split open.

Bullheads and Eels.

To skin a bullhead: cut off the ends of the spines, slit the skin behind and around the head, and then from this point along the back to the tail, cutting around the back fin. Then peel the two corners of the skin well down, sever the backbone, and, holding to the corners of the skin with one hand, pull the fish's body free from the skin with the other. To skin an eel: nail it up by the tail at a convenient height, or impale it thus on the sharpened end of a little stake; cut through the skin, around the body, just forward of the tail, work its edges loose, then pull, stripping off the skin entire.

Venison keeps a long time without curing, if the climate is cool and dry. To cure a deer's ham, hang it up by the shank, divide the muscles just above the hock, and insert a handful of dry salt. The meat of the deer tribe gets more tender and better flavored the longer it is hung up. In warm weather dust flour all over a haunch or saddle of venison, sew it up in a loose bag of cheese-cloth, and hang it in a shady place where there is a current of air. It will keep sweet for several weeks, if there is no crevice in the bag through which insects can penetrate. Ordinarily it is best not to salt meat, for salt draws the juices. Bear meat, however, requires much salt to cure it—more than any other game animal.

Curing Venison.

It is a curious fact that blow-flies work close to the ground, and will seldom meddle with meat that is hung more than ten feet above the ground. Game or fish suspended at a height of twenty feet will be immune from "blows."

To keep fish that must be carried some distance, in hot weather: clean them as soon as you can after they are caught, and *wipe them dry.* Then rub a little salt along their backbones, but nowhere else, for salt draws the juices. Do not pile them touching each other, but between layers of cheese-cloth, nettles, or basswood leaves.

Keeping Fish.

To keep fish in camp: clean, behead, and scale them; then string them by a cord through their tails, and hang them, head down, in a cool, dry, breezy place.

To dry fish for future use: split them along the back, remove the backbones and entrails, salt the fish, and hang them up on a frame over a smudge until they are well smoked. Or, make a trough by hewing out a softwood log, place the split fish in this and cover them with a weak brine for one or two nights. Make a conical bark teepee on a tripod, suspend the fish in it, and dry and smoke them over a small fire for three days and nights.

Drying Fish.

To ship rabbits, squirrels, etc.: do not skin them, but remove the entrails, wipe the insides perfectly dry, wrap in paper, and pack them back down.

Preparing for Shipment.

Never pack birds or fish in straw or grass, for in damp or warm weather this will heat or sweat them. Do not let them freeze, as they will quickly spoil after thawing. Food in a bird's crop soon sours; the crop should be removed.

To preserve birds in warm weather for shipment: draw them, wash the inside perfectly clean, dry thoroughly, and then take pieces of charcoal from the fireplace, wrap them in a thin rag, and fill the abdominal cavity with this. Also fill the bill, ears, eyes, and anal opening with powdered charcoal, to keep off flies and prevent putrefaction. Reject all pieces of charcoal that are only half-burnt or have the odor of creosote. Birds stuffed in this way will keep sweet for a week in hot weather.

If you pack birds or fish in ice, wrap them first in many thicknesses of paper or grass, so that no ice can touch them.

Colonel Park gives the following method for packing fish that are to be transported a considerable distance, and says that it is also a good way to pack venison: Kill the fish as soon as caught; wipe them clean and dry; remove the entrails; scrape the blood off from around the backbone; remove the gills and eyes; wipe dry again; split the fish through the backbone to the skin, from the inside; fill this split with salt; spread the fish over night on a board or log to cool. In the morning, before sunrise, fold the fish in dry towels, so that there is a fold of towel between each fish and its neighbor; carefully wrap the whole package in a piece of muslin, and sew it up into a tight bag, and then in woolen blanketing, sewing up the ends and sides. Now put the roll in a stout paper bag, such as a flour sack. "Fish prepared in this way can be sent from Maine to New Orleans in August, and will remain fresh and nice."

The methods of jerking venison, preparing trophies for mounting, curing pelts, and making buckskin, will be described in other chapters.

CHAPTER XI

CAMP COOKERY

"A true epicure can dine well on one dish, provided it is excellent of its kind."—*Grimod de la Reyniere.*

"There is nothing between the high art of a *cordon-bleu* and a steak toasted on a stick."—*Lord Dunraven.*

"A good cook makes a contented crew."—*Noah.*

BREAD, PORRIDGE, DRINKS

HOME cookery is based upon milk, butter, and eggs: nine-tenths of the recipes in a standard cook-book call for one or more of these ingredients. But it often happens to us campers that our "tin cow" has gone dry, our butter was finished long ago, and as for eggs—we have heard of eggs, but for us they do not exist. In such case, no ordinary cook-book is of any use to us.

When one can carry milk and butter and eggs, he can also carry a standard cook-book; * so I will not burden these pages with many recipes other than the *do-without* kind. Only such dishes are described as can be cooked with the most primitive utensils (or none at all) over an open fire, or in an earth oven dug on the spot. Let it not be thought that this spells misery, or even privation. Some of the dishes here described surpass anything that can be had at the Waldorf or the Maison Dorée. Full details are given for each dish, because I know from experience that an amateur cook needs them.

Poor cookery is not so much the result of inexperience as of carelessness and inattention to details. A man who has never cooked a meal in his life can succeed with almost any of these recipes at the first or second trial, provided he follows the directions reli-

*The best all-round treatise on camp cookery with which I am acquainted is the *Manual for Army Cooks*, which you can procure for 50 cents (stamps not accepted) from the Superintendent of Documents, Washington, D. C.

giously; but let him not discard the book and fall back upon the light of nature, which is but another name for main strength and awkwardness.

A bad mess is sure to follow from (1) a poor fire, (2) seasoning too much or too early in the game, (3) too little heat at the start, or too much thereafter, (4) handling or kneading dough made with baking powder; and it is more likely than not to result from guessing at quantities instead of measuring them.

The Cooking-Fire.

Half of cookery is the fire thereof. It is quite impossible to prepare a good meal over a higgledy-piggledy heap of smoking chunks, or over a fierce blaze, or over a great bed of coals that will warp cast-iron and melt everything else. One must have a small fire, free from smoke and flame, with coals or dry twigs in reserve; there must be some way of regulating the heat; and there must be some sort of rampart around the fire on which pots and pans will perch level and at the right elevation, and perhaps a frame from which kettles can be suspended. It is a very simple matter to build the fire aright in the first place.

An Outdoor Range.

When merely making a "one-night stand," in summer, start a small cooking-fire the moment you stop for camping, and put your kettle on. Then you will have coals and boiling water ready when you begin cooking, and the rest is easy—supper will be ready within twenty minutes. To make an outdoor range: fell a small, straight tree, and cut from it two logs, about 6 feet long and 8 or 10 inches thick. Flatten the top and one side of each with the axe. Lay these bed-logs side by side, flat sides toward each other, and about 3 inches apart at one end and 8 or 10 inches at the other. (This is provided you have no fire-irons; if you have, all that is needed is a short chunk or thick rock at each end to support the irons.) Build a fire of small sticks and bark from end to end. The bark of hemlock and of hardwoods is better fuel than wood when you want coals in a hurry.

Then plant at each end of the fire a forked stake about 4 feet high and across the forks lay a cross-stick (lug-pole) of green wood. Now cut two or three green crotches from branches, drive a nail in the small end of each, invert the crotches, and hang them on the lug-pole to suspend kettles from. These pot-hooks are to be of different lengths so that the kettle can be adjusted to different heights above the fire, first for hard boiling, and then for simmering. If kettles were hung from the lug-pole itself, this adjustment could not be made, and you would have to dismount the whole business in order to get one kettle off.*

Many and many a time I have watched old and experienced woodsmen spoil their grub, and their tempers, too, by trying to cook in front of a roaring winter camp-fire, and have marveled at their lack of common-sense. Off to one side of such a fire, lay your bed-logs, as above; then shovel from the camp-fire enough hard coals to fill the space between the logs within three inches of the top. You now have a steady, even heat from end to end; it can easily be regulated; there is level support for every vessel; and you can wield a short-handled frying-pan over such an outdoor range without scorching either the meat or yourself.

In windy weather, or where fuel is scarce, it is best to dig a trench about 18 inches wide, 12 inches deep, and 4 feet long, with a little chimney of flat stones or sod at the leeward end, to encourage draught. Build the fire in this trench with fire-irons or green sticks

* It is curious how many different names have been bestowed upon the hooks by which kettles are suspended over a fire. Our forefathers called them pot-hooks, trammels, hakes, hangers, pot-hangers, pot-claws, pot-crooks, gallows-crooks, pot-chips, pot-brakes, gibs or gib-crokes, rackan-crooks (a chain or pierced bar on which to hang hooks was called a rackan or reckon), and I know not what else besides. Among Maine lumbermen, such an implement is called a lug-stick, a hook for lifting kettles is a hook-stick, and a stick sharpened and driven into the ground at an angle so as to bend over the fire, to suspend a kettle from, is a wambeck or a spygelia—the Red Gods alone know why! The frame built over a cooking-fire is called by the Penobscots *kitchi-plak-wagn*, and the Micmacs call the lug-stick a *chiplok-waugan*, which the white guides have partially anglicized into waugan-stick. It is well to know, and heresy to disbelieve, that, after boiling the kettle, it brings bad luck to leave the waugan or spygelia standing.

If this catalogue does not suffice the amateur cook to express his ideas about such things, he may exercise his jaws with the Romany (gypsy) term for pot-hook, which is *kekauviscoe saster*.

laid across it for the frying-pan, and a frame above for the kettles.

In permanent camp, if you have no oven, a good substitute can soon be made in a clay bank or steep knoll near by. Dig down the bank to a vertical front. Back from this front, about 4 feet, drive a 4- or 5-inch stake down to what will be the bottom level of the oven. Draw the stake out, thus leaving a hole for flue. It is best to drive the stake before excavating, as otherwise it might cause the roof of your oven to cave in from the shock of driving. Now, from the bottom of the face, dig a horizontal hole back to the flue, keeping the entrance as small as you can, but enlarging the interior and arching its top. When the oven is finished, wet the whole interior, smooth it, and build a small fire in the oven to gradually dry and harden it.

Clay Oven.

To bake in such an oven: build a good fire in it of split hardwood sticks, and keep it burning hard for an hour or two; then rake out the embers, lay your dough on broad green leaves (basswood, from choice) or on the naked floor, and close both the door and the flue with flat stones or bark.

If no bank or knoll lies handy, build a form for your oven by first setting up a row of green-stick arches, like exaggerated croquet wickets, one behind the other, and cover with sticks laid on horizontally like a roof. At the rear, set up a round stake as core for the chimney. Now plaster wet clay thickly over all except the door. Let this dry naturally for a day in hot sunlight, or build a very small fire within and feed it only as needed to keep up a moderate heat. When the clay has hardened, give it another coating, to fill up the cracks that have appeared. Then give it a final firing.

When you have a bed of coals that you want to save, and there are not enough ashes in the fire, cover the coals with bark; this will leave plenty of ash on top.

BREAD

Bread is the staff of life, no less in camp than elsewhere; yet, to paraphrase Tom Hood,

Who has not met with camp-made bread,
Rolled out of putty and weighted with lead?

It need not be so. Just as good biscuit or johnny-cake can be baked before a log fire in the woods as in a kitchen range. Nor is any special knack required. The notion that a man is either a born cook or a hopeless "dodunk" at the business is all moonshine. Bread-making is a chemical process. Pay close attention to details, as a chemist does, from building the fire to testing the loaf with a sliver; then if you do fail it will be because of bad materials. As for me, I was not born a cook, nor do I like to cook; but during the past year of almost continuous camping alone, I have made some sort of bread or biscuit about every other day, and my only failure is chargeable to a razorback who nosed into camp and upset my pan of dough. Strange to say, something invisible zipped through the air just then and nipped off that pig's tail!

Biscuit.—These are best baked in a reflector (12-inch holds 1 doz., 18-inch holds 1½ doz.), unless a camp-stove is carried or an oven is dug. Build the fire high, by leaning sticks on the leeward side of a large back-log. Split wood burns better than round. Have spare dry sticks in reserve (slender ones) with which to replenish the fire. Grease the bake-pan with a bit of pork rind. For 2 doz. biscuit:

3 pints flour,
3 heaping teaspoonfuls baking powder,
1 " teaspoonful salt,
2 " tablespoonfuls cold grease,
1 scant pint cold water.

Mix thoroughly, with big spoon or wooden paddle, first the baking powder with the flour, and then the salt. Rub into this the cold grease (which may be lard, cold pork fat, drippings, or bear's grease), until there are no lumps left and no grease adhering to bottom of pan. This is a little tedious, but don't shirk it. Then stir in the water and work it with spoon until you have a rather stiff dough. Do none of the mixing with your fingers; it makes biscuit "sad." Squeeze or mold the dough as little as practicable; because the gas that makes a biscuit light is already forming and should not be pressed out. Flop the mass of dough to one side of pan, dust flour on bottom of pan, flop dough back over it, dust flour on top of loaf. Now rub some flour over the bread board, flour your hands, and gently lift loaf on board. Flour the bottle or bit of peeled sapling that you use as rolling pin, also the edges of can or can-cover used as biscuit cutter. Gently roll loaf to three-quarter-inch thickness. Stamp out the biscuit and lay them in pan. Roll out the culls (what *do* women call those remaining fragments?) and make biscuit of them too. Bake until edge of front row turns brown; reverse pan and continue until rear row is similarly done. Don't expect to brown the tops in a reflector. Time, twenty to twenty-five minutes in a reflector, ten to fifteen in a closed oven.

Different brands of baking powder vary in strength; Royal is here assumed. The amount of water required varies somewhat according to quality of flour. Too much water makes the dough sticky and prolongs the baking.

Another way to make biscuit (they taste different from the above, but are perhaps just as good) is to use enough water to make a *thick* batter, and drop this from a big spoon into the pan. Do not stir the batter more than you can help.

Dumplings.—If you are going to have boiled meat or a stew for dinner, make enough extra biscuit dough so that you can drop the culls into the pot about half an hour before the meat is done. They make capital dumplings.

Baking in Dutch Oven.—This time-honored utensil is a cast-iron pot on short legs, with heavy iron cover, the rim of which is turned up to receive coals from the fire. If it were not for its weight it ought to be in every camp outfit, for it is the best oven in the world for all kinds of baking. The delicious corn bread of the South, made from nothing but meal, salt, and water, owes its excellence to the Dutch oven, which not only bakes but cooks the dough in its own steam. The juices of meats cannot escape from such an oven. To use the Dutch oven, place it and its lid separately on the fire. Get bottom of oven moderately hot, and the lid quite hot, but not red, lest it warp so that it will never fit thereafter. Grease the bottom and sprinkle flour over it, put the bread in it, and cover. Rake a thin bed of coals out in front of the fire, stand oven on them, and cover the lid thickly with more live coals. Replenish occasionally. Have a stout hook to lift lid with, so you can inspect the progress of baking from time to time.

Army Bread.

1 quart flour,
1 teaspoonful salt,
1 tablespoonful sugar,
2 heaping teaspoonfuls baking powder.

As this is made without grease, it is easier to mix than biscuit dough. Mix the ingredients thoroughly and stir in enough cold water (about one and a half pints) to make a thick batter that will pour out level. Mix rapidly with spoon until smooth, and pour out at once into Dutch oven or bake-pan. Bake about forty-five minutes, or until no dough adheres to a sliver stuck into the loaf. Keeps fresh longer than yeast bread, and does not dry up nor mold. This is the kind of bread to bake when you are laying in a three-days' supply. It is more wholesome than biscuit, and is best eaten cold.

Frying-pan Bread.—If you have no reflector or oven, make up dough as for biscuit, but work it into flat loaves, handling as little as practicable. Grease or flour a frying-pan and put a loaf in it. Rake some embers out in front of the fire and put pan on them just long enough to form a little crust on bottom of loaf. Then remove from embers, and, with a short forked stick, the stub of which will enter hole in end of handle, prop pan up before fire at such angle that top of loaf will be exposed to heat. Turn loaf now and then, both sidewise and upside down. When firm enough to keep its shape, remove it, prop it by itself before the fire to finish baking, and go on with a fresh loaf. In this way you can soon lay in a two-days' supply. A tin plate, or a thick slab of non-resinous wood heated till the sap begins to simmer, may be used in place of frying-pan.

Unleavened Bread.—Quickly made, wholesome, and good for a change. Keeps like hardtack.

2½ pints flour,
1 tablespoonful salt,
1 " sugar.

Mix with water to stiff dough, and knead and pull until lively. Roll out thin as a soda cracker, score with knife, and bake as above. If you have no utensil, work dough into a ribbon two inches wide. Get a club of sweet green wood (birch, sassafras, maple), about two feet long and three inches thick, peel large end, sharpen the other and stick it into ground, leaning toward fire. When sap simmers wind dough spirally around peeled end. Turn occasionally. Several sticks can be baking at once. Bread for one man's meal can be quickly baked on a peeled stick as thick as a broomstick, holding over fire and turning.

Unleavened bread that is to be carried for a long time must be mixed with as little water as possible (merely dampened enough to make it adhere), for if any moisture is left in it after baking, it will mold.

To Mix Dough without a Pan.—When bark will peel, use a broad sheet of it. A sheet of canvas, or a dried hide, will do. It is easy enough, though, to mix unleavened dough in the sack of flour itself. Stand the latter horizontally where it can't fall over. Scoop a bowl-shaped depression in top of flour. Keep the right hand moving round while you pour in a little water at a time from a vessel held in the left. Sprinkle a little salt in. When a thick, adhesive dough has formed, lift this out and pat and work it into a round cake about 2½ inches thick.

Australian Damper.—Build a good fire on a level bit of ground. When it has burned to coals and the ground is thoroughly heated, mix dough as above, rake away the embers, lightly drop the loaf on the hot earth, pat it smooth, rake the embers back over the loaf until it is thickly embedded in them, and let it bake from 1½ to 2 hours, depending upon size of loaf. This is the next best thing to an ash-cake of corn meal —which is a dish fit for a king.

Sour-dough Bread, irreverently known as "pizened dog," is the stand-by of Alaska miners. Mix a pail of batter from plain flour and water, and hang it up in a warm place until the batter sours. Then add salt and soda (not baking powder), thicken with flour to a stiff dough, knead thoroughly, work into small loaves, and place them before the fire to rise. Then bake.

Salt-rising Bread.—This smells to heaven while it is fermenting, but makes wholesome and appetizing bread, which is a welcome change after a long diet of baking-powder breadstuffs.

For a baking of two or three loaves take about a pint of moderately warm water (a pleasant heat to the hand) and stir into it as much flour as will make a good batter, not too thick. Add to this ½ teaspoonful salt, not more. Set the vessel in a pan of moderately warm water, within a little distance of a fire, or in sunlight. The water must not be allowed to cool much below the original heat, more warm water being added to pan as required. In six to eight hours the whole will be in active fermentation, when the dough must be mixed with it, and as much warm water (milk, if you have it) as you require. Knead the mass till it is tough and does not stick to the board. Make up your loaves, and keep them warmly covered near the fire till they rise. They must be baked as soon as this second rising takes place; for, unless the rising is used immediately on reaching its height, it sinks to rise no more forever—selah!

To Bake Raised Bread in a Pot.—Set the dough to rise over a very few embers, keeping the pot turned as the loaf rises. When equally risen all around, put hot ashes under the pot and upon the lid, taking care that the heat be not too fierce at first.

Lungwort Bread.—On the bark of maples, and some-

The Camp in Order

Just Starting Out

times of beeches and birches, in the northern woods, there grows a green, broad-leaved lichen variously known as lungwort, liverwort, lung-lichen, and lung-moss, which is an excellent substitute for yeast. This is an altogether different growth from the plants commonly called lungwort and liverwort—I believe its scientific name is *Sticta pulmonacea.* This lichen is partly made up of fungus, which does the business of raising dough. Gather a little of it and steep it over night in lukewarm water, set near the embers, but not near enough to get overheated. In the morning, pour off the infusion and mix it with enough flour to make a batter, beating it up with a spoon. Place this "sponge" in a warm can or pail, cover with a cloth, and set it near the fire to work. By evening it will have risen. Leaven your dough with this (saving some of the sponge for a future baking), let the bread rise before the fire that night, and by morning it will be ready to bake.

It takes but little of the original sponge to leaven a large mass of dough (but see that it never freezes), and it can be kept good for months.

Flapjacks made without milk or eggs are not equal to those that mother used to make, but they fill the hiatus when a quick meal is demanded.

1 quart flour,
1 teaspoonful salt,
2 teaspoonfuls sugar (to make 'em brown),
2 level tablespoonfuls baking powder.

Rub in, dry, 2 heaped tablespoonfuls grease. If you have no grease, do without. Make a smooth batter with cold water—thin enough to pour from a spoon, but not too thin, or it will take all day to bake enough for the party. Stir well, to smoothe out lumps. Set frying-pan level over thin bed of coals, get it quite hot, and grease with piece of pork in split end of stick. Pan must be hot enough to make batter sizzle as it touches. Pour from end of a big spoon successively enough batter to fill pan within one-half inch of rim. When cake is full of bubbles and edges have stiffened, shuffle pan to make sure that cake is free below and stiff enough to flip. Then hold pan slanting in front of and away from you, go through preliminary motion of flapping once or twice to get the swing, then flip boldly so cake will turn a somerset in the air, and catch it upside down. Beginners generally lack the nerve to toss high enough. If you land a hot cake on the other fellow's eye, it serves him right for monkeying so near the cook. Grease pan anew and stir batter every time before pouring.

John's Pancakes.—Some time when you really have eggs, etc., and wish to produce something really fine, try the following recipe, which I have modified a little from Boardman's *Lovers of the Woods.* It is the invention of his guide, or helper, John.

Crumb up a thick slice of stale bread, rejecting the crust, and put it to soak in a medium-sized pail with a cupful of water. When the crumbs have soaked soft, stir in with them 1 big tablespoonful evaporated cream, or the equivalent, 2 tablespoonfuls syrup, and 2 more cupfuls water. Melt carefully, so as not to burn, butter the size of an egg; remove from fire, and stir in 2 eggs and 1 tablespoonful salt. Stir this into your crumb dope. Now stir in 1 quart flour, or enough to make the batter as thick as molasses. Just before baking, stir in 2 teaspoonfuls baking powder. Have the frying-pan snapping hot, and keep it so. Above is a meal for two or three hungry men. Such cakes rest lightly on the cook's conscience, and buoy up the whole crowd.

Plain Corn Bread.—Pone or johnny-cake is easily and quickly made, more wholesome than baking-powder bread, more appetizing than unleavened wheat bread and it "sticks to the ribs." To be eaten hot, and, like all hot breads, should be broken with the hands, never cut. Bread left over should be freshened by moistening and reheating.

The amount of water to be used depends upon whether the meal is freshly ground (moist) or old (dry), and yellow meal requires one-half more water than white.

1 quart meal,
1 teaspoonful salt,
1 pint *warm* (but not scalding) water ($1\frac{1}{2}$ pints for yellow meal).

Stir together until light. Bake to a nice brown all around, preferably in Dutch oven. Test with sliver. Done in about forty-five minutes, but improved by letting stand fifteen minutes longer, away from fire, to sweat in oven. Eat with bacon gravy.

If you have no oven, plank the bread on hot slab before a high fire, having previously formed slight under crust by laying on hot ashes; or, make ash cake by forming into balls as big as hen's eggs, roll in dry flour, lay in hot ashes and cover completely with them. Time for ash cake, fifteen to twenty minutes.

Corn Dodgers.—Salt some white corn meal to taste. Mix with cold water to stiff dough, and form into cylindrical dodgers four or five inches long and one and a half inches diameter, by rolling between the hands. Have frying-pan very hot, grease it a little, and put dodgers on as you roll them out. As soon as they have browned, put them in oven and bake thoroughly to a crisp brown.

Snow Bread.—After a fall of light, feathery snow, superior corn bread may be made by stirring together

1 quart corn meal,
$\frac{1}{2}$ teaspoonful soda,
1 " salt,
1 tablespoonful lard.

Then, in a cool place where snow will not melt, stir into above one quart light snow. Bake about forty minutes in rather hot oven. Snow, for some unknown reason, has the same effect on corn bread as eggs have, two tablespoonfuls of snow equaling one egg. It can also be used in making batter for pancakes, the batter being made rather thick, and the snow mixed with each cake just before putting in the pan.

Corn Bread with Baking Powder.—Mix together:

$1\frac{1}{2}$ pints yellow corn meal,
$\frac{1}{2}$ pint flour,
1 tablespoonful sugar,
1 teaspoonful salt,
3 heaping teaspoonfuls baking powder.

Work in a cupful of cold lard or grease. Add enough cold water or milk to make a stiff batter (about 2 pints). Grease and flour your baking-pan, frying-pan, or Dutch oven, pour the batter in, and bake forty minutes. Above makes a cake $9\frac{1}{4}$x2 inches, weighing $3\frac{3}{4}$ pounds.

Buckwheat Cakes.—Nobody knows what real buckwheat cakes are until he has eaten those baked by a Pennsylvania Dutchwoman from batter made with genuine dark-colored buckwheat flour ground in a country mill, and raised over night with yeast. There is as much difference between them and the city-restaurant kind as there is between a ripe fig and a dried codfish. However, we can't have them in camp; so here is the next best:

1 pint buckwheat flour,
$\frac{1}{2}$ " wheat flour,
2 tablespoonfuls baking powder,
$\frac{1}{2}$ teaspoonful salt.

Mix to a thin batter with milk, if you have it; otherwise water.

Rice Cakes.—When you have cold boiled rice left over, mix it half and half with flour, and proceed as with flapjacks. Cold boiled potatoes or oatmeal may be used in the same way. Rice cakes are best mixed with the water in which rice has been boiled.

Oat Cakes.—(1) Mix oatmeal with cold water and a little salt into a thick paste, pat it out as thin as possible with a spoon, and bake on the frying-pan.

(2) Mix $\frac{1}{2}$ pound oatmeal, 1 ounce butter, and a pinch of salt with enough water to make a moderately thick paste. Roll to a thickness of $\frac{1}{3}$ inch, bake in frying-pan, and give it to the Scotchman—he will bless you.

Fried Quoits.—Make dough as for frying-pan bread. Plant a stick slanting in the ground near the fire. Have another small, clean stick ready, and a frying-pan of lard or butter heated sissing hot. There must be enough grease in the pan to drown the quoits. Take dough the size of a small hen's egg, flatten it between the hands, make a hole in the center like that of a doughnut, and quickly work it (the dough, not the hole) into a flat ring of about two inches inside diameter. Drop it flat into the hot grease, turn almost immediately, and in a few seconds it will be cooked. When of a light brown color, fish it out with your little stick and hang it on the slanting one before the fire to keep hot. If the grease is of the right temperature, the cooking of one quoit will occupy just the same time as the molding of another, and the product will be crisp and crumpety. If the grease is not hot enough, a visit from your oldest grandmother may be expected before midnight. (Adapted from *Lees and Clutterbuck.*)

Stale Bread.—Biscuit or bread left over and dried out can be freshened for an hour or two by dipping quickly in and out of water and placing in the baker until heated through; or, the biscuit may be cut open, slightly moistened, and toasted in a broiler. If you have eggs, make a French toast by dipping the slices in whipped eggs and frying them. With milk, make milk toast: heat the milk, add a chunk of butter and some salt, toast the bread, and pour milk over it.

MUSH, PORRIDGE

Corn-Meal Mush.—Mix 2 level tablespoonfuls salt with 1 quart meal. Bring 4 quarts of water (for yellow meal, or half as much for fresh white meal) to a hard boil in a 2-gallon kettle. Mix the salted meal with enough *cold* water to make a batter that will run from the spoon; this is to prevent it from getting lumpy. With a large spoon drop the batter into the boiling water, adding gradually, so that water will not fall below boiling point. Stir constantly for ten minutes. Then cover pot and hang it high enough above fire to insure against scorching. Cook thus for one hour, stirring occasionally, and thinning with *boiling* water if it gets too thick.

Fried Mush.—This, as Father Izaak said of another dish, is "too good for any but very honest men." The only drawback to this gastronomic joy is that it takes a whole panful for one man. As it is rather slow to fry, let each man perform over the fire for himself. The mush should have been poured into a greased pan the previous evening, and set in a cool place over night to harden. Cut into slices $\frac{1}{3}$ inch thick, and fry in very hot grease until nicely browned. Eat with syrup, or *au naturel*.

Oatmeal Porridge.—Rolled oats may be cooked much more quickly than the old-fashioned oatmeal; the latter is not fit for the human stomach until it has been boiled as long as corn mush. To two quarts boiling water add one teaspoonful of salt, stir in gradually a pint of rolled oats, and boil ten minutes, stirring constantly, unless you have a double boiler. The latter may be extemporized by setting a small kettle inside a larger one that contains some water. "Our parritch may nae be sae gude as the laird's, but it's as hot!"

Boiled Rice.—Good precedent to the contrary notwithstanding, I contend that there is but one way to boil rice, and that is this (which I first learned from a Chinaman, but is described in the words of Captain Kenealy, whose *Yachting Wrinkles* is a book worth owning):

To cook rice so that each grain will be plump, dry, and separate, first, wash the measure of rice thoroughly in cold salted water. Then put it in a pot of *furiously boiling* fresh water, no salt being added. Keep the pot boiling hard for twenty minutes, but *do not stir.* Then strain off the water, place the rice over a very moderate fire (hang high over camp-fire), and let it swell and dry for half an hour.

Remember that rice swells enormously in cooking. Once when we camped "'way down in Arkansaw," it came Bob Staley's turn to cook. Our commissariat was low; and Bob wanted a new dish. We had rice; and a Dutchwoman had given us some "snits" (dried apples). Bob put dry rice and unsoaked snits into a pot till the vessel was almost full, poured cold water over them, and set the pot on the fire; then he went fishing. Rice and snits overflowed into White River, and White River went out of its banks that very night. Fact, I assure you!

BEVERAGES

Coffee.—There are two ways of making good coffee in an ordinary pot. (1) Put coffee in pot with cold water (one tablespoonful freshly ground to one pint, or more if canned ground) and hang over fire. Watch it, and when water first begins to bubble, remove pot from fire and let it stand five minutes. Settle grounds with a tablespoonful of cold water poured down spout. Do not let the coffee boil. Boiling extracts the tannin, and drives off the volatile aroma which is the most precious gift of superior berries. (2) (Safer.) Bring water to hard boil, remove from fire and quickly put coffee in. Cover tightly and let steep ten minutes. A better way, when you have a seamless vessel that will stand dry heat, is to put coffee in, place over gentle fire to roast until aroma begins to rise, pour boiling water over the coffee, cover tightly, and set aside.

Tea.—Pour boiling water over tea (one teaspoonful tea to the pint), cover tightly, and steep *away* from fire *four minutes by the watch.* Then strain into separate vessel. If tea is left steeping more than five or six minutes the result is a liquor that will tan skin into leather.

MEAT, GAME, AND FISH

The main secrets of good meals in camp are to have a proper fire, good materials, and then to imprison in each dish, at the outset, its natural juice and characteristic flavor. To season camp dishes as a French chef would is a blunder of the first magnitude. His art is the outcome of siege and famine, when repulsive food had to be so disguised as to cheat the palate. The raw materials used in city cuisine are often of inferior quality, from keeping in cold storage or with chemical preservatives; so their insipidity must be corrected by spices, herbs, and sauces, to make them eatable. In cheap restaurants and boarding houses, where the chef's skill is lacking, "all things taste alike," from having been penned up together in a refrigerator and cooked in a fetid atmosphere. But, in the woods, our fish is freshly caught, our game has hung out of doors, and the water and air used in cooking (most important factors) are sweet and pure. Such viands need no masking. The only seasoning required is with pepper and salt, to be used sparingly, and not added (except in soups and stews) until the dish is nearly or quite done. Remember this: salt draws the juices, no matter what may be the process of cooking.

The juices of meats and fish are their most palatable and nutritious ingredients. We extract them purposely in making soups, stews, and gravies, but in so doing we ruin the meat. Any fish, flesh, or fowl that is fit to be eaten for the good meat's sake should be cooked succulent, by first coagulating the outside (searing in a bright flame or in a very hot pan, or plunging into smoking hot grease or furiously boiling water) and then removing farther from the fire to cook gradually till done. The first process, which is quickly performed, is "the surprise." It sets the juices, and, in the case of frying, seals the fish or meat in a grease-proof envelope so that it will not become sodden but will dry crisp when drained. The horrors of the frying-pan that has been unskillfully wielded are too well known. Let us campers, to whom the frying-pan is an almost indispensable utensil, set a good example to our grease-afflicted country by using it according to the code of health and epicurean taste.

Game, and all other kinds of fresh meat, should be hung up till they have bled thoroughly and have cooled through and through—they are tenderer and better after they have hung several days.

All mammals from the 'coon size down, as well as duck and grouse, unless young and tender, should be parboiled from ten to thirty minutes, according to size, before frying, broiling, or roasting. Salt meats of all kinds should either be soaked over night in cold water or parboiled in two or three waters before cooking. Frozen meat or fish should be thawed in ice-cold water and then cooked immediately—warm water would steal their flavor. Canned meats are unwholesome at best; they should at least be heated through, and are preferably served in hash or stews. Never eat canned stuff of any kind that has been standing open in the can: it is likely to sicken you. If any is left over, remove it to a clean vessel. The liquor of canned peas, string beans, etc., is unfit for use and should be thrown away; this does not apply to tomatoes.

There is no excuse for serving hot food on cold plates. Put the plates in a pan of hot water, or fill them with boiling water. They will quickly dry themselves when emptied.

Meat, game, and fish may be fried, broiled, roasted, baked, boiled, or stewed. Frying and broiling are the quickest processes; roasting, baking, and boiling take an hour or two; a stew of meat and vegetables, to be good, takes half a day, and so does soup prepared from the raw materials. Tough meat should be boiled or braised in a pot.

Frying.

Do not try to fry over a flaming fire or a deep bed of coals; the grease would likely burn and catch aflame. Rake a thin layer of coals out in front of the fire; or, for a quick meal, make your fire of small dry sticks, no thicker than your finger, boil water over the flame, and then fry over the quickly formed coals.

If you have a deep pan and plenty of frying fat, it is much the best to completely immerse the material in boiling grease, as doughnuts are fried. Let the fat boil until little jets of smoke arise (being careful not to burn the grease) and until the violent first boil subsides. When fat begins to smoke continuously it is decomposing, and will impart an acrid taste. When a bread crumb dropped in will be crisp when taken out, the fat is of the right temperature. Then quickly drop in small pieces of the material, one at a time so as not to check the heat. Turn them once while cooking. Remove when done, and drop them a moment on coarse paper to absorb surplus grease, or hang them over a row of small sticks so they can drain. Then season. The fry will be crisp, and dry enough to handle without soiling the fingers. This is *the* way for small fish.

Travelers must generally get along with shallow pans and little grease. To fry (or, properly, to sauté) in this manner, without getting the article sodden and unfit for the stomach, heat the dry pan very hot, and then grease it only enough to keep the meat from sticking (fat meat needs none). The material must be dry when put in the pan (wipe fish with a towel) or it will absorb grease. Cook quickly and turn frequently, not jabbing with a fork; for that would let juice escape. Season when done, and serve piping hot.

Chops, fat meats, squirrels, rabbits, and the smaller birds are best sautéd or fricasseed and served with gravy.

Bacon or salt pork should be sliced *thin.* Put pan half full of water on fire; when water is warm, drop the bacon in, and stir around until water begins to simmer. Then remove bacon, throw out water, heat pan thoroughly, fry, and turn often. Remove slices while still translucent, and season with pepper. They will turn crisp on cooling.

To make gravy that is a good substitute for butter, rub into the hot grease that is left in the pan a tablespoonful of flour, keep on rubbing until smooth and brown, then add two cups boiling water and a dash of pepper. If you have milk, use it instead of water (a pint to the heaping tablespoonful of flour), and do not let the flour brown; this makes a delicious white gravy.

Birds or squirrels for frying should be cut in convenient pieces, parboiled until tender in a pot with enough water to cover, then removed, saving the liquor. Sprinkle with salt, pepper, and flour (this for the sake of the gravy), fry in melted pork fat, take out when done, then stir into the frying fat one-half cupful dry flour till a dark brown, add parboiling liquor, bring to a boil, put game in dish, and pour gravy over it.

Small fish should be fried whole, with the backbone severed to prevent curling up; large fish should be cut into pieces, and ribs cut loose from backbone, so as to lie flat in pan. Rub the pieces in corn meal, thinly and evenly (that browns them). Fry in plenty of very hot grease to a golden brown, sprinkling lightly with pepper and salt just as the color turns.

What our average camper calls "frying" is to drop any old kind of grease into a shallow pan (perhaps even into a cold pan!), slap in a thin slice of meat, or small pieces of fish or fowl, and then torture both the fry and the frier over a blazing, smoking fire. Thus the juices are all fried out of the meat, its natural flavor is lost, and the result is an indigestible mass, tasteless as a burnt chip or sodden with pork grease. This time-honored and strictly American way of frying has produced myriads of dyspeptics, even among men living otherwise wholesome lives in the open air!

Fresh meat that is tender enough to escape the boiling pot or the braising oven should either be broiled or roasted before a bed of clear, hard coals. Both of these processes preserve the characteristic flavor of the meat, and add that piquant, aromatic-bitter "taste of the fire" which no pan nor oven can impart. Broil when you are in a hurry; but, when you have leisure for a good job, roast your meat, basting it frequently with drippings from the pan below, so as to keep the surface moist and flexible, and insure that precise degree of browning which delights a gourmet.

Cut the meat at least an inch thick. Only tender pieces are fit for broiling. Venison usually requires

Broiling.

some pounding, but don't gash it in doing so. Have a bed of bright coals free from smoke, with clear flaming fire to one side. Sear outside of meat by thrusting for a moment in the flame, and turning; then broil before the fire, rather than over it, so as to catch drippings on a pan underneath. Do not season until done. A steak 1 inch thick should be broiled five minutes, 1½ inches ten minutes, 2 inches twenty minutes. Serve on hot dish with drippings poured over.

To broil enough for a party, when you have no broiler, clean the frying-pan thoroughly and get it almost red hot, so as to seal pores of meat instantly. Cover pan. Turn meat often, without stabbing. A large venison steak will be done in ten minutes. Put on hot dish, season with pepper and salt, and pour juices over it. Equal to meat broiled on a gridiron, and saves the juices.

To broil by completely covering the slice of meat with hot ashes and embers is really the best way of all.

Bacon or pork, before broiling, should be soaked in cold water an hour or longer.

Birds should be split up the back, broiled over the coals, and basted with a piece of pork on tined stick held over them. Fillets of ducks or other large birds may be sliced off and impaled on sticks with thin slices of pork.

Small fish may be skewered on a thin, straight, greenwood stick, sharpened at the end, with a thin slice of bacon or pork between every two fish, the stick being constantly turned over the coals like a spit, so that juices may not be lost.

Another way is to cut some green hardwood sticks, about three feet long, forked at one end, and sharpen the tines. Lay a thin slice of pork inside each fish lengthwise, drive tines through fish and pork, letting them through between ribs near backbone and on opposite sides of the latter—then the fish won't drop off as soon as it begins to soften and curl from the heat. Place a log lengthwise of edge of coals, lay broiling sticks on this support, slanting upward over the fire, and lay a small log over their butts.

Large fish should be planked as described under Roasting.

To Grill on a Rock.—Take two large flat stones of a kind that do not burst from heat (not moist ones), wipe them clean of grit, place them one above the other, with a few pebbles between to keep them apart, and build a fire around them. When they are well heated, sweep away the ashes, and place your slices of meat between the stones.

Roasting.

To roast is to cook by the direct heat of the fire, as on a spit or before a high bed of coals. Baking is performed in an oven, pit, or closed vessel. No kitchen range can compete with an open fire for roasting.

Build a rather large fire of split hardwood (softwoods are useless) against a high backlog or wall of rocks which will reflect the heat forward. Sear the outside of the roast (not a bird or fish) in clear flames until outer layer of albumen is coagulated. Then skewer thin slices of pork to upper end; hang roast before fire and close to it by a stout wet cord; turn frequently; catch drippings in pan or green-bark trough, and baste with them. This is better than roasting on a spit over the fire, because the heat can be better regulated, the meat turned and held in position more easily, the roast is not smoked, and the drippings are utilized.

A whole side of venison can be roasted by planting two stout forked stakes before the fire, a stub of each stake being thrust through a slit cut between the ribs and under the backbone. The forward part of the saddle is the best roasting piece. Trim off flanky parts and ends of ribs, and split backbone lengthwise so that the whole will hang flat. To roast a shoulder, peel it from side, cut off leg at knee, gash thickest part of flesh, press bits of pork into them, and skewer some slices to upper part.

When roasting a large joint, a turkey, or anything else that will require more than an hour of steady heat, do not depend upon replenishing your roasting-fire from time to time, unless you have a good supply of sound, dry hardwood sticks of stove-wood size. If green wood or large sticks must be used, build a bonfire of them to one side of your cooking-fire, and shovel coals from it as required. It will not do to check the cooking-fire.

A good way to suspend a large bird before the fire is described by Dillon Wallace in his *Lure of the Labrador Wild:*

> George built a big fire—much bigger than usual. At the back he placed the largest green log he could find. Just in front of the fire, and at each side, he fixed a forked stake, and on these rested a cross-pole. From the center of the pole he suspended a piece of stout twine, which reached nearly to the ground, and tied the lower end into a noose.

Then it was that the goose, nicely prepared for the cooking, was brought forth. Through it at the wings George stuck a sharp wooden pin, leaving the ends to protrude on each side. Through the legs he stuck a similar pin in a similar fashion. This being done, he slipped the noose at the end of the twine over the ends of one of the pins. And lo and behold! the goose was suspended before the fire.

It hung low—just high enough to permit the placing of a dish under it to catch the gravy. Now and then George gave it a twirl so that none of its sides might have reason to complain at not receiving its share of the heat. The lower end roasted first; seeing which, George took the goose off, reversed it, and set it twirling again.

A goose or a middling-sized turkey takes about two hours to roast, a large turkey three hours, a duck about forty-five minutes, a pheasant twenty to thirty minutes, a woodcock or snipe fifteen to twenty minutes.

Fish Roasted in a Reflector.—This process is simpler than baking, and superior in resulting flavor, since the fish is basted in its own juices, and is delicately browned by direct action of the fire. The surface of the fish is lightly moistened with lard (you would use butter or olive oil if you had them). Then place the fish in the pan and add two or three morsels of grease around it. Roast in front of a good fire, just as you would bake biscuit. Be careful not to overroast and dry the fish by evaporating the gravy. There is no better way to cook a large fish, unless it be planked.

Planked Fish.—More expeditious than baking, and better flavored.

Split and smoothe a slab of sweet hardwood two or three inches thick, two feet long, and somewhat wider than the opened fish. Prop it in front of a bed of coals till it is sizzling hot. Split the fish down the back its entire length, but do not cut clear through the belly. Clean, and wipe it quite dry. When plank is hot, spread fish out like an opened book, tack it, skin side down, to the plank and prop before fire. Baste continuously with a bit of pork on a switch held above it. Reverse ends of plank from time to time. If the flesh is flaky when pierced with a fork, it is done. Sprinkle salt and pepper over the fish, moisten with drippings, and serve on the hot plank. No better dish ever was set before an epicure.

Braising Meat.—Neither fish, flesh nor fowl should be baked in an oven. When baking is resorted to, let it be by one of the outdoor processes described below. Tough meat, however, is improved by braising in a Dutch oven, or a covered pot or saucepan. This process lies between baking and frying. It is pre-eminently the way to cook bear meat, venison shoulders and rounds.

Put the meat in the oven or pot with about two inches of hot water in the bottom. Add some chopped onion, if desired, for seasoning. Cover and cook, about fifteen minutes to the pound. A half hour before the meat is done, season it with salt and pepper.

The gravy is made by pouring the grease from the pot, adding a little water and salt, and rubbing flour into it with a spoon.

Baking in a Hole.—This is a modification of braising. Dig a hole in the ground, say eighteen inches square and deep. Place kindling in it, and over the hole build a cob house by laying split hardwood sticks across, not touching each other, then another course over these and at right angles to them, and so on till you have a stack two feet high. Set fire to it. The air will circulate freely, and the sticks, if of uniform size, will all burn down to coals together.

Cut the fowl, or whatever it is, in pieces, season, add a chunk of fat pork the size of your fist, put in the kettle, pour in enough water to cover, put lid on kettle, rake coals out of hole, put kettle in, shovel coals around and over it, cover all with a few inches of earth, and let it alone over night. It beats a bake-oven. In case of rain, cover with bark.

Baking an Animal in its Hide.—If the beast is too large to bake entire, cut off what you want and sew it up in a piece of the hide. Have your hole in the ground glowing hot. In this case it is best to have the hole lined with flat stones. Rake out embers, put meat in, cover first with green grass or leaves, then with the hot coals and ashes, and build a fire on top. When done, remove the skin.

A deer's head is placed in the pit, neck down, and baked in the same way: time about six hours.

Baking in Clay.—This hermetically seals the meat while cooking, and is better than baking in a kettle.

Draw the animal, but leave the skin and hair on. If it be a large bird, as a duck or goose, cut off head and most of neck, also feet and pinions, pull out tail feathers and cut tail off (to get rid of oil sac), but leave smaller feathers on. If a fish, do not scale. Moisten and work some clay till it is like softened putty. Roll it out in a sheet an inch or two thick and large enough to completely incase the animal. Cover the latter so that no feather or hair projects. Place in fire and cover with good bed of coals and let it remain with fire burning on top for about an hour, if a fish or small bird. Larger animals require more time, and had best be placed in bake-hole over night.

When done, break open the hard casing of baked clay. The skin peels off with it, leaving the meat perfectly clean and baked to perfection in its own juices.

This method has been practiced for ages by the gypsies and other primitive peoples.

Baking in the Embers.—To bake a fish, clean it—if it is large enough to be emptied through a hole in the neck, do not slit the belly—season with salt and pepper, and, if liked, stuff with Indian meal. Have ready a good bed of glowing hardwood coals; cover it with a thin layer of ashes, that the fish may not be burnt. Lay the fish on this, and cover it with more ashes and coals. Half an hour, more or less, is required, according to size. On removing the fish, pull off the skin, and the flesh will be found clean and palatable.

A bird, for example a duck, is baked in much the same way. Draw it, but do not remove the feathers. If you like stuffed duck, stuff with bread crumbs or broken biscuit, well seasoned with salt and pepper. Wet the feathers by dipping the bird in water; then bury it in the ashes and coals. A teal will require about half an hour; other birds in proportion.

The broader the pot, and the blacker it is, the quicker it boils. Fresh meats should be started in boiling water; salt or corned meats, and those intended for stews or soups in cold water. The meat (except hams) should be cut into chunks of not over five pounds each, and soup bones well cracked. Watch during first half hour, and skim off all scum as fast as it rises, or it will settle and adhere to meat. Fresh meat should be boiled until bones are free, or until a fork will pierce easily (ten pounds take about two and a half hours). Ham, bacon, and salt pork require fifteen to twenty minutes per pound. Save the broth for soup-stock. Meat that is to be eaten cold should be allowed to cool in the liquor in which it was boiled. A tablespoonful or two of vinegar added to the boiling water makes meat more tender and fish firmer. Turn the meat several times while boiling. If the water needs replenishing, do it with boiling, not cold, water. Season a short time before meat is done. If vegetables are to be cooked with the meat, add them at such time that they will just finish cooking when the meat is done (potatoes twenty to thirty minutes before the end; carrots and turnips, sliced, one to one and a half hours).

Boiling.

Remember this: put fresh meat in hard boiling water for only five minutes, to set the juices; then remove to greater height over the fire and boil very slowly—to let it boil hard all the time would make it tough and indigestible. Salt meats go in cold water at the start, and are gradually brought to a boil; thereafter they should be allowed to barely simmer.

Fish, however, should be placed in boiling salted water. This makes their flesh firmer and better flavored. They cook quickly this way, especially if vinegar is added; six to seven minutes to the pound is generally time enough.

At high altitudes it is impossible to cook satisfactorily by boiling, because water boils at a lower and lower temperature the higher we climb. The decrease is at the rate of about one degree for every 550 feet up to one mile, and one degree for 560 feet above that, when the temperature is 70°. With the air at 32° F., water boils at 202.5° at 5,000 feet, 193.3° at 10,000 feet, and 184.5° at 15,000 feet.

Stewing.—This process is slow, and should be reserved for tough meats. Use lean meat only. First brown it with some hot fat in a frying-pan; or, put a couple of ounces of chopped pork in a kettle and get it thoroughly hot; cut your meat into small pieces; drop them into the fat and "jiggle" the kettle until the surface of the meat is coagulated by the hot fat, being careful, the while, not to burn it. Add a thickening of a couple of ounces of flour, and mix it thoroughly with the fat; then a pint of water or soup-stock. Heat the contents of the kettle to boiling, and season with salt, pepper, and chopped onion. Now cover the kettle closely and hang it where it will only simmer for four or five hours. Stews may be thickened with rice, potatoes, or oatmeal, as well as with flour. Add condiments to suit the taste. A ragout is nothing but a highly seasoned stew.

The method given above is the one I have followed; but I take the liberty of adding another by Captain Kenealy, which I believe may be superior:

> Stewing is an admirable way of making palatable coarse and tough pieces of meat, but it requires the knack, like all other culinary processes. Have a hot fry-pan ready, cut the meat up into small squares and put it (without any dripping or fat) into the pan. Let it brown well, adding a small quantity of granulated sugar, and sliced onions to taste. Cook until the onions are tender and well colored. Then empty the fry-pan into a stew-pan and add boiling water to cover the meat, and let it simmer gently for two or three hours. Flavor with salt, pepper, sweet herbs, curry powder or what you will. The result will be a savory dish of tender meat, called by the French a ragout. It is easy to prepare it this way. Do not boil it furiously as is sometimes done, or it will become tough. This dish may be thickened with browned flour, and vegetables may be added—turnips, carrots, celery, etc., cut into small pieces and browned with the meat. The sugar improves the flavor vastly. The only condiments actually necessary are pepper and salt. Other flavorings are luxuries.

Steaming in a Hole.—To steam meat or vegetables: build a large fire and throw on it a number of smooth stones, not of the bomb-shell kind. Dig a hole in the ground near the fire. When the stones are red-hot, fork them into the hole, level them, cover with green or wet leaves, grass, or branches, place the meat or potatoes on this layer, cover with more leaves, and then cover all with a good layer of earth. Now bore a small hole down to the food, pour in some water, and immediately stop up the hole, letting the food steam until tender. This is the Chinook method of cooking camass.

Mammals.

The following additional details are supplementary to what has gone before, and presuppose a careful reading of the preceding pages:

Deer's Brains.—Fry them; or boil slowly half an hour.

Heart.—Remove valves and tough, fibrous tissue; then braise, or cut into small pieces and use in soups or stews.

Kidneys.—Soak in cold water one hour. Cut into small pieces, and drop each piece into cold water, as cut. Wash well; then stew.

Liver.—Carefully remove gall-bladder, if the animal has one—deer have none. Parboil the liver, and skim off the bitter scum that rises; then fry with bacon; or, put the liver on a spit, skewer some of the caul fat around it, and roast before the fire; or, cut the liver into slices ¼ inch thick, soak it one hour in cold salt water, rinse well in warm water, wipe dry, dip each slice in flour seasoned with salt and pepper, and fry.

Marrow Bones.—Cover ends with small pieces of plain dough made with flour and water, over which tie a floured cloth; place bones upright in kettle, and cover with boiling water. Boil two hours. Remove cloth and paste, push out marrow, and serve with dry toast.

Milt (Spleen).—Skewer a piece of bacon to it, and broil.

Tongue.—Soak for one hour; rinse in fresh water; put in a kettle of cold water, bring to a boil, skim, and continue boiling moderately two hours.

Venison Sausages.—Utilize the tougher parts of the deer, or other game, by mincing the raw meat with half as much salt pork, season with pepper and sage, make into little pats, and fry like sausages. Very good.

Squirrels.—Parboil, then fry in pork grease, and make gravy as directed under Frying. This dish soon palls. Then try stewing them along with any vegetables you may have. For a large party, with plenty of squirrels, prepare a

Virginia Barbecue.—Build a hardwood fire between two large logs lying about two feet apart. At each end of the fire drive two forked stakes about fifteen inches apart, so that the four stakes will form a rectangle, like the legs of a table. The forks should all be about eighteen inches above the ground. Choose young, tender squirrels (if old ones must be used, parboil them until tender but not soft). Prepare spits by cutting stout switches of some wood that does not burn easily (sassafras is best—beware of poison sumach), peel them, sharpen the points, and harden them by thrusting for a few moments under the hot ashes. Impale each squirrel by thrusting a spit through flank, belly, and shoulder, on one side, and another spit similarly on the other side, spreading out the sides, and, if necessary, cutting through the ribs, so that the squirrel will lie open and flat. Lay two poles across the fire from crotch to crotch of the posts, and across these lay your spitted squirrels. As soon as these are heated through, begin basting with a piece of pork on the end of a switch. Turn the squirrels as required. Cook slowly, tempering the heat, if needful, by scattering ashes thinly over the coals; but remove the ashes for a final browning. When the squirrels are done, butter them, and gash a little that the juices may flow.

As squirrels are usually hunted in regions where canned goods can easily be procured, I append directions for a

Brunswick Stew.—The ingredients needed, besides several squirrels, are:

1 qt. can tomatoes,
1 pt. " butter beans or limas,
1 pt. " green corn,
6 potatoes, parboiled and sliced,
½ lb. butter,
½ lb. salt pork (fat),
1 teaspoonful black pepper,
½ " Cayenne
1 tablespoonful salt,
2 tablespoonfuls white sugar,
1 onion, minced small.

Soak the squirrels half an hour in cold salted water. Add the salt to one gallon of water, and boil five minutes. Then put in the onion, beans, corn, pork (cut in fine strips), potatoes, pepper, and squirrels. Cover closely, and stew very slowly two and a half hours, stirring frequently to prevent burning. Add the tomatoes and sugar, and stew an hour longer. Then add the butter, cut into bits the size of a walnut and rolled in flour. Boil ten minutes. Then serve at once.

This is a famous huntsman's dish of the Old Dominion. One can easily see how it can be adapted to other game than squirrels.

Rabbit.—Remove the head; skin and draw; soak in cold salted water for one hour; rinse in fresh cold water, and wipe dry.

For frying, select only young rabbits, or parboil first with salt and pepper. Cut off legs at body joint, and cut the back into three pieces. Sprinkle with flour, and fry brown on both sides. Remove rabbit to a dish kept hot over a few coals. Make a gravy as follows: Put into the pan a small onion previously parboiled and minced, and add one cup boiling water. Stir in gradually one or two tablespoonfuls of browned flour; stir well, and let it boil one minute. Season with pepper, salt, and nutmeg. Pour it over the rabbit.

To roast in reflector: cut as above, lay a slice of pork on each piece, and baste frequently. The rabbit may be roasted whole before the fire.

To bake in an oven: stuff with a dressing made of bread crumbs, the heart and liver (previously parboiled in a small amount of water), some fat salt pork, and a small onion, all minced and mixed together, seasoned with pepper, salt, and nutmeg, and slightly moistened with the water in which heart and liver were parboiled. Sew up the opening closely; rub butter or dripping over rabbit, dredge with flour, lay thin slices of fat pork on back, and place it in pan or Dutch oven, back uppermost. Pour into pan a pint or more of boiling water (or stock, if you have it), and bake with very moderate heat, one hour, basting every few minutes if in pan, but not if in Dutch oven. Prepare a gravy with the pot juice, as directed above.

Rabbit is good stewed with onion, nutmeg, pepper and salt for seasoning.

Rabbits are unfit to eat in late summer, as their backs are then infested with warbles, which are the larvæ of the rabbit bot-fly.

Possum.—To call our possum an opossum, outside of a scientific treatise, is an affectation. Possum is his name wherever he is known and hunted, this country over. He is not good until you have freezing weather; nor is he to be served without sweet potatoes, except in desperate extremity. This is how to serve "possum hot."

Stick him, and hang him up to bleed until morning. A tub is half filled with hot water (not quite scalding) into which drop the possum and hold him by the tail until the hair will strip. Take him out, lay him on a plank, and pull the hair out with your fingers. Draw, clean, and hang him up to freeze for two or three nights. Then place him in a 5-gallon kettle of cold water, into which throw two pods of red pepper. Parboil for one hour in this pepper-water, which is then thrown out and the kettle is refilled with fresh water, wherein he is boiled one hour. While this is going on, slice and steam some sweet potatoes. Take the possum out, place him in a large Dutch oven, sprinkle him with black pepper, salt, and a pinch or two of sage. A dash of lemon will do no harm. Pack sweet potatoes around him. Pour a pint of water into the oven, put the lid on, and see that it fits tightly. Bake slowly until brown and crisp. Serve hot, *without* gravy. Bourbon whiskey is the only orthodox accompaniment, unless you are a teetotaler, in which case any plantation darky can show you how to make "ginger tea" out of ginger, molasses and water. Corn bread, of course.

It is said that possum is not hard to digest even when eaten cold; but the general verdict seems to be that none is ever left over to get cold.

When you have no oven, roast the possum before a high bed of coals, having suspended him by a wet string, which is twisted and untwisted to give a rotary motion, and constantly baste it with a sauce made from red pepper, salt, and vinegar.

Possum may also be baked in clay, with his hide on. Stuff with stale bread and sage, plaster over him an inch of stiff clay, and bake as previously directed. He will be done in about an hour.

Coon.—It is likewise pedantic to call this animal a raccoon. Coon he always has been, is now, and shall ever be, to those who know him best.

Skin and dress him. Remove the "kernels" (scent glands) under each front leg and on either side of spine in small of back. Wash in cold water. Parboil in one or two waters, depending upon the animal's age. Stuff with dressing like a turkey. If you have a tart apple, quarter it and add to the dressing. Roast to a delicate brown. Serve with fried sweet potatoes.

Porcupine.—I quote from Nessmuk: "And do not despise the fretful porcupine; he is better than he looks. If you happen on a healthy young specimen when you are needing meat, give him a show before condemning him. Shoot him humanely in the head, and dress him. It is easily done; there are no quills on the belly, and the skin peels as freely as a rabbit's. Take him to camp, parboil him for thirty minutes, and roast or broil him to a rich brown over a bed of glowing coals. He will need no pork to make him juicy, and you will find him very like spring lamb, only better."

The porcupine may also be baked in clay, without

skinning him; the quills and skin peel off with the hard clay covering.

Muskrat.—You may be driven to this, some day, and will then learn that muskrat, properly prepared, is not half bad. The French-Canadians found that out long ago. The following recipe is from Abercrombie & Fitch's catalogue:

"Skin and clean carefully four muskrats, being particular not to rupture musk or gall sac. Take the hind legs and saddles, place in pot with a little water, a little julienne (or fresh vegetables, if you have them), some pepper and salt, and a few slices of pork or bacon. Simmer slowly over fire until half done. Remove to baker, place water from pot in the baking pan, and cook until done, basting frequently. This will be found a most toothsome dish."

Muskrat may also be broiled over the hot coals, basting with a bit of pork held on a switch above the beastie.

Woodchuck.—I asked old Uncle Bob Flowers, one of my neighbors in the Smokies: "Did you ever eat a woodchuck?"

"Reckon I don't know what them is."

"Ground-hog."

"O la! dozens of 'em. The red ones hain't good, but the gray ones! man, they'd jest make yer mouth water!"

"How do you cook them?"

"Cut the leetle red kernels out from under their fore legs; then bile 'em, fust—all the strong is left in the water—then pepper 'em, and sage 'em, and put 'em in a pan, and bake 'em to a nice rich brown, and—then I don't want nobody there but me!"

Beaver Tail.—This tid-bit of the old-time trappers will be tested by few of our generation, more's the pity! Impale tail on a sharp stick and broil over the coals for a few minutes. The rough, scaly hide will blister and come off in sheets, leaving the tail clean, white, and solid. Then roast, or boil until tender. It is of a gelatinous nature, tastes somewhat like pork, and is considered very strengthening food. A young beaver, stuffed and baked in its hide, is good; old ones have a peculiar flavor that is unpleasant to those not accustomed to such diet.

Beaver tail may also be soused in vinegar, after boiling, or baked with beans. The liver of the animal, broiled on a stick and seasoned with butter, salt, and pepper, is the best part of the animal.

Canned Meat. Dried Fish. These are good to fall back on when game and fish fail, and you have tired of salt pork and bacon.

Corned Beef Hash.—Chop some canned corned beef fine with sliced onions. Mash up with freshly boiled potatoes, two parts potatoes to one of meat. Season highly with pepper (no salt) and dry mustard if liked. Put a little pork fat in a frying-pan, melt, add hash, and cook until nearly dry and a brown crust has formed. Evaporated potatoes and onions can be used according to directions on packages.

Stew with Canned Meat.—Peel and slice some onions. If the meat has much fat, melt it; if not, melt a little pork fat. Add onions, and fry until brown. Mix some flour into a smooth batter with cold water, season with pepper and salt, and pour into the camp kettle. Stir the whole well together. Cut meat into slices, put into the kettle, and heat through.

Stewed Codfish.—Soak over night in plenty of cold water. Put in pot of fresh, cold water, and heat gradually until soft. Do not boil the fish or it will get hard. Serve with boiled potatoes, and with white sauce made as directed under Fish.

Codfish Hash.—Prepare salt codfish as above. When soft, mash with potatoes and onions, season with pepper, and fry like corned beef hash.

Codfish Balls.—Shred the fish into small pieces. Peel some potatoes. Use one pint of fish to one quart of raw potatoes. Put them in a pot, cover with boiling water, cook till potatoes are soft, drain water off, mash fish and potatoes together, and beat light with a fork. Add a tablespoonful of butter and season with pepper. Shape into flattened balls, and fry in very hot fat deep enough to cover.

Broiled Salt Fish.—Freshen the flakes of fish by soaking for an hour in cold water. Broil over the coals, and serve with potatoes.

Smoked Herrings.—(1) Clean, and remove the skin. Toast on a stick over the coals.

(2) Scald in boiling water till the skin curls up, then remove head, tail, and skin. Clean well. Put into frying-pan with a little butter and lard. Fry gently a few minutes, dropping in a little vinegar.

Birds.

Any kind of bird may be fricasseed as follows: Cut it into convenient pieces, parboil them in enough water to cover; when tender, remove from the pot and drain. Fry two or three slices of pork until brown. Sprinkle the pieces of bird with salt, pepper, and flour, and fry to a dark brown in the pork fat. Take up the bird, and stir into the frying fat half a cup, more or less, of dry flour, stirring until it becomes a dark brown; then pour over it the liquor in which the bird was boiled (unless it was a fish-eater), and bring the mixture to a boil. Put the bird in a hot dish, and pour gravy over it.

Wild Turkey, Roasted.—Pluck, draw, and singe. Wipe the bird inside and out. Stuff the crop cavity, then the body, with either of the dressings mentioned below, allowing room for the filling to swell. Tie a string around the neck, and sew up the body. Truss wings to body with wooden skewers. Pin thin slices of fat pork to breast in same way. Suspend the fowl before a high bed of hardwood coals, as previously described, and place a pan under it to catch drippings. Tie a clean rag on the end of a stick to baste with. Turn and baste frequently. Roast until well done (two to three hours).

Meantime cleanse the gizzard, liver, and heart of the turkey thoroughly in cold water; mince them; put them in a pot with enough cold water to cover, and stew gently until tender; then place where they will keep warm until wanted. When the turkey is done, add the giblets with the water in which they were stewed to the drippings in pan; thicken with one or two tablespoonfuls of flour that has been stirred up in milk or water and browned in a pan; season with pepper and salt, and serve with the turkey.

Stuffing for Turkey.—(1) If chestnuts are procurable, roast a quart of them, remove shells, and mash. Add a teaspoonful of salt, and some pepper. Mix well together, and stuff the bird with them.

(2) Chop some fat salt pork very fine; soak stale bread or crackers in hot water, mash smooth, and mix with the chopped pork. Season with salt, pepper, sage, and chopped onion.

No game bird save the wild turkey should be stuffed, unless you deliberately wish to disguise the natural flavor.

Boiled Turkey.—Pluck, draw, singe, wash inside with warm water, and wipe dry. Cut off head and neck close to backbone, leaving enough skin to turn over the stuffing. Draw sinews from legs, and cut off feet just below first joint of leg. Press legs into sides and skewer them firmly. Stuff breast as above. Put the bird into enough hot water to cover it. Remove scum as it rises. Boil gently one and one-half to two hours. Serve with sauce.

Waterfowl have two large oil glands in the tail, with which they oil their feathers. The oil in these glands imparts a strong, disagreeable flavor to the bird soon after it is killed. Hence the tail should always be removed before cooking.

To Cook a Large Bird in a Hurry.—Slice off several fillets from the breast; impale them, with slices of pork, on a green switch; broil over the coals.

Baked Duck.—The bird should be dry-picked, and the head left on. Put a little pepper and salt inside the bird, but *no other dressing.* Lay duck on its back in the bake-pan. Put no water in the pan. The oven must be hot, but not hot enough to burn; test with the hand. Baste frequently while cooking. A canvas-back requires about thirty minutes; other birds according to size. When done, the duck should be plump, and the flesh red, not blue.

This is the way to bring out the distinctive flavor of a canvasback. Seasoning and stuffing destroy all that.

Stewed Duck.—Clean well and divide into convenient pieces (say, legs, wings, and four parts of body). Place in pot with enough cold water to cover. Add salt, pepper, a pinch of mixed herbs, and a dash of Worcestershire sauce. Cut up fine some onions and potatoes (carrots, too, if you can get them). Put a few of these in the pot so they may dissolve and add body to the dish (flour or corn starch may be substituted for thickening). Stew slowly, skim and stir frequently. In forty-five minutes add the rest of the carrots, and in fifteen minutes more add the rest of the onions and potatoes, also turnips, if you have any. Stew until meat is done.

A plainer camp dish is to stew for an hour in water that has previously been boiled for an hour with pieces of salt pork.

Fish-eating Ducks.—The rank taste of these can be neutralized, unless very strong, by baking with an onion inside. Use plenty of pepper, inside and out.

Mud-hens and Bitterns.—Remove the breast of a coot or rail, cut slits in it, and in these stick thin slices of fat salt pork; broil over the embers.

The broiled breast of a young bittern is good.

Fish.

Fish caught in muddy streams should be cut up and soaked in strong salted water. Never put live fish on a stringer and keep them in water till you start for home. Does it not stand to reason that fish strung through the gills must breathe with difficulty and be tormented? Why sicken your fish before you eat them? Kill every fish as soon as caught and bleed it through the throat.

Fish Chowder.—Clean the fish, parboil it, and reserve the water in which it was boiled. Place the dry pot on the fire; when it is hot, throw in a lump of butter and about six onions sliced finely. When the odor of onion arises, add the fish. Cover the pot closely for fish to absorb flavor. Add a very small quantity of potatoes, and some of the reserved broth. When cooked, let each man season his own dish. Ask a blessing and eat. (*Kenealy.*)

Roasted Eel.—Cut a stick about three feet long and

an inch thick; split it about a foot down from one end; draw the eel, but do not skin it; coil it between the two forks of the stick, and bind the top of split end with green withes; stick the other end in the ground before a good fire, and turn as required.

Stewed Eel.—Skin the eel, remove backbone and cut the eel into pieces about two inches long; cover these with water in the stew-pan, and add a teaspoonful of strong vinegar or a slice of lemon, cover stew-pan and boil moderately one half hour. Then remove, pour off water, drain, add fresh water and vinegar as before, and stew until tender. Now drain, add cream enough for a stew, season with pepper and salt (no butter), boil again for a few minutes, and serve on hot, dry toast. (*Up De Graff.*)

Fish Roe.—Parboil (merely simmer) fifteen minutes; let them cool and drain; then roll in flour, and fry.

Frog Legs.—First after skinning, soak them an hour in cold water to which vinegar has been added, or put them for two minutes into scalding water that has vinegar in it. Drain, wipe dry, and cook as below:

To fry: roll in flour seasoned with salt and pepper and fry, not too rapidly, preferably in butter or oil. Water cress is a good relish with them.

To grill: Prepare 3 tablespoonfuls melted butter, ½ teaspoonful salt, and a pinch or two of pepper, into which dip the frog legs, then roll in fresh bread crumbs, and broil for three minutes on each side.

Turtles.—All turtles (aquatic) and most tortoises (land) are good to eat, the common snapper being far better than he looks. Kill by cutting throat or (readier) by shooting the head off. This does not kill the brute immediately, of course, but it suffices. The common way of killing by dropping a turtle into boiling water I do not like. Let the animal bleed. Then drop into a pot of boiling water for a few seconds. After scalding, the outer scales of shell, as well as the skin, are easily removed. Turn turtle on its back, cut down middle of under shell from end to end, and then across. Throw away entrails, head, and claws. Salt and pepper it inside and out. Boil a short time in the shell. Remove when the meat has cooked free from the shell. Cut up the latter and boil slowly for three hours with some chopped onion. If a stew is preferred, use less water, and add some salt pork cut into dice.

Crayfish.—These are the "craw-feesh!" of our streets. Tear off extreme end of tail, bringing the entrail with it. Boil whole in salted water till the crayfish turns red. Peel and eat as a lobster, dipping each crayfish at a time into a saucer of vinegar, pepper, and salt.

VEGETABLES, ETC.

The general rules for cooking vegetables are few and simple.

(1) Do not wash fresh vegetables until just before they are to be cooked or eaten. They lose flavor quickly after being washed. This is true even of potatoes.

(2) Green vegetables go into boiling salted water. Salt prevents their absorbing too much water. The water should be boiling fast, and there should be plenty of it. They should be boiled rapidly, with the lid left off the pan. If the water is as hot as it should be, the effect is similar to that which we have noted in the case of meats: the surface is coagulated into a waterproof envelope which seals up the flavor instead of letting it be soaked out. In making soup, the rule is reversed.

(3) Dried vegetables, such as beans and peas, are to be cooked in unsalted water. If salted too soon they become leathery and difficult to cook. Put them in cold, fresh water, gradually heated to the boiling point, and boil slowly.

(4) Desiccated vegetables are first soaked in cold water, according to directions on package—potatoes require long soaking, and they should be boiled in three waters. Place in boiling water slightly salted, and proceed as with fresh vegetables.

To clear cabbage, etc., from insects, immerse, stalk upward, in plenty of cold water salted in the proportion of a large tablespoonful to two quarts; vinegar may be used instead of salt. Shake occasionally. The insects will sink to bottom of pan.

To keep vegetables, put them in a cool, dry place (conditions similar to those of a good cellar). Keep each kind away from the other, or they will absorb each other's flavor.

Potatoes, Boiled.—Pick them out as nearly as possible of one size, or some will boil to pieces before the others are done; if necessary, cut them to one size. Remove eyes and specks, and pare as thinly as possible, for the best of the potato lies just under the skin. As fast as pared, throw into cold water, and leave until wanted. Put in furiously boiling salted water, then hang kettle a little higher where it will boil moderately, but do not let it check. Test with a fork or sliver. When the tubers are done (about twenty minutes for new potatoes, thirty to forty minutes for old ones) drain off all the water, dust some salt over the potatoes (it absorbs the surface moisture), and let the pot stand uncovered close to the fire, shaking it gently once or twice, till the surface of each potato is dry and powdery. Never leave potatoes in the water after they are done; they would become watery.

Potatoes, Boiled in their Jackets.—After washing thoroughly, and gouging out the eyes, snip off a bit from each end of the potato; this gives a vent to the steam and keeps potatoes from bursting open. I prefer to put them in cold water and bring it gradually to a boil, because the skin of the potato contains an acid poison which is thus extracted. The water in which potatoes have been boiled will poison a dog. Of course we don't "eat 'em skin and all," like the people in the nursery rhyme; but there is no use in driving the bitterness into a potato. Boil gently, but continuously, throw in a little salt now and then, drain, and dry before the fire.

Mashed Potatoes.—After boiling, mash the potatoes, and work into them some butter and cream, gin you have any. Then beat them up light with a fork. However it may be with "a woman, a dog, and a walnut tree," it is true of mashed potatoes, that "the more you beat 'em, the better they be."

Potatoes, Steamed.—After you have once learned the knack, you will find that the best of all ways to cook potatoes is by steaming in a hole in the ground, as directed in the last chapter. No danger of them being watery then.

Baked Potatoes.—Nessmuk's description cannot be improved: "Scoop out a basin-like depression under the fore-stick, three or four inches deep, and large enough to hold the tubers when laid side by side; fill it with bright hardwood coals, and keep up a strong heat for half an hour or more. Next, clean out the hollow, place the potatoes in it, and cover them with hot sand or ashes, topped with a heap of glowing coals, and keep up all the heat you like. In about forty minutes commence to try them with a sharpened hard-wood sliver; when this will pass through them they are done, and should be raked out at once. Run the sliver through them from end to end, to let the steam escape, and use immediately, as a roast potato quickly becomes soggy and bitter."

Fried Potatoes.—Boiled or steamed potatoes that have been left over may be sliced $\frac{1}{4}$ inch thick, and fried. They are better *à la Lyonnaise:* fry one or more sliced onions until they are turning yellowish, then add sliced potatoes; keep tossing now and then until the potatoes are fried somewhat yellow; salt to taste.

Potatoes, Fried Raw.—Peel, and slice into pieces $\frac{1}{2}$ inch thick. Drop into cold water until frying-pan is ready. Put enough grease in pan to completely immerse the potatoes, and get it very hot, as directed under Frying. Pour water off potatoes, dry a slice in a clean cloth, drop it into the sizzling fat, and so on, one slice at a time. Drying the slices avoids a splutter in the pan and helps to keep from absorbing grease. If many slices were dropped into the pan together, the heat would be checked and the potatoes would get soggy with grease. When the slices begin to turn a faint brown, salt the potatoes, pour off the grease at once, and brown a little in the dry pan. The outside of each slice will then be crisp and the insides white and deliciously mealy.

Sweet Potatoes, Boiled.—Use a kettle with lid. Select tubers of uniform size; wash; do not cut or break the skins. Put them in boiling water, and continue boiling until, when you pierce one with a fork, you find it just a little hard in the center. Drain by raising the cover only a trifle when kettle is tilted, so as to keep in as much steam as possible. Hang the kettle high over the fire, cover closely, and let steam ten minutes.

Sweet Potatoes, Fried.—Skin the boiled potatoes and cut them lengthwise. Dust the slices with salt and pepper. Throw them into hot fat, browning first one side, then the other. Serve very hot.

Potatoes and Onions, Hashed.—Slice two potatoes to one onion. Parboil together about fifteen minutes in salted water. Pour off water, and drain. Meantime be frying some bacon. When it is done, remove it to a hot side dish, turn the vegetables into the pan, and fry them to a light brown. Then fall to, and enjoy a good thing!

Beans, Boiled.—Pick out all defective beans, and wash the rest. It is best to soak the beans over night; but if time does not permit, add $\frac{1}{4}$ teaspoonful of baking soda to the parboiling water. In either case, start in fresh cold water, and parboil one pint of beans (for four men with hearty appetites) for one-half hour, or until one will pop open when blown upon. At the same time parboil separately one pound fat salt pork. Remove scum from beans as it rises. Drain both; place beans around the pork, add two quarts boiling water, and boil slowly for two hours, or until tender. Drain, and season with salt and pepper.

It does not hurt beans to boil all day, provided boiling water is added from time to time, lest they get dry and scorch. The longer they boil the more digestible they become.

Baked Beans.—Soak and parboil, as above, both the beans and the pork. Then pour off the water from the pork, gash the meat with a knife, spread half of it over the bottom of the kettle, drain the beans, pour them into the kettle, put the rest of pork on top, sprinkle not more than $\frac{1}{2}$ teaspoonful of salt over the beans, pepper liberally, and if you have molasses, pour a tablespoonful over all; otherwise a tablespoonful of sugar. Hang the kettle high over the fire where it will not scorch, and bake six hours; or, better, add a little of the water that the beans were boiled in, place kettle in bake-hole as elsewhere directed, and bake all night.

Baked beans are strong food, ideal for active men in cold weather. One can work harder and longer on pork and beans, without feeling hungry, than on any other food with which I am acquainted, save bear meat. The ingredients are compact and easy to transport; they keep indefinitely in any weather. But when one is only beginning camp life he should be careful not to overload his stomach with beans, for they are rather indigestible until you have toned up your stomach by hearty exercise in the open air.

Onions, Boiled.—More wholesome this way than fried or baked. Like potatoes, they should be of as uniform size as possible, for boiling. Do not boil them in an iron vessel. Put them in enough boiling salted water to cover them. Cover the kettle and boil gently, lest the onions break. They are cooked when a straw will pierce them (about an hour). If you wish them mild, boil in two or three waters. When cooked, drain and season with butter or dripping, pepper, and salt.

Green Corn.—If you happen to camp near a farm in the "roasting-ear" season, you are in great luck.

The quickest way to roast an ear of corn is to cut off the butt of the ear closely, so that the pith of the cob is exposed, ream it out a little, impale the cob lengthwise on the end of a long hardwood stick, and turn over the coals.

To roast in the ashes: remove one outer husk, stripping off the silk, break off about an inch of the silk end, and twist end of husks tightly down over the broken end. Then bake in the ashes and embers as directed for potatoes. Time, about one hour.

To boil: prepare as above, but tie the ends of husks; this preserves the sweetness of the corn. Put in enough boiling salted water to cover the ears. Boil thirty minutes. Like potatoes, corn is injured by over-boiling. When cooked, cut off the butt and remove the shucks.

Cold boiled corn may be cut from the cob and fried, or mixed with mashed potato and fried.

Greens.—One who camps early in the season can add a toothsome dish, now and then, to his menu by gathering fresh greens in the woods and marshes. Many of these are mentioned in my chapter on *The Edible Plants of the Wilderness.* They may be prepared in various ways; here are a few:

As a salad (watercress, peppergrass, dandelion, sorrel, etc.): wash in cold salted water, if necessary, although this abstracts some of the flavor; dry immediately and thoroughly. Break into convenient pieces, rejecting tough stems. Prepare a simple French dressing, thus:

1 tablespoonful vinegar,
3 tablespoonfuls best olive oil,
½ teaspoonful salt,
¼ " black pepper.

Put salt and pepper in bowl, gradually add oil, rubbing and mixing till salt is dissolved; then add by degrees the vinegar, stirring continuously one minute. In default of oil, use cream and melted butter; but plain vinegar, salt and pepper will do. Pour the dressing over the salad, turn the latter upside down, mix well and serve.

A scalded salad is prepared in camp by cutting bacon into small dice, frying, adding vinegar, pepper, and a little salt to the grease, and pouring this, scalding hot, over the greens.

Greens may be boiled with salt pork, bacon, or other meat. To boil them separately: first soak in cold salted water for a few minutes, then drain well, and put into enough boiling salted water to cover, pressing them down until the pot is full. Cover, and boil steadily until tender, which may be from twenty minutes to an hour, depending upon kind of greens used. If the plants are a little older than they should be, parboil in water to which a little baking soda has been added; then drain, and continue boiling in plain water, salted.

Some greens are improved by chopping fine after boiling, putting in hot frying-pan with a tablespoonful of butter and some salt and pepper, and stirring until thoroughly heated.

Poke stalks are cooked like asparagus. They should not be over four inches long, and should show only a tuft of leaves at the top; if much older than this, they are poisonous. Wash the stalks, scrape them, and lay in cold water for an hour; then tie loosely in bundles, put in a kettle of boiling water and boil three-fourths of an hour, or until tender; drain, lay on buttered toast, dust with pepper and salt, cover with melted butter, and serve.

Jerusalem artichokes must be watched when boiling and removed as soon as tender; if left longer in the water, they harden.

Dock and sorrel may be cooked like spinach: pick over and wash, drain, shake and press out adhering water; put in kettle with one cup water, cover kettle, place over moderate fire, and steam thus twenty minutes; then drain, chop very fine, and heat in frying-pan as directed above.

Mushrooms.—Every one who camps in summer should take with him a mushroom book, such as Gibson's, Atkinson's, or Nina Marshall's. (Such a book in pocket form, with *colored* illustrations, is a desideratum.) Follow recipes in book. Mushrooms are very easy to prepare, cook quickly, and offer a great variety of flavors.

Canned Tomatoes.—When you can get butter, try this: To a pint of tomatoes add butter twice the size of an egg, some pepper, very little salt, and a tablespoonful of sugar. Boil about five minutes. Put some bread crumbs or toast in a dish, and pour tomatoes over them.

Canned Sweet Corn.—Same as tomatoes, but omitting sugar and bread. Add a cup of cream, if convenient.

Jambolaya.—This is a delicious Creole dish, easily prepared. Cut up any kind of small game into joints, and stew them. When half done, add some minced ham or bacon, $\frac{1}{4}$ pint rice, and season with pepper and salt. If rabbit is used, add onions. Serve with tomatoes as a sauce.

Pot Pie.—Take $\frac{1}{2}$ teaspoonful baking powder to $\frac{1}{2}$ pint of flour, sift together, and add 1 teaspoonful lard or butter by rubbing it in, also a pinch of salt. Make a soft biscuit dough of this, handling as little as possible, and being careful not to mix too thin. Roll into a sheet, and cut into strips about $1\frac{1}{2}$ inch wide and 3 inches long, cutting two or three little holes through each to let steam escape. Meantime you have been boiling meat or game, and have sliced some potatoes. When the meat is within one-half hour of being done, pour off the broth into another vessel and lift out most of the meat. Place a layer of meat and potatoes in bottom of kettle, and partially cover with strips of the dough; then another layer of meat and vegetables, another of dough, and so on until the pot is nearly full, topping off with dough. Pour the hot broth over this, cover tightly, and boil one-half hour, without lifting the pot cover, which, by admitting cold air, would make the dough "sad." Parsley helps the pot, when you can get it.

Slumgullion.—When the commissariat is reduced to bacon, corned beef, and hardtack, try this sailor's dish, described by Jack London: Fry half a dozen slices of bacon, add fragments of hardtack, then two cups of water, and stir briskly over the fire; in a few minutes mix in with it slices of canned corned beef; season well with pepper and salt.

Soups.

When Napoleon said that "soup makes the soldier," he meant thick, substantial soup—soup that sticks to the ribs—not mere broths or meat extracts, which are fit only for invalids or to coax an indifferent stomach. "Soup," says Nessmuk, "requires time, and a solid basis of the right material. Venison is the basis, and the best material is the bloody part of the deer, where the bullet went through. We used to throw this away; we have learned better. Cut about four pounds of the bloody meat into convenient pieces, and wipe them as clean as possible with leaves or a damp cloth, but don't wash them. Put the meat into a five-quart kettle nearly filled with water, and raise it to a lively boiling pitch. Let it boil for two hours. Have ready a three-tined fork made from a branch of birch or beech, and with this test the meat from time to time; when it parts readily from the bones, slice in a large onion. Pare six large, smooth potatoes, cut five of them into quarters, and drop them into the kettle; scrape the sixth one into the soup for thickening. Season with salt and white pepper to taste. When, by skirmishing with the wooden fork, you can fish up bones with no meat on them, the soup is cooked, and the kettle may be set aside to cool."

Any kind of game may be used in a similar way, provided that none but lean meat be used. Soup is improved by first soaking the chopped-up meat in cold water, and using this water to boil in thereafter. Soup should be skimmed for some time after it has started simmering, to remove grease and scum.

Bean Soup.—Boil with pork, as previously directed, until the beans are tender enough to crack open; then take out the pork and mash the beans into a paste. Return pork to kettle, add a cup of flour mixed thin with cold water, stirring it in slowly as the kettle simmers. Boil slowly an hour longer, stirring frequently so that it may not scorch. Season with little salt but plenty of pepper.

Pea Soup.—Wash well one pint of split peas, cover with cold water, and let them soak over night. In the morning put them in a kettle with close-fitting cover. Pour over them 3 quarts cold water, adding $\frac{1}{2}$ pound lean bacon or ham cut into dice, 1 teaspoonful salt, and some pepper. When the soup begins to boil, skim the froth from the surface. Cook slowly three to four hours, stirring occasionally till the peas are all dissolved, and adding a little more boiling water to keep up the quantity as it boils away. Let it get quite thick. Just before serving, drop in small squares of toasted bread or biscuits, adding quickly while the bread is hot. Vegetables may be added one-half hour before the soup is done.

Dried Fruit.—Soak over night in cold water, just enough to cover—too much water makes them insipid. They are quite eatable then, without cooking. Add half a cup of sugar and some spice; simmer until done. Fruit should not be cooked in an iron vessel, nor in tin, if it can be avoided.

Snits und Knepp.—This is a Pennsylvania-Dutch dish, and a good one for campers. Take some dried apples (not evaporated ones, which are tasteless, but the old-fashioned dried apples of the country) and soak them over night. Boil until tender. Prepare knepp as directed for pot-pie dough, only make a thick batter of it instead of a dough. It is best to add an egg and use no shortening. Drop the batter into the pan of stewing apples, a large spoonful at a time, not fast enough to check the boiling. Boil about one-half hour. Season with butter, sugar, and cinnamon.

Desserts.

Plain Plum Duff.—Put into a basin one pound of flour, one heaping teaspoonful of baking powder, one pound raisins (stoned, if possible), three-quarters of a pound of fat of salt pork (well washed and cut into small dice, or chopped), and two tablespoonfuls of sugar. Add half a pint of water and mix well together. Dip a cloth bag large enough to hold the pudding into boiling water, wring it out, and apply flour well to the inside. Put in the pudding and fasten it up, leaving a little room in the bag for the pudding to swell. Now place the whole in enough boiling water to cover the bag, and boil two hours, turning the bag several times to prevent its scorching against the bottom or sides of the pot. If necessary, add boiling water to keep the bag covered. When done take the pudding from the pot, plunge it into cold water for an instant, and then turn it out to be eaten. Suet may be used to advantage instead of pork fat. Spices and molasses also, if you have them, and want a richer duff. (*Kenealy.*)

Pie.—It is not to be presumed that a mere male camper can make a good pie-crust in the regular way; but it is easy to make a wholesome and very fair pie-crust in an irregular way, which is as follows: Make a glorified biscuit dough by mixing thoroughly 1 pint flour, 1 teaspoonful baking powder, ½ teaspoonful salt, rubbing in 4 heaped tablespoonfuls of lard, and making into a soft dough with cold water. In doing this, observe the rules given under Biscuit. The above quantity is enough for a pie filling an 8x12 reflector pan. Roll the dough into a thin sheet, as thin as you can handle, and do the rolling as gently as you can. From this sheet cut a piece large enough for bottom crust and lay it in the greased pan. The sheet should be big enough to lap over edge of pan. Into this put your fruit (dried fruit is previously stewed and mashed), and add sugar and spice to taste. Then, with great circumspection and becoming reverence, lay on top of all this your upper crust. Now, with your thumb, press the edges of upper and lower crust together all around, your thumb-prints leaving scallops around the edge. Trim off by running a knife around edge of pan. Then prick a number of small slits in the top crust, here and there, to give a vent to the steam when the fruit boils. Bake as you would biscuits.

Note that this dough contains baking powder, and that it will swell. Don't give the thing a name until it is baked; then, if you have made the crust too thick for a pie, call it a cobbler or a shortcake, and the boys, instead of laughing at you, will ask for more.

Doughnuts.—Mix one quart of flour with one teaspoonful of salt, one tablespoonful of baking powder and one pint of granulated sugar, and half a nutmeg grated. Make a batter of this with four beaten eggs and enough milk to make smoothe. Beat thoroughly and add enough flour to make a soft dough. Roll out into a sheet half an inch thick and cut into rings or strips, which may be twisted into shape. Fry in very hot fat; turn when necessary. Drain and serve hot

Or, mix with less water into a stiff dough, and manipulate as explained under Fried Quoits.

And now, having done my share, I will loll back at mine ease and smoke mine pipe, while the other fellow does the dish-washing!

Scullionry.

Gilbert Hamerton, in his *Painter's Camp*, dwells lovingly upon all the little details of camp life, excepting this:

> 5 P. M. Cease painting for the day. Dine . . . After dinner the woeful drudgery of cleaning-up! At this period of the day am seized with a vague desire to espouse a scullery-maid, it being impossible to accommodate one in the hut without scandal, unless in the holy state of matrimony: hope no scullery-maid will pass the hut when I am engaged in washing-up, as I should be sure to make her an offer.

There is a desperately hard and disagreeable way of washing dishes, which consists, primarily, in "going for" everything alike with the same rag, and wiping grease off one dish only to smear it on the next one. There is another, an easier, and a cleaner way: First, as to the frying-pan, which generally is greasiest of all: pour it nearly full of water, place it level over the coals, and let it boil over. Then pick it up, give a quick flirt to empty it, and hang it up. Virtually it has cleaned itself, and will dry itself if let alone. Greasy dishes are scraped as clean as may be, washed with scalding water, and then wiped. An obdurate pot is cleaned by first boiling in it some wood ashes, the lye of which makes a sort of soap of the grease; or it may be scoured out with sand and hot water. Greasy dishes can even be cleaned without hot water, if first wiped with a handful or two of moss, which takes up the grease; use first the dirt side of the moss as a scourer, then the top. To scour greasy knives and forks, simply jab them once or twice into the ground. Rusty ones can be burnished by rubbing with a freshly cut potato dipped in wood ashes. The scouring rush (*Equisetum hymenale*), which grows in wet places and along banks throughout the northern hemisphere, has a gritty surface that makes an excellent swab. It is the tall, green, jointed, pipe-stem-like weed that children amuse themselves with, by pulling the joints apart. In brief, the art of dish-washing consists in first cleaning off nearly all the grease before using your dish-cloth on it. Then the cloth will be fit to use again. Dish-cloths are the supplies that first run short in an average outfit.

CHAPTER XII

PESTS OF THE WOODS

SUMMER twilight brings the mosquito. In fact, when we go far north or far south, we have him with us both by day and night. Rather I should say that we have *her;* for the male mosquito is a gentleman, who sips daintily of nectar and minds his own business, while madame his spouse is a whining, peevish, venomous virago, that goes about seeking whose nerves she may unstring and whose blood she may devour. Strange to say, not among mosquitoes only, but among ticks, fleas, chiggers, and the whole legion of bloodthirsty, stinging flies and midges, it is only the female that attacks man and beast. Stranger still, the mosquito is not only a bloodsucker but an incorrigible winebibber as well—she will get helplessly fuddled on any sweet wine, such as port, or on sugared spirits, while of gin she is inordinately fond.

Such disreputable habits—the querulous sing-song, the poisoned sting, the thirst for blood, and the practice of getting dead drunk at every opportunity, are enough of themselves to make the mosquito a thing accursed; but these are by no means the worst counts in our indictment against her. We have learned, within the past few years, that all the suffering and mortality from malaria, yellow fever, and filariasis (including the hideous and fatal elephantiasis of the tropics) is due to germs that are carried in no other way than by mosquitoes. Flies spread the germs of typhoid fever and malignant eye diseases; fleas carry the bubonic plague; the sleeping-sickness of Africa is transmitted by insects. There is no longer any guesswork about this: it is demonstrated fact. Professor Kellogg, summing up what is now known of the life history of malaria-bearing mosquitoes (*Anopheles*) says: "When in malarial regions, avoid the bite of a mosquito as you would that of a rattlesnake—one can be quite as serious in its results as the other."

The worst of it, from a sportsman's view-point, is that the farther we push toward the arctics or the tropics, the worse becomes this pest of dangerous insects. It is into just such countries that, nowadays and in future, we must go in order to get really first-class hunting and fishing. Consequently the problem of how best to fight our insect enemies becomes of ever increasing importance to all who love to hunt over and explore the wild places that are still left upon the earth.

Mosquitoes are bad enough in the tropics, but they are at their worst in the coldest regions of the earth.

Mosquitoes.

Harry de Windt reports that at Verkhoyansk, in Siberia, which is the arctic pole of cold (where the winter temperature often sinks to–75° Fahr., and has been known to reach–81°) the mosquitoes make their appearance before the snow is off the ground, and throughout the three summer months, make life almost unbearable to the wretched natives and exiles. The swamps and shoaly lakes in the surrounding country breed mosquitoes in such incredible hosts that reindeer, sledge-dogs, and sometimes even the natives themselves, are actually tormented to death by them.

Throughout a great part of central and western Canada, and Alaska, there are vast tundras of bog moss, called by the Indians muskegs, which in summer are the breeding-grounds of unending clouds of mosquitoes whose biting powers exceed those of any insects known in the United States. Even if the muskeg land were not a morass, this plague of mosquitoes would forever render it uninhabitable in summer. The insects come out of their pupæ at the first sprouting of spring vegetation, in May, and remain until destroyed by severe frosts in September. In Alaska, all animals leave for the snow-line as soon as the mosquito pest appears, but the enemy follows them even to the mountain tops above timber-line. Deer and moose are killed by mosquitoes, which settle upon them in such amazing swarms that the unfortunate beasts succumb from literally having the blood sucked out of their bodies. Bears are driven frantic, are totally blinded, mire in the mud, and starve to death. Animals that survive have their flesh discolored all through, and even their marrow is reduced to the consistency of blood and water. The men who penetrate such regions are not the kind that would allow toil or privation to break their spirit, but they become so unstrung from days and nights of continuous torment inflicted by enemies insignificant in size but infinite in number, that they become savage, desperate, and sometimes even weep in sheer helpless anger.

In regions so exceptionally cursed with mosquitoes no mere sportsman has any business until winter sets in.

Preventives. But even in the more accessible woodlands north and south of us the insect pest is by far the most serious hardship that fishermen and other summer outers are obliged to meet. Headnets and gauntlets are all very well in their way, but one can neither hunt, fish, paddle, push through the brush, nor even smoke, when so accoutered. Consequently everybody tries some kind or other of "fly-dope," by which elegant name we mean any preparation which, being rubbed over the exposed parts of one's skin, is supposed to discourage insects from repeating their attacks.

Fly-Dopes. The number of such dopes is legion. They may be classified in two groups:

(1) Thick ointments that dry to a tenacious glaze on the skin, if the wearer abstain from washing;

(2) Liquids or semi-fluid unguents that are supposed to protect by their odor alone, and must be renewed several times a day.

The latter vary a great deal. It is safe to say that everything in the pharmacopœia that seemed in the least promising has been tried. The oils of pennyroyal, cloves, lavender, citronella, verbena and lemongrass are often used singly; eucalyptol is favored by some, others find the tincture of *ledum palustre* (a

European relative of our Labrador tea) efficacious; while mixtures of camphor (1) and paraffin oil (3), or of sweet oil (16) and carbolic acid (1), or of creosote and glycerin, each has its coterie that swears by it. The personal equation seems to cut some figure in such matters: what works satisfactorily with some people is of no avail with others. A crushed dock or caribou leaf gives temporary relief.

Among the glazes, Nessmuk's recipe, published in his *Woodcraft*, is perhaps as well known and as widely used as any. He says this about it:

> I have never known it to fail: 3 oz. pine tar, 2 oz. castor oil, 1 oz. pennyroyal oil. Simmer all together over a slow fire, and bottle for use. You will hardly need more than a 2-oz. vial full in a season. One ounce has lasted me six weeks in the woods. Rub it in thoroughly and liberally at first, and after you have established a good glaze, a little replenishing from day to day will be sufficient. And don't fool with soap and towels where insects are plenty. A good safe coat of this varnish grows better the longer it is kept on—and it is cleanly and wholesome. If you get your face or hands crocky or smutty about the camp-fire, wet the corner of your handkerchief and rub it off, not forgetting to apply the varnish at once wherever you have cleaned it off. Last summer I carried a cake of soap and a towel in my knapsack through the North Woods for a seven weeks' tour, and never used either a single time. When I had established a good glaze on the skin, it was too valuable to be sacrificed for any weak whim connected with soap and water . . . It is a soothing and healing application for poisonous bites already received.

Aside from my personal tests of many dopes, I have had some interesting correspondence on this topic with sportsmen in various parts of the world. I quote from one letter, received last year from Col. Norman Fletcher of Louisville:

> Upon the swampy trout streams of Michigan on a warm May day . . . when the insects are abundant and vicious . . . pure pine tar is by far the best repellant when properly used. I give two recipes:
>
> (1) Pure pine tar. . . . . . . .1 ounce,
> Oil pennyroyal. . . . . . .1 "
> Vaselin . . . . .3 ounces.
>
> Mix cold in a mortar. If you wish, you can add 3 per cent. carbolic acid to above. Sometimes I make it 1½ oz. ta..

(2) Pure pine tar........2 ounces,
Castor oil...........3 "
Simmer for half an hour, and when cool add
Oil pennyroyal.......1 ounce.

There are many others of similar nature, but the above are as good as any . . . Now as to use of above: apply freely and frequently to all exposed parts of person, and *do not wash off until leaving* the place where the pests abound. You can wash your eyes in the morning, and wash the palms of your hands as often as may be necessary, but if you wish to be immune, don't wash any other exposed parts . . . When you get accustomed to it you will find some compensating comfort . . . I have had to contend with mosquitoes, deer-flies, black-flies, and midges . . . and have found "dope" with tar in it the best. I know that where mosquitoes are not very bad, oil of citronella, oil of verbena or of lemon-grass or of pennyroyal mixed with vaselin will keep them off, if the mixture is applied frequently. These essential oils are quickly evaporated, however, by the heat of the body. Camphorated oil is also used by some; this is simply sweet oil with gum camphor dissolved in it: the camphor is volatile and soon evaporates . . . Now I don't much like tar dope because I can not wash my face and hands as often as I could wish; but when it is necessary to get some trout, without being worried too much by the insects, I can stand the tar for a few days.

The fruit of my own experiments thus far is that tar dopes are the most effective ones in comparatively cool climates, but that they are of little avail in hot countries, because when one perspires freely both by night and day, there is no chance for a glaze to be established.

Fleas.

In the high mountains of North Carolina and adjoining states there are no mosquitoes, at least none that sting or bite; but if a man sits down on a log, it may be five miles from any house, the chance is good that he will arise covered with fleas. I have been so tormented by these nimble allies of Auld Reekie, when spending a night in a herder's cabin on the summit of the Smokies, that I have arisen in desperation and rubbed myself from head to foot with kerosene. That settled the fleas, and almost settled me. Here I may offer a bit of a discovery, not copyrighted, that I believe is new:

fleas can't swim. When you catch one, don't try to crush him or examine him (*her*, I should say), but keep a tight grip until you get your thumb and finger into some water; then let go, and she will sink, and drown, and go to meet her reward, which, let us hope, is a warm one.

Blood-sucking Flies.

In northern forests we have several species of flies that attack man. The deer-fly or "bull-dog" is a small gad-fly that drives her dagger-like mandibles into one's skin so viciously that she takes out a bit of flesh and makes the blood flow freely. The black-fly (*Similium molestum*) is a stout, humpbacked, black termagent with transparent wings, from one-sixth to one-quarter inch long. This creature is a common nuisance of the forests and along the streams of northern New England, the Adirondacks, the Lake region, and Canada. She keeps busy until late in the afternoon, poisoning everything that she attacks, and raising a painful lump as big as a dime at every bite. Closely related species are the buffalo-gnat and turkey-gnat of the South, which sometimes appear in incredible numbers, driving animals frantic and setting up an inflammatory fever that may prove fatal. Black-flies and their ilk are easily driven away by smudges.

Blow-Flies.

Worst of all flies, though fortunately rare in the North (it has been known to reach Canada), is the screw-worm fly (*Compsomyia macellaria*), a bright metallic-green insect with golden reflections and four black stripes on the upper part of the body. This is a blow-fly which has the sickening habit of laying its eggs in wounds, and even in the nostrils of sleeping men. Several fatalities from this cause have been reported in our country; they have been much more numerous in South America. The *gusanéro* of tropical America is described by a traveler as "a beast of a fly that attacks you, you know not when, till after three or four months you know that he has done so by the swelling up of the bitten part into a fair-sized boil, from which issues a maggot of perhaps an inch and a half in length." Another

Amazonian fly of similar habits is the *birni*, whose larva generates a grub in one's skin that requires careful extraction, lest it be crushed in the operation, "and then," said a native, "gentlemen often go to *o outro mundo*" (the other world). The *motûca* of Brazil has ways similar to those of our black-fly, and, like it, can easily be killed with one's fingers.

Pests of the Tropics.

While I am on this topic, it may add a little to the contentment of those outers who are unable to seek adventure in faraway lands, but must needs camp within a hundred miles or so of home, if I transcribe from the pages of a well-known naturalist the following notes on some of the impediments to travel in the tropics:

But the most numerous and most dreaded of all animals in the middle Amazons are the insects. Nearly all kinds of articulate life here have either sting or bite. The strong trade wind keeps the lower Amazons clear of the winged pests; but soon after leaving Manãos, and especially on the Marañon in the rainy season, the traveler becomes intimately acquainted with half a dozen insects of torture:

(1) The sanguinary mosquito. . . . There are several species, most of them working at night; but one black fellow with white feet is diurnal. Doctor Spruce experimented upon himself, and found that he lost, by letting the blood-letters have their own way, three ounces of blood per day. . . . The ceaseless irritation of these ubiquitous creatures makes life almost intolerable. The great Cortez, after all his victories, could not forget his struggles with these despicable enemies he could not conquer. Scorpions with cocked tails, spiders six inches in diameter, and centipedes running on all dozens, are not half so bad as a cloud of mosquitoes. . . .

(2) The *piúm*, or sand-fly, a species of *trombidium* called mosquito in Peru. It is a minute, dark-colored dipter with two triangular, horny lancets, which leave a small, circular red spot on the skin. It works by day, relieving the mosquito at sunrise. It is the great scourge of the Amazons. Many a paradisaic spot is converted into an inferno by its presence. There are several species, which follow one another in succession through the day, all of them being diurnal. Their favorite region is said to be on the Cassiquiare and upper Orinoco.

(3) The *maruim*, which resembles the *piúm*. They are infinitely numerous on the Juruá. Humboldt estimated there were a million to a cubic foot of air where he was.

(4) The *mutúca*, called *tábono* on the Marañon (*Hadaus*

lepidotus), resembling a small horse-fly, of a bronze-black color, with the tips of the wings transparent, and a formidable proboscis. . . .

(5) The *moquím* . . . a microscopic scarlet *acarus*, resembling a minute crab under the glass. It swarms on weeds and bushes, and on the skin causes an intolerable itching. An hour's walk through the grassy streets of Teffé was sufficient to cover my entire body with myriads of *moquíms*, which it took a week, and repeated bathing with rum, to exterminate.

(6) *Carapátos*, or ticks (*ixodes*), which mount to the tips of blades of grass, attach themselves to the clothes of passers-by, and bury their jaws and heads so deeply in the flesh that it is difficult to remove them without leaving the proboscis behind to fret and fester. In sucking one's blood they cause no pain; but serious sores, even ulcers, often result. . . .

These few forms of insect life must forever hinder the settlement of the valley. . . . Besides these there are ants . . . innumerable in species and individuals, and of all sizes, from the little red ant of the houses to the mammoth *tokandéra*, an inch and a half long. . . . The latter . . . bites fiercely, but rarely causes death. . . . Doctor Spruce likens the pain to a hundred thousand nettles. . . . On the Tapajós lives the terrible fire-ant . . . whose sting is likened to the puncture of a red-hot needle. The *saübas* are not carnivorous, but they make agriculture almost impossible. . . . There are black and yellow wasps. . . . The large, hairy caterpillars should be handled with care, as the irritation caused by the nettling hairs is sometimes a serious matter. Cockroaches are great pests in the villages. Lice find a congenial home on the unwashed Indians of every tribe, but particularly the Andean. Jiggers and fleas prefer dry, sandy localities; they are accordingly most abounding on the mountains. The Pacific slope is worthy of being called flea-dom.—ORTON, *The Andes and the Amazons*, pp. 484–487.

Northern Chiggers.

The *moquím* mentioned above answers the description of our own chigger, jigger, red-bug, as she is variously called, which is an entirely different beast from the real chigger or chigoe of the tropics. I do not know what may be the northern limit of these most unladylike creatures, but have made their acquaintance on Swatara Creek in Pennsylvania. They are quite at home on the prairies of southern Illinois, exist in myriads on the Ozarks, and throughout the lowlands of the South, and are perhaps worst of all in some parts of Texas. The chigger, as I shall call her, is invisible on one's skin, unless you know just what to look for.

Get her on a piece of black cloth, and you can distinguish what looks like a fine grain of red pepper. Put her under a microscope, and she resembles, as Orton says, a minute crab. She lives in the grass, and on the under side of leaves, dropping off on the first man or beast that comes her way. Then she prospects for a good place, where the skin is thin and tender, and straightway proceeds to burrow, not contenting herself, like a tick, with merely thrusting her head in and getting a good grip, but going in body and soul, to return no more. The victim is not aware of what is in store for him until he goes to bed that night. Then begins a violent itching, which continues for a week or two. I have had two hundred of these tormenting things in my skin at one time.

If one takes a bath in salt water every night before retiring, he can keep fairly rid of these unwelcome guests; but once they have burrowed underneath the skin, neither salt, nor oil, nor turpentine, nor carbolized ointment, nor anything else that I have tried will kill them, save mercurial ointment or the tincture of stavesacre seed, both of which are dangerous if incautiously used. After much experiment, I found that chloroform, dropped or rubbed on each separate welt, will stop the itching for about six hours. It is quite harmless, and pleasant enough to apply. The country people sometimes rub themselves with salty bacon-rind before going outdoors, and claim that this is a preventive; also that kerosene will do as well. If one keeps an old suit of clothes expressly for chigger-time, puts the suit in a closet, and fumigates it thoroughly with the smoke of burning tobacco stems, no chigger will touch him. Alas! that the preventives should all be so disagreeable.

Tropical Chigoes.

The chigoe or sand-flea of Mexico, Central America, and South America, is a larger and more formidable pest than our little red-bug. It attacks, preferably, the feet, especially underneath the nail of the great toe, and between the toes. The insect burrows there, becomes encysted, swells enormously from the development of her young, and thus sets up an intolerable itching in the victim's skin. If the female is crushed or ruptured in the tumor she has formed, the result is likely to be amputation of the toe, if nothing worse. She should be removed entire by careful manipulation with a needle. This chigoe is a native of tropical America, but seems to be gradually spreading northward. About 1872 it was introduced into Africa, and spread with amazing rapidity over almost the entire continent. It will probably soon invade southern Europe and Asia.

Ticks. The wood-ticks that fasten on man are, like the chiggers, not true insects, but arachnids, related to the scorpions and spiders. They are leathery-skinned creatures of about the same size and shape as a bedbug, but of quite different color and habits. They "use" on the under side of leaves of low shrubs, and thence are detached to the person of a passer-by just as chiggers are. They also abound in old mulchy wood, and are likely to infest any log that a tired man sits on. They hang on like grim death, and if you try to pull one out of your skin, its head will break off and remain in the epidermis, to create a nasty sore. The way to get rid of them is to drop oil on the bug, or clap a quid of moistened tobacco on her, or touch her with nicotine from a pipe, or stand naked in the dense smoke of a green wood fire, or use whiskey externally, or hot water, or flame; in either case the tick will back its way out. Preventive measures are the same as for chiggers. The meanest ticks to get rid of are the young, which are known as "seed-ticks." They are hard to discover until they have inflamed the skin, and then are hard to remove because they are so small and fragile. The ticks that infest birds, bats, sheep, and horses, are true insects, in no wise related to the wood-ticks, dog-ticks, and cattle-ticks. The cattle-tick is responsible for the fatal disease among cattle that is known as Texas fever.

Punkies. The punky or "no-see-um" of the northeastern wildwoods, and her cousin the stinging midge of western forests, are minute bloodsuckers that, according to my learned friend Professor Comstock, live, "under the bark of decaying branches, under fallen leaves, and in sap flowing from wounded trees."

With all due deference to this distinguished entomologist, I must aver that they don't live there when I am around; they seem particularly fond of sap flowing from wounded fishermen. Dope will keep them from biting you, but it won't keep them out of your eyes. Punkies are particularly annoying about sunset. Oil of citronella is the best preventive of their attacks.

Insects in Camp.

If you want mosquitoes to leave your tent in a hurry, explode a little black gunpowder in it. Burning insect powder in the tent is also effective, but it is not so prompt nor so sportsmanlike. The best way, though, is to keep them out from the first, by the device mentioned in White's book *The Forest:* have an inside tent of cheese-cloth, which is hung up out of the way in the daytime, and can be dropped and made snug all around the bottom before you turn in.

If ants are troublesome about a permanent camp, pour kerosene on their runways. They will not cross a broad line drawn with chalk or charcoal. Oil of sassafras sprinkled about will keep flies and ants out of a cabin. The fresh leaves of the Kentucky coffee tree, bruised and sweetened, are good to poison flies. Black walnut leaves will drive fleas out of a bed; the leaves, soaked in water for some hours, then boiled, and applied to the skins of horses or other animals, will prevent their being worried by flies. To get rid of flies, if you have milk, add to 1 pint of milk $\frac{1}{4}$ lb. of sugar and 2 oz. ground pepper; place in a shallow dish; the flies will eat greedily, and choke to death.

Smudges.

A good smudge is raised by using cedar "cigars," made as follows: Take long strips of cedar bark and bunch them together into a fagot six or eight inches in diameter, about one strip in three being dry and the others water-soaked; bind them with strips of the inner bark of green cedar. Ignite one end at the camp-fire, and set up two or more such cigars on different sides of the camp, according as the wind may shift. Punky wood piled on a bed of coals is also good. The ammoniacal vapors from a smudge of dried cow-dung is particularly effective. I have elsewhere referred to smudges made of dried toadstools; these are peculiarly repellent to punkies. A toadstool as large as one's two fists will hold fire for six or eight hours. A piece of one can be carried suspended by a string around one's neck, the burning end out. If the fungus is too damp at first, it can soon be dried out before the fire.

The pain or itching caused by insect bites is quickly relieved by rubbing the spot with a lump of indigo, or by touching it with glycerin or ammonia, or by rubbing a bit of raw onion over it.

Scorpions.

Scorpions are not uncommon as far north as Missouri. I often used to find them in the neighborhood of St. Louis—little red fellows about 4 inches long. In the southwest, where they abound, they grow to a length of 6 or 7 inches. They hide by day under flat rocks, in dead trees, and in moist, dark places generally, and do their foraging at night. They are very belligerent, always fighting to the death. They carry their tails curled upward and forward, and can only strike upward and backward. They are sometimes unpleasantly familiar around camp, especially in rainy weather, having a penchant for crawling into bedding, boots, coat sleeves, trousers' legs, etc. The sting of a small scorpion is about as severe as that of a hornet; that of a large one is more serious, but never fatal, so far as I know, except to small children. After a person is stung a few times he is inoculated, and proof against the poison thereafter. If you get stung, take a hollow key or small tube, press the hollow with force over the puncture, causing the poison and a little blood to exude, hold firmly in place for several minutes, and, if the scorpion was a large one, you have a good excuse for drinking all the whiskey you want. Ordinarily a quid of moist tobacco locally applied eases the pain and reduces the swelling. Tobacco juice, by the way, is fatal to scorpions, tarantulas, and centipedes, and will set a snake crazy.

I first witnessed the leaping powers of a tarantula one night when I was alone in a deserted log cabin in southern Missouri. The cabin had not been occupied for fifteen years, and there was no furniture in it. I had scarcely made my bed on the board floor when a tornado struck the forest. It was a grand sight, but scared me stiff. Well, the electric plant was working finely, just then, the lightning being almost a continuous glare. A tarantula that spread as broad as my hand jumped out of the straw that I was lying on and—it was hard to tell which was quicker, he or the lightning. He seemed disturbed about something. Not being able to fight the tornado, I took after the big spider with an old stumpy broom that happened to be in the cabin. When the broom would land at one side of the room, the tarantula would be on the other side. I was afraid he would spring for my face, but presently he popped into a hole somewhere, and vanished. The cabin somehow stuck to terra firma, and I returned to my pallet.

Tarantulas.

The tarantula's habits are similar to the scorpion's. The fangs are in its mouth. The bite is very severe, but not fatal to an adult. Cases of men being injured by either of these venomous arachnids are extremely rare, considering the abundance of the pests in some countries, and their habit of secreting themselves in clothes and bedding. If you want to see a battle royal, drop a scorpion and a tarantula into the same box. They will spring for each other in a flash, and both are absolutely game to the last.

Centipedes.

I have had no personal experience with centipedes. Paul Fountain says:

> The centipedes were an intolerable nuisance for they had a nasty habit of hiding among the bed-clothes and under the pillows, attracted there to prey on the bugs, as I suppose: one evil as a set-off to another. But the centipedes were something more than a mere nuisance. It is all very well to be blandly told by gentlemen who think they know all about it that the

bites of centipedes and scorpions are not dangerous. It may not be particularly dangerous to have a red-hot wire applied to your flesh, but it is confoundedly painful. Yet that is to be preferred to a centipede bite, which will not only make you dance at the time of infliction, but leave a painful swelling for many days after, accompanied by great disturbance of the system.

CHAPTER XIII

FOREST TRAVEL—KEEPING A COURSE

Quand na pas choual, monté bourique;
Quand na pas bourique, monté cabri;
Quand na pas cabri, monté jambe.
(When you have no horse, you ride a donkey;
When you have no donkey, you ride a goat;
When you have no goat, you ride your legs.)
—*Creole Saying.*

IN walking through a primitive forest, an Indian or a white woodsman can wear out a town-bred athlete, although the latter may be the stronger man. This is because a man who is used to the woods has a knack of walking over uneven and slippery ground, edging through thickets, and worming his way amid fallen timber, with less fret and exertion than one who is accustomed to smooth, unobstructed paths.

How to Walk.

There is somewhat the same difference between a townsman's and a woodsman's gait as there is between a soldier's and a sailor's. It is chiefly a difference of hip action, looseness of joints, and the manner of planting one's feet. The townsman's stride is an up-and-down knee action, with rather rigid hips, the toes pointing outward, and heels striking first. The carriage is erect, the movement springy and graceful, so long as one is walking over firm, level footing—but beware the banana-peel and the small boy's sliding-place! This is an ill-poised gait, because one's weight falls first upon the heel alone, and at that instant the walker has little command of his balance. It is an exhausting gait as soon as its normally short pace is lengthened by so much as an inch.

A woodsman, on the contrary, walks with a rolling motion, his hips swaying an inch or more to the stepping side, and his pace is correspondingly long. This hip action may be noticed to an exaggerated degree in the stride of a professional pedestrian; but the latter walks with a heel-and-toe step, whereas an Indian's or sailor's step is more nearly flat-footed. In the latter case the center of gravity is covered by the whole foot. The poise is as secure as that of a rope-walker. The toes are pointed straight forward, or even a trifle inward, so that the inside of the heel, the outside of the ball of the foot, and the smaller toes, all do their share of work and assist in balancing. Walking in this manner, one is not so likely, either, to trip over projecting roots, stones, and other traps, as he would be if the feet formed hooks by pointing outward. The necessity is obvious in snowshoeing.

A fellow sportsman, H. G. Dulog, once remarked: "If the Indian were turned to stone while in the act of stepping, the statue would probably stand balanced on one foot. This gait gives the limbs great control over his movements. He is always poised. If a stick cracks under him it is because of his weight, and not by reason of the impact. He goes silently on, and with great economy of force. . . . His steady balance enables him to put his moving foot down as gently as you would lay an egg on the table."

There is another advantage in walking with toes pointing straight ahead instead of outward: one gains ground at each stride. I have often noticed that an Indian's stride gains in this manner, as well as from his rolling motion on the hips. The white man acquires this habit, if he ever gets it, but an Indian is *molded* to it in the cradle. If you examine the way in which a papoose is bound to its cradle-board, this will be made clear. Immediately after birth the infant is stretched out on the board, its bowlegged little limbs are laid as straight as possible, and the feet are placed exactly perpendicular and close together before being swaddled. Often the squaw removes the bandages and gently drags and works on the baby's limbs and spine to make them as straight as possible. Then, in rebandaging, care is always taken that the toes shall point straight forward.

The custom of wearing moccasins also increases the normal stride beyond what it would be if one wore boots.

Over-Strain.

When carrying a pack on your back, do not over-exert yourself. Halt whenever your breathing is very labored or exertion becomes painful. Rig your pack at the start so that it can be flung off whenever you sit down for a moment's rest; it pays. Nobody who understands horses would think of driving them ahead when they show signs of distress, and there is quite as much common sense in treating yourself with the same consideration, if you want to travel far. Over-exertion is particularly disastrous in mountain-climbing.

Care of the Feet.

One who is unused to long marches may get along pretty well the first day, but on the second morning it will seem as if he could not drag one foot after the other. This is the time when the above remarks do not apply; for if one uses the gad and goes ahead he will soon limber up. But by the morning of the third day it is likely that complications will have set in. The novice by this time is worn, not only from unaccustomed exertion, but from loss of sleep—for few men sleep well the first night or two in the open. He is probably constipated from change of diet, and from drinking too much on the march. More serious still, he probably has sore feet. This latter ailment is not so much due to his feet being tender at the start as from his not having taken proper care of them. Aside from the downright necessity of seeing that one's shoes and stockings fit well, and that the shoes were well broken in before starting, there are certain rules of pedestrian hygiene that should be observed from the word "go." Every morning before starting, dust some talc powder inside your stockings, or rub some vaselin, tallow, or soap on the inside of them. Then wash your feet every evening, preferably in hot salted water, and, if they feel strained, rub them with whiskey. The underwear should also be dusted inside with powdered soapstone, or otherwise treated like the stockings, at all places where the garments are likely to chafe. Socks should be washed every other day.

If a blister has formed on the foot, do not merely prick it and squeeze the water out, but thread a needle with soft cotton or worsted, draw the latter partly through the blister, snip off the ends about one-fourth inch from the blister, and leave the thread there to act as a drainage tube. Then cover the part with a soft, clean rag greased with vaselin, or tallow rubbed up with a little whiskey. This will prevent the skin being rubbed off, and a consequent painful wound. Corns may be removed by a plaster of pine turpentine (not spirits, but the raw sap of the tree).

Thirst.

In warm weather, one's first few days in the open air will bring an inordinate thirst, which is not caused by the stomach's demand for water, but by a fever of the palate. This may be relieved somewhat by chewing a green leaf, or by carrying a smooth, non-absorbent pebble in the mouth; but a much better thirst-quencher is a bit of raw onion carried in the mouth. One can go a long time without drinking if he has an onion with him; this also prevents one's lips from cracking in alkali dust.

Drink as often as you please, but not very much at a time. If the water is cold, sip it slowly so as not to chill the stomach. Never try to satisfy thirst by swallowing snow or ice; melt the snow first by holding it in the mouth, if no fire can be made.

Rough Travel.

The way to find game, or to get the best of anything else that the forest hides, is not to follow well-beaten paths. One must often make his own trails, and go where the going is hardest. As he travels through the unbroken woods he may come, now and then, to a glade where the trees do not crowd each other, where the undergrowth is sparse, and the view so unobstructed that he can see to shoot for a hundred yards in any direction; such spots may be about as common, relatively, as are safe anchorages and deep-water harbors along the coast. But, most of the time, a wanderer in the forest primeval must pick a way for his feet over uneven

Crude, but Comfortable

Down the Snow-white Alleys

ground that is covered with stubs, loose stones, slippery roots, crooked saplings, mixed downwood, and tough, thorny vines. He is forever busy seeking openings, parting bushes, brushing away cobwebs, fending off springy branches, crawling over or under fallen trees, working around impenetrable tangles, or trying to find a foot-log or a ford. There is no such thing as a short-cut. It is beyond the power of man to steer a straight course, or to keep up a uniform cadence of his steps. Unless the traveler knows his ground there is no telling when he may come to a "windfall" where several acres of big timber have been overthrown by a hurricane and the great trees lie piled across each other in an awkward snarl. Or maybe there is an alder thicket or a cedar swamp in the way, or a canebrake or a cypress slough, or a laurel or rhododendron "slick," wherein a man will soon exhaust his strength to no purpose, if he be so unwise as to try to force a passage.

A *brûlé* or burnt-wood is a nasty place to pass through. Every foot of ground that is not covered by charred snags, or fallen trunks and limbs, bristles with a new growth of fireweed, blackberry and raspberry briers, young red cherries, white birches, poplars, quaking aspens, scrub oaks, or gray pines. Where the fire has occurred on one of those barren ridges that was covered with dwarfish oaks (post, black, or blackjack), the sharp, fire-hardened stubs of limbs protrude, like bayonets, at the height of one's face, menacing his eyes. An old "lumber works," where the trees have been chopped out, leaving nothing but stumps, tree-tops, and other débris, grows up with the same rank tenants as a burnt-wood, and is as mean to flounder through. As a general rule, a mile and a half an hour of actual progress is "making good time" in the woods.

Use of Divides.

Rivers are often spoken of as having been man's natural highways in the days before railroads. This was true only to a limited extent. A few great rivers such as the Hudson, the Ohio, the Mississippi, and the Missouri, were highways for down-stream travel, and smaller waterways were, and still are, used in summer in the *muskeg* country of the North, where land travel is impracticable until everything freezes up. But the general rule of aboriginal travel was to keep away from streams and follow the ridges between them. This rule still holds good when a party travels afoot or with

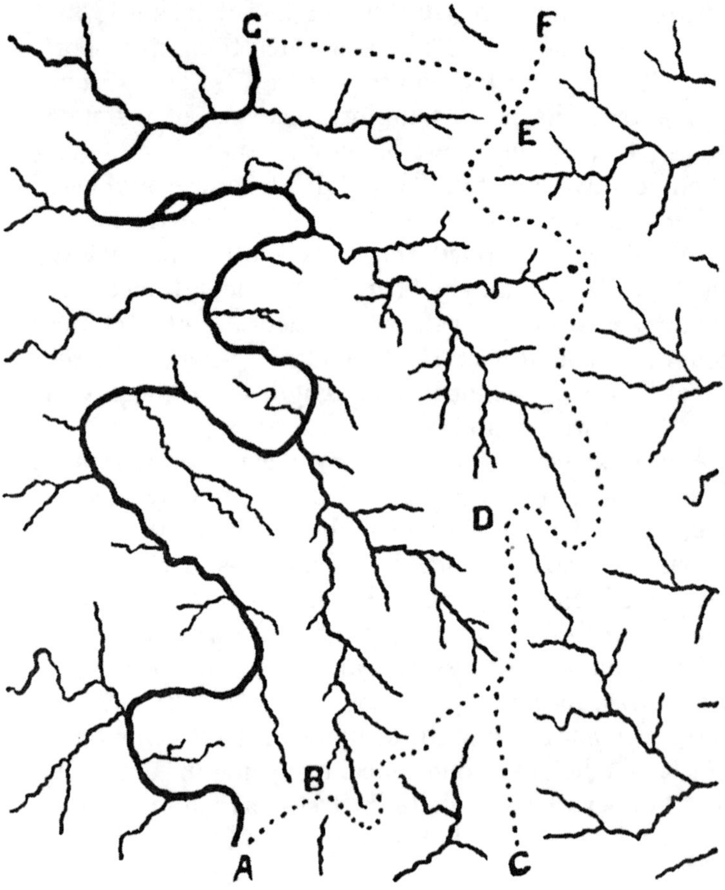

FIG. 8.

pack-train in a country where there are no bridges. A glance at the accompanying diagram will show why.

In this figure, *AG* represents a river, and *CF* the main divide or summit of watershed separating it from another river basin. It is assumed that a party afoot or with horses desires to advance from *A* to *G*. Evidently, if they try to follow either bank of the main stream, they will have many fords to make, not only crossing tributaries here and there, but fording or swimming the main stream itself, many times, where cliffs, bogs, or impenetrable thickets make one of the banks impassable. If the region through which the river runs is wide bottom-land, the mouths of its tributaries are likely to be deep, or to run over fathomless mud as dangerous as quicksand, and this will necessitate long detours. The vegetation up to the very bank of the river will be exceedingly rank, a wretched tangle of bushes, vines, briars, and tall grass, and fallen trees will be plentiful and large. At any time a heavy rainstorm may send the river out of its banks, and the party may find itself marooned where it can neither go forward nor backward. On the other hand, if the river runs through a mountainous country, it is probable that the travelers will come to a cañon that will compel them to retreat. In any case, the party will never have an outlook; it will never know what lies beyond the next bend of the river.

A comparatively easy way around all of these difficulties is shown by the dotted line *ABDEG*. Leaving the river by a ridge that leads to the main divide, and following the crest to a similar abutting ridge that runs down to the valley at the objective point, there will be no fords to make, the footing will be much better because vegetation is thinner on the more sterile, windswept heights, the fallen trees will be smaller, there will be no mud or quicksand or miry bogs, and every here and there a coign of vantage will be climbed from which a far outlook can be had over the surrounding country.

The chief precaution to be observed in trying to follow a divide where there is no trail, or where there are many intersecting trails, is not to stray off on some abutting ridge. Thus, at the points *B* and *D* there may be in each case a gap between knolls or peaks, and the lead to the left might easily be mistaken for the main divide. If the party were enticed along either of these leads, on account of its trending in the desired direction, they would soon find themselves in a *cul de sac.*

The city man's gait, to which I have already referred, is peculiarly exhausting in mountain-climbing. He is accustomed to spring from the toe of the lower foot, in going uphill. That throws nearly the whole weight of the body upon the muscles of the calf of the leg, a misadjustment of strain that would soon wear out even a native mountaineer. The latter walks uphill with a woodsman's gait, planting the whole foot on the ground, and swinging or rolling the hip at each stride, thus not only gaining an inch or two in his pace, but distributing the strain between several groups of muscles.

Mountain-Climbing.

In Dent's *Mountaineering* are given some useful hints to climbers that I take the liberty of condensing here:

> In walking up a steep hill, go slowly and steadily. If you cannot talk without catching your breath, it is a sure sign that you are going too fast.
>
> If you slip on a loose stone, do not try to recover your lost ground quickly, but slip away until your foot is checked a few inches below. Thus keep up the rhythm of your footfall.
>
> On an average mountain, where the slope is tolerably uniform, and the climber has no long journey before him, an ascent of 1,000 ft. in an hour is quick walking. In beginning a long climb, 800 ft. of vertical ascent in an hour is good work. On a good trail, for a moderate distance, 1,500 ft. an hour is quick walking. Under favorable conditions a good climber can ascend from a height of 7,000 ft. to 14,000 ft. in seven hours; at greater altitudes the pace will slacken.
>
> In descending a mountain, the pace, however slow, should be continuous. To remain stationary, even for a moment, not only necessitates a fresh start, but demands an adjustment of balance which implies an unnecessary outlay of muscular effort. To descend rapidly and safely without exertion, a certain looseness of joints should be cultivated. On a steep slope one should descend sideways, so that the whole length of the foot can be planted fairly on any hold that offers.
>
> A man will never sprain his ankle when he expects to do so at any moment, nor will he be likely to slip if he is always prepared to fall.

If you have to cross a deep, rocky ravine or dangerous mountain stream by passing over a high foot-log or fallen tree, then, if the log is tilted at an uncomfortable angle, or if its surface is wet, or icy, or treacherous with loose bark, or if, for any reason, you fear dizziness or faintness, don't

Foot-Logs.

be ashamed to get down and straddle the log, hunching yourself along with hands and thighs. Let your companions laugh, if they will. It is not nice to break a limb or a jaw when you are in a country so rough that your comrades may have to pack you out, by each, in turn, carrying you on his own back and crawling with you.

Breaking a Trail.

When a man ventures into strange woods far from settlements, he should blaze a tree here and there along his course, and, between the blazes, every now and then he should bend a green bush over *in the direction he is going*, snapping the stem or clipping it with the hatchet, but letting it adhere by the bark so that the

FIG. 9.

FIG. 10.

under side of the bushy top will "look at him" when he returns. The under side of the leaves, being of lighter shade than the upper, makes such a bush-sign conspicuous in the woods. Marks like these can be made without slacking one's pace. Have it mutually understood that a single blaze on a tree is always to be made on the side away from camp, and that if the side toward camp is marked at all it should be with two blazes. Even when a man is bewildered he can remember "*A* blaze means *a-way* from; *two* blazes mean *to-ward*."

Never leave your bed without making sure that you have your pocketbook, jackknife, watch, and your waterproof matchbox *filled.* Make a practice of loading the latter, if it needs it, every night when you wind your watch. In cold weather do not leave camp without your hunting hatchet. If you leave a boat for the purpose of hunting along the bank while the boat drifts on her way, have it understood by your companions that you will blaze a tree on the bank about every half mile. Then they can keep on down-stream as long as they pass fresh blazes.

Signals.

In a treeless country piles of rock or freshly upturned earth can be used; or signals that will attract attention from a great distance can be made with smoke; from one to three smudges being made, according to a prearranged code. The distress signal with a gun is a shot, a pause, and then two shots in quick succession. It is disregarded until after, say, 4 P.M., at which hour the campkeeper (in a fixed camp) should blow his horn.

This gunshot code is reversed in some countries. Learn what is the custom in the land where you travel; but, in any case, have *some* signal agreed upon so that your comrades will understand it.

Sameness of the Forest.

All dense woods look much alike. Trees of all species grow very tall in a forest that has never been cut over, their trunks being commonly straight and slender, with no branches within, say, forty feet of the ground. This is because they cannot live without sunlight for their leaves, and they can only reach sunlight by growing tall like their neighbors that crowd around them. As the young tree shoots upward, its lower limbs atrophy and drop off. To some extent the characteristic markings of the trunk that distinguish the different species when they grow in the open, and to a greater extent their characteristic habits of branching, are neutralized when they grow in dense forest. Consequently a man who can readily tell one species from another, in open country, by their bark and branching habits, may be puzzled to distinguish them in aboriginal forest. Moreover, the lichens and mosses that cover the boles of trees, in the deep shade of a primitive wood, give them a sameness of aspect, so that there is some excuse for the novice who says that "all trees look alike" to him.

The knowledge of trees that can be gained, first from books and secondly from studies of trees themselves in city parks or in country wood-lots, must be supplemented by considerable experience in the real wilderness before one can say with confidence, by merely glancing at the bark, "that is a soft maple, and the other is a sugar tree." And yet, I do not know any study that, in the long run, would be more serviceable to the amateur woodsman than to get a good manual of American trees and then go about identifying the species in his neighborhood. Having gained some facility in this, then let him turn to studying peculiarities of individual growth. Such self-training, which can be carried out almost anywhere, will make him observant of a thousand and one little marks and characteristics that are sign-boards and street-numbers in the wilds.

Sense of Direction.

This sort of knowledge has direct bearing upon the art of following a course, or retracing one's course, in the wilderness. We hear much about the "extraordinary bump of locality," the "phenomenal memory of landmarks," the "preternatural sense of direction," of certain woodcraftsmen. I do not like those phrases, if by them is meant that certain men are born with a "gift," a sixth sense, that is denied to others. I do not believe that any man is a "born woodsman." In the art of wilderness travel, as in other things, some men are more adept than others who have had equal advantages, and a few possess almost uncanny powers, amounting to what we call genius. To my notion this means nothing more than that some individuals are quicker to observe than others, reason more surely from cause to effect, and keep their minds more alert; and I believe that this is far more due to their taking unusual interest in their surroundings than to any partiality of Mother Nature in distributing her gifts.

After a novice has had some preliminary training of the kind I have indicated, so that all things in the woods no longer look alike to him, he will meet another difficulty. His memory will be swamped! It is utterly impossible for any man, whether he be red, white, black, or piebald, to store up in his mind all the woodland marks and signs that one can see in a mile's tramp, to say nothing of the infinite diversity that he encounters in a long journey. Now, here is just where a skilled woodcraftsman has an enormous advantage over any and all amateurs. He knows what is common, and pays no attention to it; he knows what is uncommon, it catches his eye at once, and it interests him, so that he need make no effort to remember the thing. This *disregard for the common* eliminates at once three-fourths, perhaps nine-tenths, of the trees, plants, rocks, etc., from his consideration; it relieves his memory of just that much burden. He will pass a hundred birch trees without a second glance, until his eye is riveted by a curly birch. Why riveted? Because curly birch is valuable. In the bottom lands he will scarcely see a sour gum, or a hundred of them; but let him come across one such tree on top of the ridge, and he will wonder how it chanced to stray so far from home. And so on, through all categories of woodland features. A woodsman notices such things as infallibly, and with as little conscious effort, as a woman notices the crumbs and lint on her neighbor's carpet.

What to Notice.

A compass is like a pistol, seldom used, but invaluable in an emergency. Ordinarily a traveler in the forest does not use a compass—in fact I never knew a native of the wilderness who ever used one—he relies chiefly on the sun and the general lay of the land to guide him. In thick woods, canebrakes, swamps, big thickets, and other places where the course is necessarily very tortuous, a compass is of no use while one is on the march. Wherever the traveler can get an outlook he fixes on some landmark in advance, notes how the sun strikes him when facing the mark, and thenceforth

Averaging Windings.

averages up his windings as well as he can. The compass is only of service when he can no longer see the sun, and is in doubt as to the direction he is traveling in.

In the wilderness one never knows when he may want to retrace his steps. Hence, when passing any-

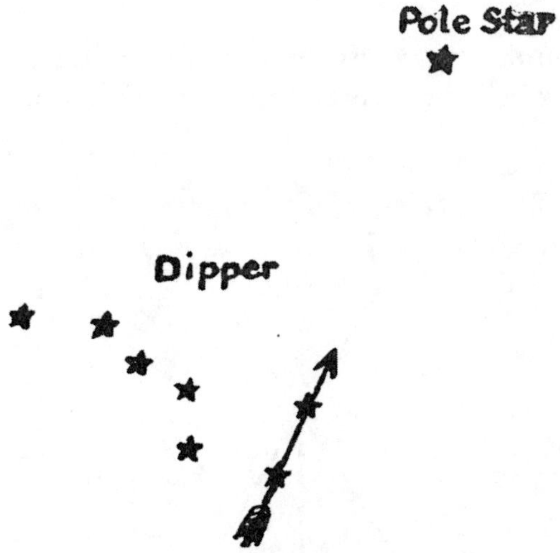

FIG. 11.

thing that has particularly caught his eye, let him turn and see how it looks from the other side.

Celestial Guides.

To find the sun on a cloudy day: hold a knife-blade perpendicularly on the thumb-nail, or on a watch-case, and slowly twirl it around. It will cast a faint shadow, unless the day is very dark. Choose an open spot in the woods for this, rather than under the trees, and don't try it near noon, when scarcely any shadow would be cast anyway.

To determine the points of the compass from a watch: The watch being set by local (sun) time, then, when the sun is shining, turn the face of the watch to the sun in such position that the hour-hand shall point to the sun. Half-way between the hour-hand and 12 o'clock will then be the *south* point. South of the equator this would indicate the north point. When the sun is near the zenith this method is of little use.

To find the pole star: In the constellation of the Great Bear, the seven stars called the "Dipper" never set. The two stars forming the front of the dipper's bowl point toward a conspicuously bright star almost in line with them, and higher, which is Polaris, the north star.

When rough-and-ready methods of determining the meridian are not precise enough for one's purpose, the

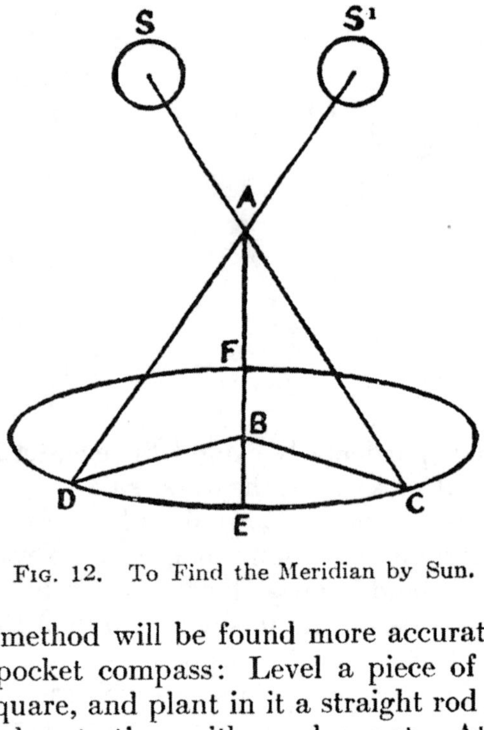

FIG. 12. To Find the Meridian by Sun.

following method will be found more accurate than an ordinary pocket compass: Level a piece of ground a few feet square, and plant in it a straight rod *AB*, truly perpendicular, testing with a plummet. At an hour or two before noon (say at 10:30 A.M.) mark accurately the extremity *C* of the shadow *BC* thrown by the rod, the sun being at *S*. Then from the base *B* as a center, with the radius *BC*, describe with a string a circle *CDF* on the ground. As the sun's altitude increases, the shadow of the rod will gradually grow shorter until noon, after which it will grow longer until, when the sun has reached the position *S'*, the shadow will again reach the circumference of the circle, at *D*. Divide the arc *CD* into two equal parts, and from *E*, a point equidistant from *C* to *D*, draw the line *BE*. This line will approximate closely to the true meridian, *E* being, of course, *north*, in north latitude.

When traveling in the dark, torches may be needed. If a dead pine tree can be found, chop off one of the old stubs of limbs, cutting deep into the trunk at the joint, so as to get as much of the heavy resinous bulb as you can. Cut a few splinters on this big end, if necessary, and light it.

Torches.

A bark torch is made by peeling several strips of birch bark four or five inches wide; double or fold them two or three times if the strips are long, and place these bunches in the split end of a stick, for handle.

A good torch is made by winding cotton yarn or rags around a forked stick, in the form of a ball, and soaking in oil or melted tallow.

To make a "pig-afire," cut a piece of fat pork about 1x1x4 inches, slit each end about 1½ inches, drive a sharpened stick through the center of the strip, and light the slit ends. It does not last long, but makes a good enough temporary flare.

Southern Indians, when exploring caves, used joints of cane filled with deer's tallow and supplied with wicks.

CHAPTER XIV

BLAZES—SURVEY LINES—NATURAL SIGNS OF DIRECTION

THE chief difficulty in forest travel, especially in flat lands that are heavily timbered, is the lack of natural outlooks from which one could get a view of distant landmarks. Although there are plenty of marks in the woods themselves by which a trained woodsman can follow a route that he traversed not long before, yet these signs are forever changing, vanishing, being superseded by others. Not only do new growths spring up, but old ones are swept away, sometimes suddenly, as by flood or fire. Hence, when men have once picked out a course through the woods that they intend to follow again, they leave permanent marks along the way for future guidance. The most conspicuous and durable waymarks that can easily be made are blazes on the trees. It is of no little consequence to a traveler in the wilds that he should know something about blazes and the special uses made of them in the backwoods.

Blazes.

On a thin-barked tree, a blaze is made by a single downward stroke, the axe being held almost parallel with the trunk; but if the bark is thick. an upward and a downward clip must be made, perhaps several of them, because, in any case, the object usually is to expose a good-sized spot of the whitish sapwood of the tree, which, set in the dark framework of the outer bark, is a staring mark in the woods, sure to attract attention, at least while fresh. Outside of white birch forests, white is the most conspicuous color in the woods, until snow falls.

If a blaze is made merely on the outer bark, it will not show so plainly by contrast. This kind of blaze, however, may be preferred for some purposes; for example, by a trapper who does not want to call everybody's attention to where his traps are set. A bark-blaze has the peculiarity that it lasts unaltered, so long as the bark itself endures, preserving its original outlines and distinctness, no matter how much the tree may grow. But if a wound, however slight, be made through the bark into the sapwood of the tree, so that the sap, which is the tree's blood, exudes, a healing process will at once set in, and the injury, in time, will be covered over. So, as soon as a blaze is made that exposes the wood, the tree begins at once to cover up its scar. This is a slow process. First the edges of the cut will widen, then a sort of lip of smoothe new inner bark will form, and this will gradually spread inward over the gash. Once this new skin has formed, the wound will be covered by new annual layers of wood, as well as by new outer bark. Years after the blaze was made, nothing will show on the surface but a slight scar, a sign that takes practised eyes to detect and read.

Old blazes that are completely grown over can only be proven by chopping into the wood until they are uncovered. The original marks of the axe are then plainly visible, and the age of a blaze can be determined to within, at most, a few years, by the number of rings that have grown over it, except in the case of tupelo and winged elm trees, the fiber of which is very irregular.

A blaze always remains at its original height above the ground, and, where two or more spots have been cut in the same tree, they will always stand at the same distance apart. This is because a tree increases its height and girth only by building on top of the previous growth, not by stretching it.

Following a Line.

An old line of blazes on spruce or pine trees is much easier to follow than if made on non-resinous trees, because the resin deposited by the oozing sap leaves a very noticeable and durable mark. Similarly, when an inscription has been penciled or painted on a fresh blaze on a pine tree, the sap glazes over the mark and makes it almost imperishable.

In searching out a line of blazes, one should keep his eyes glancing horizontally along a plane about breast-high, because that is the height at which surveyors leave their marks, and others usually follow the custom, unless the line has been spotted by a man on horseback, or from a boat during time of overflow.

When a blazed line turns abruptly, so that a person following might otherwise overrun it, a long slash is made on that side of the tree which *faces* the new direction.

It is difficult to follow a line of blazes when snow is falling, because the wind drives the damp flakes against the tree, where they adhere, and must be brushed away to find the blaze.

Now, it is often of much consequence to a traveler to remember such facts as these. For example, there is nothing more common in the annals of misadventure than for a novice to stray off on a deer trail, or, in southern forests, on a cattle trail, which, although seductively plain at first, leads nowhere in particular and soon dwindles to nothing. When undecided, look for blazes along the path. In heavily timbered regions, such as we are now considering, any trail that is, or ever has been, used as a highway by white men is almost sure to have been blazed.

Again, it is often of moment to determine, when one strikes a strange trail, what its nature is—for what purpose it was made—and thus be able to figure out whether it is likely to lead directly to a settlement or camp. This ought not to be very difficult when one knows what classes of men have preceded him in this particular forest. Generally speaking, a line spotted in a wide forest that as yet has no farmers' clearings is likely to have been made by either (1) a trapper, (2) a lumberman or timber-looker, or (3) a surveyor.

A Trapper's Line usually leads from one stream or lake to another. The blazes are likely to be inconspicuous. The line probably meanders a good deal, but not to escape ordinary obstacles, not disdaining a steep climb for a short-cut. Along its course, at intervals of eight or ten miles, there are probably rude shanties containing supplies, or the ruins of such shacks, if the line is no longer used. Such a line does not lead to any settlement, and can seldom be of any use to a wayfarer.

Timber-lookers may or may not leave evidence of their wanderings—more likely not, for, like other seekers after bonanzas, they may have excellent reasons for not doing so. At most, they would merely mark the easiest route for a prospective road from the river to some "bunch" of timber.

A Lumberman's Line. Where logging operations have already begun, then, wherever a stump stands it will not be hard to determine the direction in which the logs were twitched to the nearby "lizard road," where they were loaded on lizards (forks of timber used as sleds), or on wagons, and dragged to the river or sawmill. (I am assuming primitive operations in a remote wilderness.) The lizard road was blazed when first laid out. Logs are never dragged uphill if that can be avoided; consequently the trend of the road will be downhill, or on a level. The lizard road will show ruts, trees barked along the way by whiffle-trees, and other characteristic marks. Once the old lumbercamp site is reached, even though it be deserted, the signs of an old "tote road" can be discerned, leading toward a settlement from which supplies were transported.

A Surveyor's Line is always absolutely straight. When it reaches an impassable obstacle, such as a swamp or a cliff, an offset is made to right or left; but this offset is also a straight line, at right angles, of course, to the main one, the latter being continued in the original direction as soon as the obstacle has been passed. For this, and other reasons that presently will appear, a surveyor's line can never be mistaken for any other.

If one understands the merest rudiments of public surveying, and has a township map of the locality he is in, then, whenever he runs across a section line, he can soon tell just where he is, and what is the most direct route to any other point in the neighborhood. In those parts of the United States that are still wild enough to offer attractions to campers, the method of numbering, subdividing, and marking township sections is usually that adopted by the public land surveys, a brief description of which follows:

Township and Section Lines.

The public lands of the United States are generally divided into townships of six miles square (23,040 acres), as nearly as convergence of meridians allows. A township is subdivided into thirty-six sections, each one mile square, as nearly as may be, which, as a general rule, are numbered as shown in the first diagram here given, and are legally subdivided as indicated in the second diagram.

Starting from an established corner, all trees that stand directly on the line of survey have two chops or notches cut on each side of them, without any other marks whatever. These are called "sight trees" or "line trees" (sometimes "fore and aft trees"). Since there may not be enough trees actually intercepting the line of sight to make such a line conspicuous, a sufficient number of other trees standing within not more than two rods of the line, on either side of it, are blazed on two sides diagonally, or quartering toward the line, or coinciding in direction with the line where the trees stand very near it. Blazes are not omitted where trees two inches or more in diameter are found.

Bushes on or near the line are bent at right angles therewith, and receive a blow with the axe at the usual height of blazes from the ground, sufficient to leave them in a bent position, but not to prevent growth.

When the course is obstructed by swamps, lakes, or other impassable objects, the line is prolonged across by taking the necessary right angle offsets, or by traverse, etc., until the line is regained on the opposite side. At the intersection of lines on both margins, a post is set for a witness point, and two trees on opposite sides of the line are here marked with a blaze and notch facing the post; but on the margins of navigable

6	5	4	3	2	1
7	8	9	10	11	12
18	17	16	15	14	13
19	20	21	22	23	24
30	29	28	27	26	25
31	32	33	34	35	36

Plan for Numbering Sections of a Township.

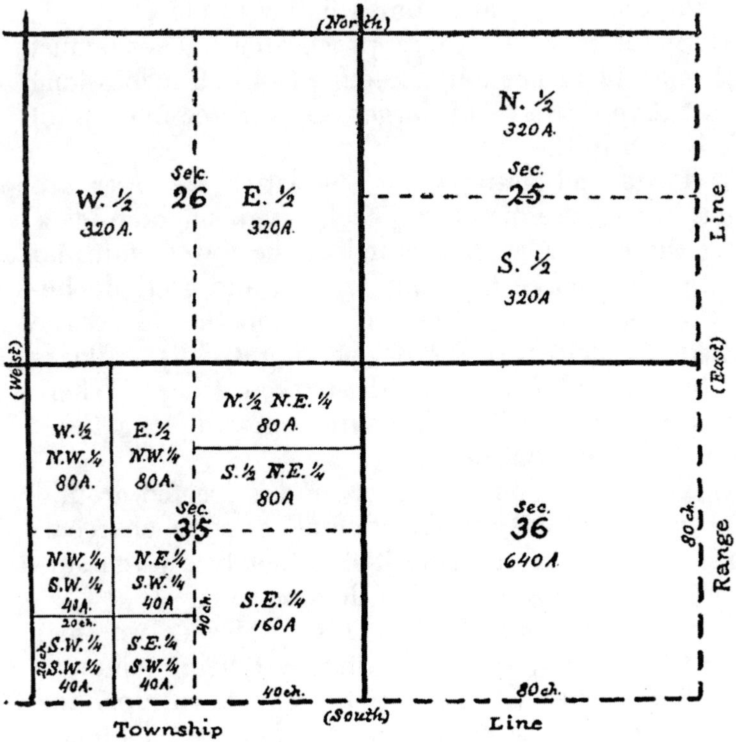

Sections 25, 26, 35 and 36 Divided.

PLATE II. Subdivision of a Township.

rivers or lakes the trees are marked with the number of the fractional section, township, and range. Arabic figures are used exclusively.

The following corners are marked:

(1) For township boundaries, at intervals of every six miles.

Corner Marks.

(2) For section boundaries, at intervals of every mile.

(3) For quarter-section boundaries, at intervals of one-half mile (with exceptions).

(4) Meander corners, wherever lines intersect banks of rivers, etc., directed to be meandered.

Witness corners bear the same marks as those of true corners, plus the letters *W. C.*

Four different modes of perpetuating corners are employed, in the following order of choice:

(1) Corner trees, when a tree not less than five inches in diameter stands immediately in place.

(2) Stone corners, where procurable. These must be at least 14 inches long. Stones 14 to 18 inches long are set two-thirds and larger ones three-fourths of their length in the ground.

(3) Posts and witnesses. The latter are trees adjacent, in opposite directions, each with a smoothe blaze facing the corner, with a notch at the lower end, and with the number of township, range, and section; below this, near the ground, on a smoothe blaze are marked the letters *B. T.* ("bearing tree"). Blazes may be omitted from smoothe-barked trees. Where there are no trees, witness pits are dug, two feet square, and at least one foot deep.

(4) Posts and mounds. A mound is erected around the corner post, and a marked stone, or some charcoal, or a charred stake, is deposited a foot below the surface on the side toward which the line runs.

Township Corner Post.—This projects two feet above the ground, the projecting part being squared. When the corner is common to four townships, the post is set cornerwise to the lines, and on each flattened side is marked the number of the township, range, and section, thus: *T.* 1 *S.*; *R.* 2 *W.*; *S.* 36.

This example reading "Township 1 South, Range 2 West, Section 36." *Six notches* are cut on each of the four edges.

If the post is on a closing corner, where the line does not continue straight ahead, but is offset to allow for convergence of meridians, this closing corner being common to two townships south of the base line, six notches are cut on each of the east, south, and west sides, but none on the north, and *C. C.* ("closing corner") is cut on the surface.

The position of *all* township corner posts is witnessed by four "bearing trees," or pits, or stones. Bearing trees are marked like the post; stones are merely notched.

Section Corners.—When the corner is common to four sections, the post is set cornerwise to the lines, the numbers of sections being marked on the surfaces facing them, and on the northeast face the number of township and range is inscribed. All mile-posts on township lines have as many notches on the two corresponding edges as they are miles distant from the respective township corners. Section posts in the interior of a township have as many notches on the south and east edges as they are miles from the south and east boundaries of the township, but none on the north and west edges. All section posts are "witnessed" as above. Section corner stones are merely notched.

Quarter-section Corners.—These are merely marked $\frac{1}{4}$ and "witnessed."

Red chalk is used to make marks more conspicuous.

In older sections of the United States, and in Canada, other systems of marks may be used; but the general principles are much the same. On arriving in a new country, it pays to inquire about the methods of marking survey lines that are there in vogue.

Are there any natural signs of direction that will give a man his bearings when the sky is obscured?

Natural Signs of Direction.

This is a question on which there has been much discussion in the sportsmen's press. Every one has heard, for example, that "moss grows thickest on the north side of a tree," and nearly every one has heard this as flatly contradicted. The general opinion seems to be that such signs are "important if true." The Indians and white frontiersmen of fiction never have any difficulty in finding their way by noting where moss grows thickest on the trees; but when our novel-reader goes into the woods, compass in hand, and puts the thing to actual test, he will probably be disgusted to find that, in densely shaded primeval forest, there seems to be no regularity in the growth of moss, one tree having a thick layer of it on the north side, another on the east, another on the south, and so on. He is then ready to declare that the old saying is a "fake."

I shall endeavor to show that there is more in this matter than is generally credited. There are certain signs of direction that are fairly constant in given regions, so that by their help a native, or even a stranger who has good powers of observation, some patience, and a fair knowledge of the life habits of trees and plants, can steer his course without a compass, and without help from sun or stars. But let us clearly understand what is involved in this use of nature's compass-marks.

No universal rule can be established from such signs as the growth of moss on trees, the preponderance of branches on one side of a tree, or the direction toward which the tips of tall conifers point. Such things are modified by prevailing winds, shadows and shelter of nearby mountains, depth or sparseness of forest growth, and other local conditions. Everywhere exceptions will be found; if there were none, it would be child's play, not woodcraft, to follow such signs.

No one sign is infallible. A botanist can tell the north side of a steep hill from the south side by examining the plant growth; but no one plant of itself will tell him the story. So a woodsman works out his course by a system of *averaging* the signs around him. It is this averaging that demands genuine skill. It takes into account the prevailing winds of the region, the lay of the land, the habits of shade-loving and moisture-loving plants (and their opposites), the tendency of certain plants to point their leaves or their tips persistently in a certain direction, the growth of tree bark as influenced by sun and shade, the nesting habits of certain animals, the morning and evening flight of birds, and other natural phenomena, depending upon the general character of the country traversed. Moreover, in studying any one sign, a nice discrimination must be exercised. Let us glance at a few examples:

Moss on Trees.

First, as to the time-honored subject of moss—not confusing real moss with the parasitic lichens that incrust rocks and trees. Moss favors that part of a tree that holds the most moisture; not necessarily the part that receives the most moisture, but the part that *retains* it longest. Consequently it grows more abundantly on the upper side of a leaning tree than on the under side, on rough bark than on smooth bark, on top of projecting burls rather than on the lower side, and in the forks of trees, and on their buttressed bases. These factors are, of course, independent of the points of the compass.

Does it follow, then, that exposure has nothing to do with the growth of moss? Not at all. It merely follows that a competent woodcraftsman, seeking a sign of direction from the moss on trees, would *ignore* leaning trees, uncommonly rough bark, bossy knots, forks of limbs, and the bases of tree trunks, just as he would give no heed to the growth on prostrate logs. He would single out for examination the straight shafted old trees of rather smooth bark, knowing that on them there would be fairly even lodgment for moisture all around, and that the wet would evaporate least from the north and northeast sides of the tree, as a general rule, and, consequently, that on those sides the moss would preponderate. He would expect to find such difference more pronounced on the edge of thick forests than in their densely shaded interior. He would give special heed to the evidence of trees that were isolated enough to get direct sunlight throughout a good portion of the day, while those that were in the shade of cliffs or steep mountains so that they could only catch the sunbeams in the morning or the afternoon would be ruled out of court.

You see how much more swiftly and surely such a man could reach a decision than could one who tried to take into account all kinds and conditions of trees, regardless of surroundings, and how much less he would have to puzzle over contradictory evidence. Among a hundred trees he might only examine ten, but those ten would be more trustworthy for his purpose than their ninety neighbors. This is woodcraft —the genuine article—as distinguished from the mysterious and infallible "sixth sense" of direction that, I think, exists nowhere outside of Leatherstocking Tales.

Tips of Conifers.

A rule that holds good in the main, wherever I have had a chance to study it, is that the feathery tip, the topmost little branch, of a towering pine or hemlock, points toward the rising sun, that is to say, a little south of east. There are exceptions, of course, but I have generally found this to be the case in three-fourths of the trees examined, leaving out of consideration those growing in deep, narrow valleys, or on wind-swept crests. I do not know whether it is characteristic of all conifers, throughout their ranges; but I commend this peculiar phenomenon to travelers, for observation.

Bark and Annual Rings.

The bark of *old* trees is generally thicker on the north and northeast sides than on the other sides. A more reliable indicator of direction, though one that a traveler seldom has opportunity to test, is the thickness of annual rings of wood growth, which is more pronounced on the north than on the south side of a tree. This has been noted in widely separated parts of the earth, and has been known for many centuries. More than four hundred years ago it was mentioned by Leonardo da Vinci, that universal genius who was scarcely less celebrated as an engineer and scientist than as an artist and litterateur. "The rings of trees," wrote Leonardo, "show how many years they have lived, and their greater or smaller size shows whether the years were damper or drier. They also show the direction in which they were turned, because they are *larger on the north side than on the south*, and for this reason the center of the tree is nearer the bark on the south than on the north side." In 1893 this matter was put to a definite test by the New York State Forest Commission, which directed its foresters to examine the regularity of the northward thickening of annual rings in the black spruce of the Adirondacks. The foresters examined 700 trees, of varying exposure, noting in each case the compass-point toward which the longest radius of wood growth pointed. The result was:

North	471	South	1
Northeast	81	Southeast	0
East	106	West	27
		Southwest	6
Total north and east	658	Northwest	8
	94%		
		Total south and west	42
			6%

These figures deserve more than a passing glance.

Compass-Plants.

Some plants show a decided polarity in their habit of growth. The compass-plant or rosin-weed (*Silphium laciniatum*) that once abounded on the prairies of the Mississippi valley, from Minnesota to Texas, is a conspicuous example. It is a tall plant with long, stiff leaves, that do not grow horizontally but with their edges perpendicular. Its natural habitat is the open, shadeless prairie. If plants are examined that grow thus in the open, especially those in the little swales where they are not fully exposed to fierce winds, it will be found that the great majority of them present their radical leaves *north and south*. The large flower heads on short, thick stems point, like the hemlock's "finger," to the eastward, and show no such tendency to follow the sun towards the west as is characteristic of many plants. I have often used the compass-plant as a guide, and never was led astray by it; in fact, the old settlers on the prairies, if they chanced to get lost on a dark night, would get their bearings by feeling the leaves of the compass-plant.

The closely related prairie dock (*Silphium terebinthinaceum*) and that troublesome weed known as prickly lettuce (*Lactuca scariola*), show a similar polarity. This characteristic is lost if the plants are grown where they receive much shade. Of course, terrestrial magnetism has nothing to do with the polarity of plants; it is the sunlight, received on the two sides of the leaves alternately, that determines their position.

Lost Arts.

I am of the opinion that there are natural compass-signs in the forest, and on the plain, that we are ignorant of, but that were well known to savages in a state of nature. Such men, dependent from childhood upon close observation of their environment, but observation urged by entirely different motives from those of our naturalists, and directed toward different ends, would inevitably acquire a woodland lore different from ours, but quite as thorough in its own way. That they should develop keen perceptive faculties is no more remarkable than that a carpenter should hit a nail instead of the thumb that steadies it. That they should notice and study signs that no modern hunter or scientist would bother his head about is a matter of course. Unquestionably we have lost many arts of wildcraft that were daily practised by our ancestors of the stone age, just as we have lost their acquaintance with the habits of animals now extinct. Probably no white man of the future will ever equal Jim Bridger as a trailer; and it is but natural to suppose that Bridger himself had superiors among the savages from whom he learned his craft. It is a superficial judgment to rate as an old-wives' tale every story of exploits in the past that we cannot at present duplicate. However, we need not go to novelists to find out how such things were done. There is much pleasure to be gained in seeking to recover some of the lost arts of a primitive age; and, I believe, some profit as well.

CHAPTER XV

GETTING LOST—BIVOUACS

Quesla selva selvaggia, aspra e forte!

WHEN a man fixes up his pack and strikes out alone into strange woods, just for a little adventure, not caring where he may come out, he may be lost all the time, in one sense, but in a better sense he is at home all the time. Not for a moment does he worry about the future; he is exploring new territory —that is all.

But if one sets out for a certain destination, expecting to reach it by a given time, and loses the trail, he will be anxious at once, and the longer this continues, the more it will get on his nerves. Still we would hardly call him lost, so long as he retains a good idea of the general direction in which he should travel.

A man is really lost when, suddenly (it is always suddenly), there comes to him the thudding consciousness that he cannot tell, to save his life, whether he should go north, east, south, or west. This is an unpleasant plight to be in, at any time; the first time that it is experienced the outlook will seem actually desperate. Instantly the unfortunate man is overwhelmed by a sense of utter isolation, as though leagues and leagues of savage forest surrounded him on all sides, through which he must wander aimlessly, hopelessly, until he drops from exhaustion and starvation. Nervously he consults his compass, only to realize that it is of no more service to him now than a brass button. He starts to retrace his steps, but no sign of footprint can he detect. He is seized with a panic of fear, as irrational but quite as urgent as that which swoops upon a belated urchin while he is passing a country graveyard at night. It will take a mighty effort of will to rein himself in and check a headlong stampede.

In such predicament as this, a man is really in serious peril. The danger is not from the wilderness, which, pitiless niggard though it be to the weak-minded or disabled, can yet be forced to yield food and shelter to him who is able-bodied and who keeps his wits about him. No: the man's danger is from himself. We hear it said that no one ever was lost for more than twenty-four hours without suffering a derangement of mind. This is not true; thousands of wayfarers have been lost for much longer periods than that without losing their self-command. But it is literally true that a lost man who permits panic to conquer him is likely either to perish or to come out of the woods a gibbering idiot. If that does happen, it is the victim's own fault. There is no valid excuse for an able-bodied man losing heart from being lost, so long as he has a gun and ammunition, or even a few matches and a jackknife.

Panic.

I have heard old woodsmen say that there is no use in offering advice to novices about what they should do if they get lost, because a lost man is an insane man, anyway, and will remember nothing that has been told him. From my own experience I know that this is a mistake. The first time that I was lost, I was rattled and shook all over. Something seemed to tell me that camp lay in a certain direction, and I felt the same impulse to rush madly toward it that one feels to dash for the door when there is a cry of "fire!" in a theater. But I did remember what old Barnes had told me: "If you get lost, *sit down!*—sit down and give yourself half an hour to think it over." I sat down, and for five minutes could not think of anything, except cold, and rain, and hunger. Then I got to drawing diagrams on the ground. Making no headway at this, I began considering how to pass the night if I remained just where I was. This cleared my mind, robbed the woods of their spooks, and presently I was myself again. Then the actual situation flashed upon me. I saw just how I had got into this scrape, and knew that if I made a circuit of 200 yards radius I would strike the trail. Before this it had seemed at least two miles away. Well, I found it, all right. Had I listened to the demon of flight, in the first place, I would have plunged into one of the worst canebrakes in all Arkansas, and might have struggled there till I died—all within a mile and a half of my own camp.

The Risk. I have been lost several times since then—twice in canebrakes, twice in the laurel, twice in flat woods, once in fog, once above the clouds (in the sense that I did not know on which side to descend from an *aiguille* or bare pinnacle of rock), and three times in caverns. The latter experiences were hair-raising, but the others were only incidents to chuckle over in retrospect, although I have scorched the back of more than one coat from lying too near a bivouac fire. A bad record, you will say, for one who pretends to tell others how to keep from getting lost! Well, maybe so; but the fact that I am still on deck may be some excuse for offering a little counsel as to what to do if you should get lost.

I do not think that one can get the best of wild life if he does not often "go it alone." Men who are interested in the guiding business may say otherwise. If one does go it alone, he may as well take it for granted that, sooner or later, he will get lost and have to stay out over night, or for several nights, alone. There is no man, white or red, who is not liable to lose his bearings in strange woods if he is the least bit careless. If an Indian is seldom at fault as to his course it is because he pays close attention to business; he does not lose himself in reverie, nor is his mind ever so concentrated on an object of pursuit that he fails to notice irregular or uncommon things along the way. And yet, even Indians and white frontiersmen sometimes get lost. I have been with a first-class woodsman when he got mixed up on his own home hunting-ground—an overflow from the Mississippi, flooding sixty miles inland, had swept away old landmarks, replaced them with new ones, and changed the appearance of the country; then, subsiding, it had even altered the drainage of the land. In fog or snowstorm anybody can get lost. You may take a professional guide from New Brunswick, let us say, or from Florida—it matters not where—place him in a country where outlooks are few, and where the vegetation, the rocks and soil, and the general features of the country, are strange to him, and, if he does not get lost, it will be because he thinks more about avoiding it than he does about anything else. Those who scout the idea of their ever losing bearings are such as have traveled little in "strange londes," or have never ventured far without a native guide. Personally, I would rather get lost now and then than be forever hanging on to a guide's coat-tail. It is a matter of taste. Anyway, I shall never again have the willyjigs as I had 'em that first time, when I was actually within forty rods of a plain trail.

In the Mountains.

There is little excuse for getting lost, in fair weather, in a mountainous or undulating country where there are plenty of watercourses, unless one gets on the wrong side of a divide that separates two streams which do not run into each other. Thus, in Fig. 13, let *ABC* be a main divide, *BD* a spur to the southward separating two streams that eventually flow in opposite directions, and let *X* be the location of the camp. A stranger who had spent the day on the upper mountains might return toward evening to *B*, and, thinking to follow the creek from *f* to *X*, might turn down at *e*, by mistake, and travel a considerable distance before he realized that he was going in the wrong direction.

Flat Woods.

In flat woods, where the watercourses are few and very meandering, the vegetation rank and monotonously uniform in appearance, and landmarks rare, a man may return within 200 yards of his own camp and pass by it, going ahead with hurrying pace as he becomes more and more anxious. In Fig. 14 a man leaves camp *X* in the morning, going in the direction indicated by the dotted line. He consults his compass at intervals during the day, tries to allow for his windings, and, returning in the evening, strikes the river at *Z*. If he follows its bank in either direction, he is likely to spend the night alone in the woods. If the camp were at *A*, and the homeward-bound hunter should reach the stream at

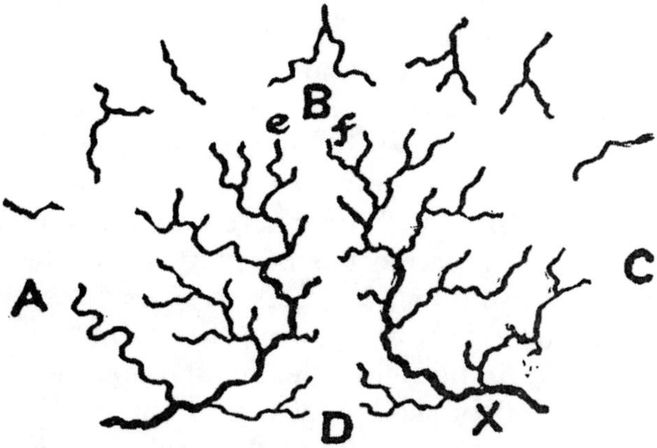

FIG. 13.

B, he would be dumfounded to find himself, apparently, on the wrong bank of the river.

Another easy way to get bewildered is as follows: In Fig. 14 we will assume that the current runs from *A* toward *Z*, that a party unfamiliar with the river is descending it in a boat, and that one of the men leaves the boat at *A*, going ashore to hunt along the bank. At *X* he comes to the mouth of a deep creek, or some other obstruction, or he starts game that leads him back into the woods. Not long afterward he reaches the river again at *Z*, and, after hallooing and firing a shot or two, but getting no answer, he hurries on down stream, thinking that the boat got ahead of him while he was making his detour. The boat, meanwhile, has been rounding a great ox-bow curve, and may be a couple of miles behind the man ashore.

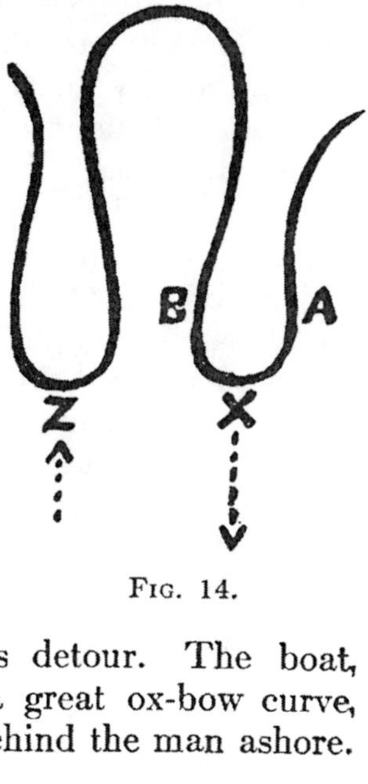

FIG. 14.

In each of these examples the country is assumed to be fairly easy to traverse, and in each case the misadventure might have been avoided by a little forethought. A bush bent over, here and there, a blaze on a tree where the underbrush was dense, would have saved all that. Without such precautions, there are places where a good man can get badly muddled in a forty-acre tract. This is no exaggeration. One of my companions was once lost from early morning until after nightfall in a thirty-acre patch of blue cane. He struggled until almost completely exhausted, and when we found him he looked like a scarecrow. At no time had he been half a mile from the cabin.

Thickets.

A canebrake is bad enough, but it is not so bad as those great tracts of rhododendron which, in the region between Clingman Dome and the Balsam Mountains (Tennessee and North Carolina) cover mile after mile of steep mountainside where no white man, at least, has ever been. The natives call such wastes "laurel slicks," "woolly heads," "lettuce beds," "yaller patches," and "hells." The rhododendron is worse than laurel, because it is more stunted and grows much more densely, so that it is quite impossible to make a way through it without cutting, foot by foot; and the wood is very tough. Two powerful mountaineers starting from the Tennessee side to cross the Smokies were misdirected and proceeded up the slope of the Devil's Court House, just east of Thunderhead. They were two days in making the ascent, a matter of three or four miles, notwithstanding that they could see out all the time and pursued the shortest possible course. I asked one of them how they managed to crawl through the thicket. "We couldn't crawl," he replied, "we swum," meaning that they sprawled and floundered over the top. These men were not lost at all. In another slick not very far away, an old hunter and trapper who was born and bred in these mountains, was lost for three days, although the slick was not more than a mile square. His account of it gave it the name that it bears to-day, "Huggins's hell." I could give many such instances, but these will suffice to show that there is still virgin ground in some of our oldest states. If one is ambitious in such matters, he might tackle the Everglades. Swamps are the worst places of all, above ground.

The first thing that one should do when he realizes that he has lost his bearings is to *stop* and sit down.

What to Do.

Think how long it was since you were where you were sure of your location. Probably not a long time. One does not go far before he realizes that he is off his course. Suppose you have traveled half an hour after leaving a known landmark. What is half an hour in the woods? You are not more than three-quarters of a mile from that place. So keep your shirt on. Don't take one more step until you have recovered your wits so that you can trace on the ground with a stick your probable course since leaving camp, and mark on it the estimated location of such watercourses and other landmarks as you have passed. Then make up your mind that if you must stay out all night, alone in the woods, it is no killing matter, but rather an interesting adventure. Having recovered your mental balance, then take note of the lay of the land around you, the direction of its drainage, the character of its vegetation, and the hospitalities that it offers to a night-bound traveler, in the way of drinking-water, sound downwood, natural shelter, and browse. Then blaze a tree on four sides—make big blazes that can be seen from any direction. Do this even though there be several hours of daylight ahead, and although you have no present intention of staying here; for you *do* know that this spot is only so many hours from camp by back trail, and that you may have good reason to return to it. This blazed tree will be of great assistance to your camp-mates in searching for you, if you should not turn up before morning.

If you start out to recover a trail, make bush-marks as you go along, for it will otherwise be the easiest thing in the world to lose that blazed tree, and that you must not do. In searching for a trail, do not look close to your feet, but fifteen or twenty feet ahead of you, for a faint trail is more readily seen at that angle than by looking straight down upon it. Cast your eyes, also, from side to side, bearing in mind what a trail ought to look like when you walk parallel with it, as well as when approaching at right angles.

But we will suppose that you find no trail. Now try to get an outlook over the surrounding country. In flat woods this will be difficult. If you can risk climbing a tall tree, do so. Select one that has a slender tree growing beside it from which to clamber into the limbs of the larger one. If necessary (and you have a hatchet) chop partly through one side of the slender tree and lodge it against the other. A tree trunk of large girth can be climbed by twisting a withe of hickory or other tough wood, putting it around the tree, and holding the ends. It will assist the feet if you make from some part of your clothing a strong band with a loop in each end for a stirrup (the feet should fit tightly, so as not to slip through), wet the band, fix the feet in the stirrups, spread the legs a little, get your withe in position with a good grip as high up as you can reach, then, raising your legs, press the band against the tree, some inches above the ground, stand in the stirrups, and so go clambering up. The descent is in reverse order.

Getting an Outlook.

Having gained your outlook, note the compass direction of watercourses and other landmarks, mapping them on a bit of paper, for a lost man's memory is treacherous. The courses of small streams show where the main valley lies. If the creeks are very meandering, or if their banks are very brushy, look for a divide. Decide where to go, take the compass direction, note how the sun strikes it, and descend.

Now, as you travel, make bush-marks and blazes along your course. Do not neglect this; for it may be important thereafter to return to the place where you first realized that you were lost. Consult your compass every ten minutes, or oftener if the timber and underbrush are thick, average up your windings, allow for the westward motion of the sun, and steer for your destination. Do not venture aside into one of those attractive woodland trails that, as Nessmuk says, "peters out into a squirrel track, runs up a tree, and disappears into a knot-hole."

Fog or Snow-storm.

No signs nor compass can aid a man if he does not know in what direction his destination lies; nor is it possible to keep a course by compass when the fog is thick or a blizzard is raging. In such case, bivouac where you are, and wait for clearing weather. This is no hardship in warm weather; but when the temperature is below freezing, or when an all-night rain is coming, it may put one to his trumps.

Bivouacs.

Look first for a wind-break—it may be a cliff, a large rock, a fallen tree; if you cannot find one ready-made, construct one by piling up a two-foot wall of rocks, or by driving stakes into the ground and piling against them several saplings or sticks of downwood five or six inches thick and seven feet long. If it threatens to rain, lay some poles over this backing, slanting sharply upward and projecting over your bed, and shingle them with sheets of bark, or with browse, on top of which lay other poles to hold the roof in place. The best kinds of bark for such purpose are paper birch, basswood, slippery elm, spruce, chestnut, pignut hickory, balsam fir, hemlock, white elm, white ash, cottonwood. I have never seen a rain-proof roof of browse. If one has an axe he can soon rive enough boards or slabs from cedar, spruce, arbor-vitæ, ash, basswood, chestnut, balsam, or other easily split wood, to make a good shelter. Build your fire on the leeward side of this wind-break and within about four feet of it (if the weather be cold). Build this fire above the level that you sleep on, for the higher it is (within reason) the more good it will do you, and the less smoke you will get. Stake a couple of backlogs behind the fire. Have ready some evergreen boughs to plant in front of you as a screen if the fire gets too hot. Now get in plenty of long poles for night-wood, make a bed of browse or boughs in front of the wind-break, or at least lay some poles or a couple of logs there, and lie parallel with the fire. A very small fire, if it is kept up, will keep a man warm in bitterly cold weather if he lies lengthwise with it, close to it, and has browse underneath and a log behind him. Such preparations take an hour of smart work; hence do not struggle on until dark in the hope of finding camp.

In very cold weather, build a fire first against the wind-break. After it has burned down, rake the embers forward, rebuild the fire in front, spread boughs where the first fire was, and lie on them over the hot ground. This can be done several times alternately through the night. There is no danger whatever of freezing.

If the snow is deep, you must shovel down to the ground, using the toe of a snowshoe, or a riven board, for a shovel. Dig out a triangular space of about seven feet base and eight feet long. At the smaller end, which should be downhill, build the fire. Make a bed at the upper end. The walls of snow make an excellent wind-break all around. If it be snowing, lay poles over the wide end and cover with browse.

On a prairie where there is no wind-break, build two fires at right angles to the wind, and get between them. The smoke will then have a tendency to blow away in columns parallel with your body.

A hollow log is about the last place I would think of crawling into to spend the night. Even though no snake nor skunk had preëmpted the den, it would surely be alive with insects, and the draught through it would be most unwholesome. The Indians of dime novels often sleep in hollow logs, but I think they must be drunk.

A standing hollow tree is all right, provided there is no prospect of a high wind. I have spread my blanket inside a hollow cypress where three men could have stretched out at ease. But don't light a fire in such a place; the inside of a dead tree is very inflammable.

CHAPTER XVI

EMERGENCY FOODS—LIVING OFF THE COUNTRY

But mice and rats, and such small deer,
Have been Tom's food for seven long year.

WHEN men go to explore an untracked wilderness, with no equipment but what they must carry on their own backs a good part of the time, there can be no such thing as a trifle in their outfit. Every article in it, and every part of every article, has weight; and that weight, small though it be, should be sternly challenged as to whether it is indispensable, whether something more essential might not be substituted for it. The very buckle on one's belt may some day be balanced, in tortured imagination, against its weight in meal.

I have tried several kinds of army emergency rations, but have not found any that is suitable for explorers' use, save as an accessory. When used continuously they make one's stomach rebel. The best of them, I think, is the pea-meal sausage that is known by its German name of *Erbswurst;* but, although it makes a good soup or porridge for an occasional quick meal, as an article of steady diet it is not as palatable nor as wholesome as an equal weight of bacon and hardtack.

The problem of an emergency ration is not merely one of condensing the utmost nutriment into the least bulk and weight. One cannot live on Swiss cheese or the yolks of hard-boiled eggs, however nutritious they may be in theory. The stuff must be digestible; it must neither nauseate nor clog the system. When a man is faint from hunger his stomach must not be forced to any uncommon stunts. And so I hold that a half ration of palatable food that is readily assimilated does more good than a full quota of stuff that taxes a man's gastric strength. Military precedent in such matters is not a safe guide for explorers, who may be cut off from their base of supplies, not for a few days only, but for weeks and months at a time. Canned meat, for example, is unfit for the human stomach, and is likely to sicken the man who persists in using it as a steady diet. For those who go far from civilization, the only emergency food worthy the name is such as is nutritious and wholesome to a man who has been weakened by much toil and fasting, and such as can be eaten with relish at the hundredth consecutive serving. It is my opinion that the best efforts of army commissary and medical departments in this respect fall far below the emergency foods that have been used by the Indians of North and South America for many thousands of years. These latter preparations, in the forms of parched meal, jerked meat, and pemmican, have also been the mainstays of all our white frontiersmen and explorers who became adept in wildcraft.

The first European settlers in this country were ignorant of the ways of the wilderness. Some of them had been old campaigners in civilized lands, but they did not know the resources of American forests, nor how to utilize them. The consequence was that many starved in a land of plenty. The survivors learned to pocket their pride and learn from the natives, who, however contemptible they might seem in other respects, were past masters of the art of going "light but right." An almost naked savage could start out alone and cross from the Atlantic to the Mississippi, without buying or begging from anybody, and without robbing, unless from other motives than hunger. This was not merely due to the abundance of game. There were large tracts of the wilderness where game was scarce, or where it was unsafe to hunt. The Indian knew the edible plants of the forest, and how to extract good food from roots that were rank or poisonous in their natural state; but he could not depend wholly upon such fortuitous findings. His mainstay on long journeys was a small bag of parched and pulverized maize,

The Old, Old Story,—

But a Good Day's Luck Lands Them

a spoonful of which, stirred in water, and swallowed at a draught, sufficed him for a meal when nature's storehouse failed.

Parched Indian Meal.

All of our early chroniclers praised this parched meal as the most nourishing food known. In New England it went by the name of "nocake," a corruption of the Indian word *nookik.* William Wood, who, in 1634, wrote the first topographical account of the Massachusetts colony, says of nocake that "It is Indian corn parched in the hot ashes, the ashes being sifted from it; it is afterwards beaten to powder and put into a long leatherne bag trussed at the Indian's backe like a knapsacke, out of which they take three spoonsful a day." Roger Williams, the founder of Rhode Island, said that a spoonful of nocake mixed with water made him "many a good meal." Roger did not affirm, however, that it made him a square meal, nor did he mention the size of his spoon.

In Virginia this preparation was known by another Indian name, "rockahominy" (which is not, as our dictionaries assume, a synonym for plain hominy, but a quite different thing). That most entertaining of our early woodcraftsmen, Colonel Byrd of Westover, who ran the dividing line between Virginia and North Carolina in 1728–29, speaks of it as follows:

> Rockahominy is nothing but Indian corn parched without burning, and reduced to Powder. The Fire drives out all the Watery Parts of the Corn, leaving the Strength of it behind, and this being very dry, becomes much lighter for carriage and less liable to be Spoilt by the Moist Air. Thus half a Dozen Pounds of this Sprightful Bread will sustain a Man for as many Months, provided he husband it well, and always spare it when he meets with Venison, which, as I said before, may be Safely eaten without any Bread at all. By what I have said, a Man needs not encumber himself with more than 8 or 10 Pounds of Provisions, tho' he continue half a year in the Woods. These and his Gun will support him very well during the time, without the least danger of keeping one Single Fast.

The best of our border hunters and warriors, such as Boone and Kenton and Crockett, relied upon this

Indian dietary when starting on their long hunts, or when undertaking forced marches more formidable than any that regular troops could have withstood. So did Lewis and Clark on their ever-memorable expedition across the unknown West. Modern explorers who do their outfitting in London or New York, and who think it needful to command a small army of porters and gun-bearers when they go into savage lands, might do worse than read the simple annals of that trip by Lewis and Clark, if they care to learn what real pioneering was.

In some parts of the South and West the pulverized parched corn was called "coal flour" or "cold flour." By the Delawares it was called *citamon*. The Indians of Louisiana gave it the name of *gofio*. In Mexico it is known as *pinole* (Spanish pronunciation, *pee*-no-lay; English, pie-*no*-lee). It is still the standby of native travelers in Spanish-American countries, and is used by those hardy hunters, "our contemporary ancestors," in the Southern Appalachians. Quite recently, one of my camp-mates in the Great Smoky Mountains expressed his surprise that any one should be ignorant of so plain a necessity of the hunter's life. He claims that no other food is "so good for a man's wind" in mountain climbing.

Some years ago Mr. T. S. Van Dyke, author of *The Still Hunter* and other well-known works on field sports, published a very practical article on emergency rations in a weekly paper, from which, as it is now buried where few can consult it, I take the liberty of making the following quotation:

> *La comida del desierto*, the food of the desert, or *pinole*, as it is generally called, knocks the hind sights off all American condensed food. It is the only form in which you can carry an equal weight and bulk of nutriment on which alone one can, if necessary, live continuously for weeks, and even months, without any disorder of stomach or bowels. . . . The principle of *pinole* is very simple. If you should eat a breakfast of corn-meal mush alone, and start out for a hard tramp, you will feel hungry in an hour or two, though at the table the dewrinkling of your abdomen may have reached the hurting point. But if, instead of distending the meal so much with water and heat, you had simply mixed it in cold water and

drunk it, you could have taken down three times the quantity in one-tenth of the time. You would not feel the difference at your waistband, but you would feel it mightily in your legs, especially if you have a heavy rifle on your back. It works a little on the principle of dried apples, though it is quite an improvement. There is no danger of explosion; it swells to suit the demand, and not too suddenly.

Suppose, now, instead of raw corn-meal, we make it not only drinkable but positively good. This is easily done by parching to a very light brown before grinding, and grinding just fine enough to mix so as to be drinkable, but not pasty, as flour would be. Good wheat is as good as corn, and perhaps better, while the mixture is very good. Common rolled oats browned in a pan in the oven and run through a spice mill is as good and easy to make it out of as anything. A coffee mill may do if it will set fine enough. Ten per cent. of popped corn ground in with it will improve the flavor so much that your children will get away with it all if you don't hide it. Wheat and corn are hard to grind, but the small Enterprise spice mill will do it. You may also mix some ground chocolate with it for flavor, which, with popped corn, makes it very fine. . . . Indigestible? Your granny's nightcap! . . . You must remember that it is "werry fillin' for the price," and go slow with it until you have found your coefficient. . . .

Now for the application. The Mexican rover of the desert will tie a small sack of *pinole* behind his saddle and start for a trip of several days. It is the lightest of food, and in the most portable shape, sandproof, bug and fly proof, and everything. Wherever he finds water he stirs a few ounces in a cup (I never weighed it, but four seem about enough at a time for an ordinary man), drinks it in five seconds, and is fed for five or six hours. If he has jerky, he chews that as he jogs along, but if he has not he will go through the longest trip and come out strong and well on *pinole* alone.—*Shooting and Fishing*, Vol. xx, p. 248.

Not having any spice mill, I pulverize the corn in a hominy-mortar, which is only a three-foot cut off of a two-foot log, with a hole burnt and gouged in the top, and a wooden pestle. The hole in the mortar is of smaller diameter at the bottom than at the top, so that each blow of the pestle throws most of the corn upward, and thus it is evenly pulverized. I often carry a small bag of this parched meal when mountaineering. Four heaping tablespoonfuls (4 ounces) stirred in a pint of water is enough to fill the stomach. A few raisins, or a chunk of sweet chocolate or maple sugar, make the meal quite satisfactory. Generally I prefer to use only half the above quantity at a time, and take it oftener during the day.

Jerked Venison.

"Jerky" or jerked meat has nothing to do with our common word "jerk." It is an anglicized form of the Spanish *charqui*, which is itself derived from the Quichua (Peruvian) *ccharqui*, meaning flesh cut in flakes and dried without salt. It is the same as the African *biltong*. Those who have not investigated the matter may be surprised to learn that the round of beef is 61 per cent. water, and that even the common dried and smoked meat of the butcher shops contains 54 per cent. water. The proportions of water in some other common foods are bacon 17 per cent., fat salt pork 8, corn-meal 12½, wheat flour 12, wheat bread 35, dried beans 12½, fresh potatoes 63. To condense the nutritive properties of these substances, the water, of course, must be exhausted. In ordinary dried beef this is only partially done, because the pieces are too thick. To jerk venison or any other kind of lean meat, proceed as follows:

If you can afford to be particular, select only the tender parts of the meat; otherwise use all of the lean. Cut it in strips about half an inch thick. If you have time, you may soak them a day in strong brine. If not, place the flakes of meat on the inside of the hide, and mix with them about a pint and a half of salt for a whole deer, or two or three quarts for an elk or moose; also some pepper. These condiments are not necessary, but are added merely for seasoning. Cover the meat with the hide, to keep flies out, and let it stand thus for about two hours to let the salt work in. Then drive four forked stakes in the ground so as to form a square of eight or ten feet, the forks being about four feet from the ground. Lay two poles across from fork to fork, parallel, and across these lay thin poles about two inches apart. Lay the strips of meat across the poles, and under them build a small fire to dry and smoke the meat. Do not let the fire get hot enough to cook the meat, but only to partially cook it, so that the flesh becomes dry as a chip. The best fuel is birch, especially black birch, because it imparts a pleasant flavor.

This will reduce the weight of the meat about one-half, and will cure it so that it will keep indefinitely. You may have to keep up the fire for twenty-four hours. The meat of an old bull will, of course, be as tough as sole leather; but, in any case, it will retain its flavor and sustenance. When pounded pretty fine, jerky makes excellent soup; but it is good enough as it is, and a man can live on it exclusively without suffering an inordinate craving for bread.

In the dry air of the plains, meat does not putrefy, even when unsalted, and it may be dried in the sun, without fire. Elk flesh dried in the sun does not keep as well as that of deer.

Pemmican.

The staple commissary supply of arctic travelers, and of hunters and traders in the far Northwest, is pemmican. This is not so palatable as jerky, at least when carelessly prepared; but it contains more nutriment, in a given bulk, and is better suited for cold climates, on account of the fat mixed with it.

The old-time Hudson Bay pemmican was made from buffalo meat, in the following manner: First a sufficient number of bags, about 2x1½ feet, were made from the hides of old bulls that were unfit for robes. The lean meat was then cut into thin strips, as for jerky, and dried in the sun for two or three days, or over a fire, until it was hard and brittle. It was then pounded to a powder between two stones, or by a flail on a sort of hide threshing-floor with the edges pegged up. The fat and marrow were then melted and mixed with the powdered lean meat to a paste; or, the bags were filled with the lean and then the fat was run in on top. After this the mass was well rammed down, and the bags were sewed up tight. No salt was used; but the pemmican thus prepared would keep sweet for years in the cool climate of the North. A piece as large as one's fist, when soaked and cooked, would make a meal for two men. When there was flour in the outfit, the usual allowance of pemmican was 1¼ to 1½ pounds a day per man, with one pound of flour added. This was for men performing the hardest labor, and whose appetites were enormous. Service berries were sometimes added. "Officers' pemmican" was made from buffalo humps and marrow.

Pemmican nowadays is made from beef. Bleasdell Cameron gives the following details: A beef dressing 698 pounds yields 47 pounds of first-class pemmican, 47 pounds of second-class pemmican, and 23 pounds of dried meat, including tongues, a total of 117 pounds, dried. The total nutritive strength is thus reduced in weight to one-sixth that of the fresh beef. Such pemmican costs the Canadian government about forty cents a pound, equivalent to six pounds of fresh beef.

Pemmican is sometimes eaten raw, sometimes boiled with flour into a thick soup or porridge called *robiboo;* or, mixed with flour and water and fried like sausage, it is known as *rascho.* The pemmican made nowadays for arctic expeditions is prepared from the round of beef cut into strips and kiln-dried until friable, then ground fine and mixed with beef suet, a little sugar, and a few currants. It is compressed into cakes, and then packed so as to exclude moisture.

Ordinary beef extract is not a food. If a man tried to subsist on it he would starve to death. But there is a way of concentrating much of the nourishment of beef or veal in the form of little cubes of a gluey consistency from which a strengthening soup can quickly be prepared. It is superior to the concentrated soups sold in our markets. Take a leg of young beef, veal, or venison (old meat will not jelly easily). Pare off every bit of fat and place the lean meat in a large pot. Boil it steadily and gently for seven or eight hours, until the meat is reduced to rags, skimming off, from time to time, the grease that arises. Then pour this strong broth into a large, wide stew-pan, place it over a moderate fire, and let it simmer gently until it comes to a thick jelly. When it gets so thick that there may be danger of scorching it, place the vessel over boiling water, and stir it very frequently until, when cold, it will have the consistency of glue. Cut this substance into small cubes and lay them singly where they can

Concentrated Meat.

become thoroughly dry. Or, if you prefer, run the jelly into sausage skins and tie up the ends. A cube or thick slice of this glaze, dissolved in hot water, makes an excellent soup. A small piece allowed to melt in one's mouth is strengthening on the march. This is a very old recipe, being mentioned in Byrd's *History of the Dividing Line*, and recommended along with rockahominy. The above can be made in camp, when opportunity offers, thus laying in enough concentrated soup stock to last a month, which is quite convenient, as it takes at least half a day to make good soup from the raw materials, and these are not always at hand when most wanted.

It has been demonstrated times without number that civilized men, no less than savages, can keep in good health and perform the hardest kind of work on a diet of either meat alone or cereals alone, a cold climate being more favorable for the former, and a hot one for the latter.

Personally, if I were going afoot into an uninhabited land, I would cut out all utensils save a small aluminum pail and a tin cup, and would carry no provisions other than some rockahominy in a waterproof silk bag, some tea, and a little hoard of salt. I would carry no meat at all, for, if by the time my meal was half gone I had not found game or fish, it would be time to retreat.

“Meat Straight.”

When a man deliberately stakes his life upon the chance of finding food in an unknown land, he should begin early in the game to habituate his digestive organs to whatever nutriment the country may afford, thereby hoarding his packed rations, rather than fall back upon unaccustomed food as a last extremity when his stomach has been seriously weakened by starvation. He should especially get used to living on “meat straight.” This will at first cause some bowel troubles, as every one knows who has partaken freely of venison as soon as he got to the woods; but this soon wears off when one's system is in a healthy condition. It is a curious fact that a man who has been eating nothing but game and fish for several months is unable, at first, to assimilate the food of civilization when he returns to it. Even though he eats more sparingly than his appetite demands, he will be troubled with indigestion for a week or more; bread and vegetables will lie on his stomach like lead, and he will suffer from constipation.

"Small Deer."

It goes without saying that men traveling through a barren region cannot be fastidious in their definition of "game." All's meat that comes to a hungry man's pot. A few words here may not be amiss as to the edible qualities of certain animals that are not commonly regarded as game, but which merit an explorer's consideration from the start; also as to some that are not to be recommended.

Probably most sportsmen know that 'coon is not bad eating, especially when young, if it is properly prepared; but how many would think to remove the scent-glands before roasting a 'coon? These glands should be sought for and extracted from all animals that have them, before the meat is put in the pot. Properly dressed, and, if necessary, parboiled in two or three waters, even muskrats, woodchucks, and fish-eating birds can be made palatable. Prairie-dog is as good as squirrel. The flesh of the porcupine is good, and that of the skunk is equal to roast pig. Beaver meat is very rich and cloying, and in old animals is rank; but the boiled liver and tail are famous tid-bits wherever the beaver is found. A man would have to be hard pressed to tackle any of the other fur-bearers as food, excepting, of course, bear and 'possum.

The flesh of all members of the cat tribe, wildcats, lynxes, and panthers, is excellent. Doctor Hart Merriam declares that panther flesh is better than any other kind of meat. The Englishman Ruxton, who lived in the Far West in the time of Bridger and the Sublettes and Fitzpatrick, says: "Throwing aside all the qualms and conscientious scruples of a fastidious stomach, it must be confessed that dog meat takes a high rank in the wonderful variety of cuisine afforded to the gourmand and the gourmet by the prolific mountains. Now, when the bill of fare offers such tempting viands as buffalo beef, venison, mountain mutton, turkey, grouse, wildfowl, hares, rabbits, beaver-tails, etc., etc., the station assigned to dog as No. 2 in the list can be well appreciated—No. 1, in delicacy of flavor, richness of meat, and other good qualities, being the flesh of panthers, which surpasses every other, and all put together."

Lewis and Clark say of dog flesh: "The greater part of us have acquired a fondness for it. . . . While we subsisted on that food we were fatter, stronger, and in general enjoyed better health than at any period since leaving the buffalo country." Again they say: "It is found to be a strong, healthy diet, preferable to lean deer or elk, and much superior to horse flesh in any state." They reported that horse flesh was "unwholesome as well as repellant." Many other travelers and residents in the early West commended dog meat; but the animals that they speak of were such as had been specially fattened by the Indians for food, and not starved and hard-worked sledge animals.

One who was driven by starvation to eat wolf's flesh says that it "tastes exactly as a dirty, wet dog smells, and it is gummy and otherwise offensive." But it seems that tastes differ, or, more likely, that all wolves are not alike. Ivar Fosheim of Sverdrups second Norwegian polar expedition says: "They were two she-wolves in very much better condition than beasts of prey usually are, with the exception of bears. The fat really looked so white and good that we felt inclined to taste it, and if we did that, we though we might as well try the hearts at the same time. Although most people will consider this a dish more extraordinary than appetizing, I think prejudice plays a large part here; as, at any rate, we found the meat far better than we expected."

I am assured by more than one white man who has eaten them that the flesh of snakes and lizards is as good as chicken or frogs' legs. One of my friends, however, draws the line at the prairie rattler. Once when he was on the U. S. Geological Survey he came near starving in the desert, and had to swallow his scruples along with a snake diet. "Probably," he said, "a big, fat diamond rattler might be all right, but the little prairie rattler is too sweetish for my taste; it's no comparison to puff-adder; puff-adder, my boy, is out of sight!"

This much I can swallow, by proxy; but when Dan Beard speaks approvingly of hellbenders as a side dish, I must confess that I'm like Kipling's elephant when the alligator had him by the nose: "This is too buch for be!" If Dan ever really ate a hellbender he is the most reckless dare-devil I ever heard of.

Another of my acquaintances declares that the prejudice against crow (real *Corvus*) is not well founded. The great gray owl is good roasted, despite what it may be when "biled." The flesh of the whippoorwill is excellent. Turtles' eggs are better than those of the domestic fowl (soft-shell turtles deposit their eggs on sandbars about the third week in June).

It is the testimony of gourmets who survived the siege of Paris that cats, rats, and mice are the most misprized of all animals, from a culinary point of view. "Stewed puss," says one of them, "is by far more delicious than stewed rabbit. . . . Those who have not tasted *couscoussou* of cat have never tasted anything."

Anyway, who are we, to set up standards as to the fitness or unfitness of things to eat? We shudder with horror at the idea of eating dog or cat, but of such a downright filthy animal as the pig we eat ears, nose, feet, tail, and intestines. How about our moldy and putrid cheeses, our boiled cabbage and sauerkraut, raw Hamburgers, lambfries, and "high" game? The hardihood of him who first swallowed a raw oyster! And if snails are good, why not locusts, dragon flies, and grubs? I tell you from experience that when you get to picking the skippers out of your pork, and begrudge them the holes they have made in it, you will agree that any kind of fresh, wild meat that is not carrion is clean and wholesome. Caspar Whitney, after describing his menu of frozen raw meat in the Barren Grounds, says: "I have no doubt some of my readers will be disgusted by this recital; and as I sit here at my desk writing, with but to reach out and press a button for dinner, luncheon—what I will—I can hardly realize that only a few months ago I choked an Indian until he gave up a piece of muskox intestine he had stolen from me. One must starve to know what one will eat."

I trust that none of my readers may be cast down by reading this somewhat lugubrious chapter. After all, it is not so bad to learn new dishes; but think of the predicament of that poor wight—he was a missionary to the Eskimo, I believe—who, being cast adrift on an ice floe, and essaying to eat his boots, did incontinently sneeze his false teeth into the middle of Baffin's Bay!

Perhaps the greatest privation that a civilized man suffers, next to having no meat, is to lack salt and tobacco. In the old days they used to burn the outside of meat and sprinkle gunpowder on it in lieu of salt; but in this age of smokeless powder we are denied even that consolation. The ashes of plants rich in nitre, such as tobacco, Indian corn, sunflower, and the ashes of hickory bark, have been recommended. Coville says that the ash of the palmate-leaf sweet coltsfoot (*Petasites palmata*) was highly esteemed by western Indians as a substitute for salt. "To obtain the ash the stem and leaves were first rolled up into balls while still green, and after being carefully dried they were placed on top of a very small fire on a rock, and burned." Many Indians, even civilized ones like the Qualla Cherokees, do not use salt to this day. Strange to say, the best substitute for salt is sugar, especially maple sugar or syrup. One soon can accustom himself to eat it even on meat. Among some of the northern tribes, maple syrup not only takes the place of salt in cooking, but is used for seasoning the food after it is served. Wild honey, boiled, and the wax skimmed off, has frequently served me in place of sugar in my tea, in army bread, etc.

Substitutes for Salt.

Kinnikinick.

Men who use tobacco can go a good while hungry without much grumbling, so long as the weed holds out.

Thou who, when cares attack,
Bidd'st them avaunt! and Black
Care, at the horseman's back
Perching, unseatest!

But let tobacco play out, and they are in a bad way! Substitutes for it may be divided into those that are a bit better than nothing and those that are worse. Among the latter may be rated: Tea. Yes, tea is smoked by many a poor fellow in the far North! It is said to cause a most painful irritation in the throat, which is aggravated by the cold air of that region. Certainly it can have no such effect on the nerves as tobacco, for it is full of tannin, and tannin destroys nicotin.

Kinnikinick is usually made of poor tobacco mixed with the scrapings or shavings of other plants, although the latter are sometimes smoked alone. Chief of the substitutes is the red osier dogwood (*Cornus stolonifera*) or the related silky cornel (*C. sericea*) commonly miscalled red willow. These shrubs are very abundant in some parts of the North. The dried inner bark is aromatic and very pungent, highly narcotic, and produces in those unused to it a heaviness sometimes approaching stupefaction. Young shoots are chosen, or such of the older branches as still keep the thin, red outer skin. This skin is shaved off with a keen knife, and thrown away. Then the soft, brittle, green inner bark is scraped off with the back of the knife and put aside for use; or, if wanted immediately, it is left hanging to the stem in little frills and is crisped before the fire. It is then rubbed between the hands into a form resembling leaf tobacco, or is cut very fine with a knife and mixed with tobacco in the proportion of two of bark to one of the latter.

A more highly prized kinnikinick is made from the leaves of the bear-berry or uva-ursi (*Arctostaphylos uva-ursi*), called *sacacommis* by the Canadian traders, who sell it to the northern Indians for more than the price of the best tobacco. The leaves are gathered in the summer months, being then milder than in winter. Inferior substitutes are the crumbled dried leaves of the smoothe sumac (*Rhus glabra*) and the fragrant

A Stray Goose Wanders Near

Where Lurks the Lusty Trout

sumac (*R. aromatica*), which, like tea, contain so much tannin that they generally produce bronchial irritation or sore throat.

In my chapters on *Camp Cookery* are described many processes for cooking without utensils; but, it may be asked, how could one *boil water* without a kettle? There are two ways of doing this. One of them, which many have heard of, but few have seen, is to split a log, chop out of it a trough, pour water in, heat a number of stones red hot, pick them up, one at a time, with a forked stick (or with one beathed in the fire, at its middle, and bent into hairpin shape), and drop them one by one into the water. To do this successfully, one must choose such stones as will neither burst in the fire nor shiver to pieces when dropped in the water.

Boiling Water without a Kettle.

Another way, which will be news to many, is to boil the water in a bucket made of birch bark, heated by direct action of the fire. The only difficulty about this is in so fastening the sheet of bark, below the waterline, that it will not leak.

Take a thin sheet of birch bark, free from knots or "eyes," and make a trough-shaped bucket, as illustrated in another chapter. Pin the folds with green twigs *below the waterline.* Pour the water in, set the bucket on a bed of fresh coals that do not flame, pile coals around it up almost to the waterline, and let it hum.

It might seem impossible to melt snow in such a bark utensil, but the thing can be done when you know how. Place the bucket in the snow before the fire, so it will not warp from the heat. In front of it set a number of little forked sticks, slanting backward over the bucket, and on each fork place a snowball. Thus let the snowballs melt into the bucket until the vessel is filled above the pins that hold it together. Then set the bucket on the coals, and the water will boil in a few moments.

CHAPTER XVII

EDIBLE PLANTS OF THE WILDERNESS

THERE is a popular notion that our Indians in olden times varied their meat diet with nothing but wild roots and herbs. This, in fact, was the case only among those tribes that pursued a roving life and had no settled abodes, such as the "horse Indians" and "diggers" of the Far West—and not all of them. The "forest Indians" east of the Mississippi and south of the Great Lakes, particularly such nations as the Iroquois and Cherokees, lived in villages and cultivated corn, beans, squashes and pumpkins. Still, wild plants and roots were often used even by these semi-agricultural peoples, in the same way that garden vegetables are used by us, and, in time of famine or invasion, they were sometimes almost the sole means of sustenance.

To-day, although our wild lands, such as are left, produce all the native plants that were known to the redmen, there is probably not one white hunter or forester in a thousand who can pick out the edible plants of the wilderness, nor who would know how to cook them if such were given to him. Nor are many of our botanists better informed. Now it is quite as important, in many cases, to know how to cook a wild plant as it is to be able to find it, for, otherwise, one might make as serious a mistake as if he ate the vine of a potato instead of its tuber, or a tomato vine instead of the fruit.

Take, for example, the cassava or manioc, which is still the staple food of most of the inhabitants of tropical America and is largely used elsewhere. The root of the bitter manioc, which is used with the same impunity as other species, contains a milky sap that is charged with prussic acid and is one of the most virulent vegetable poisons known to science. The Indians somehow discovered that this sap is volatile and can be driven off by heat. The root is cleaned, sliced, dried on hot metal plates or stones, grated, powdered, the starch separated from the meal, and the result is the tapioca of commerce, or farina, or Brazilian arrowroot, as may be, which we ourselves eat, and feed to our children and invalids, not knowing, perchance, that if it had not been for the art of a red savage, the stuff taken into our stomachs would have caused almost instant death.

Another example, not of a poisonous but of an extremely acrid root that the Indians used for bread, and which really is of delicious flavor when rightly prepared, is the common Indian turnip. Every country schoolboy thinks he knows all about this innocent looking bulb. He remembers when some older boy grudgingly allowed him the tiniest nibble of this sacred vegetable, and how he, the recipient of the favor, started to say "Huh! 'tain't bad"—and then concluded his remark with what we good, grown-up people utter when we jab the black-ink pen into the red-ink bottle!

However, not all of our wild food-plants are acrid or poisonous in a raw state, nor is it dangerous for any one with a rudimentary knowledge of botany to experiment with them. Many are easily identified by those who know nothing at all of botany. I cannot say that all of them are palatable; but most of them are, when properly prepared for the table. Their taste in a raw state, generally speaking, is no more of a criterion than is that of raw beans or asparagus.

To give a detailed account of the edible wild plants of the United States and Canada, with descriptions and illustrations sufficing to identify them, would require by itself a book at least as large as this. I have only space to give the names and edible properties of those that I know of which are native to, or, as wild plants, have become naturalized in the region north of the southern boundary of Virginia and east of the Rocky Mountains. Besides those mentioned below, there are others which grow only in the southern or western states, among the more important being the palmetto, palm, yam, cacti, aloe, Spanish bayonet, mesquite, wild sago, orcoontie, tule plant, western camass, kouse root, bread root, screw bean, pimple mallow, manzañita, piñons, juniper nuts, many pine seeds, squaw berry, lycium berry—but the list is long enough. Those who wish further details should examine the publications of the U. S. Department of Agriculture, and especially those of one of its officers, Mr. F. V. Coville, who has made special studies in this subject.

I have given the botanical name of every plant cited herein, because without it there would be no guarantee of identification. The nomenclature adopted is that of Britton and Brown in their *Illustrated Flora of the Northern States and Canada* (Scribner's Sons, New York), which, as it contains an illustration of every plant, is of the first assistance to an amateur in identifying. Wherever Gray's nomenclature differs, it is added in parentheses.

The months named under each plant are those in which it flowers, the earlier month in each case being the flowering month in the plant's southernmost range, and the later one that of the northernmost. In the case of wild fruits, the months are those in which the fruit ripens. It is necessary to remember that most of the edible plants become tough and bitter when they have reached full bloom.

SUBSTANTIAL FOODS

Acorns.—The eastern oaks that yield sweet mast are the basket, black jack, bur, chestnut, overcup, post, rock chestnut, scrub chestnut, swamp white, and white oaks, the acorns of chestnut and post oaks being sweetest; those producing bitter mast are the black, pin, red, scarlet, shingle, Spanish, water, and willow oaks, of which the black and water oak acorns are most astringent.

None of these can be used raw, as human food, without more or less ill effect from the tannin contained. But there are tribes of western Indians who extract the tannin from even the most astringent acorns and make bread out of their flour. The process varies somewhat among different tribes, but essentially it is as follows:

The acorns are collected when ripe, spread out to dry in the sun, cracked, and stored until the kernels are dry, care being taken that they do not mold. The kernels are then pulverized in a mortar to a fine meal, with frequent siftings to remove the coarser particles, until the whole is ground to a fine flour, this being essential. The tannin is then dissolved out by placing the flour in a filter and letting water percolate through it for about two hours, or until the water ceases to have a yellowish tinge. One form of filter is contrived by laying a coarse, flat basket or strainer on a pile of gravel with a drain underneath. Rather fine gravel is now scattered thickly over the bottom and up the sides of the strainer, and the meal laid thickly over the gravel. Water is added, little by little, to set free the tannin. The meal is removed by hand as much as possible, then water is poured over the remainder to get it together, and thus little is wasted. The meal by this time has the consistency of ordinary dough.

The dough is cooked in two ways: first, by boiling it in water as we do corn-meal mush, the resulting porridge being not unlike yellow corn-meal mush in appearance and taste; it is sweet and wholesome, but rather insipid. The second mode is to make the dough into small balls, which are wrapped in green corn leaves. These balls are then placed in hot ashes, some green leaves of corn are laid over them, and hot ashes are placed on the top, and the cakes are thus baked.

Acorns possess remarkable fattening power, and their nutritive value, when the tannin has been removed, is high.

(Coville, *Contrib. to U. S. Herbarium*, VII, No. 3.—Palmer, in *Amer. Naturalist*, XII, 597. Another method, used by the Pomo Indians, who add 5 per cent. of red earth to the dough, is described by J. W. Hudson in the *Amer. Anthropologist*, 1900, pp. 775–6.)

NUTS.—Among the Cherokees, and also in Italy and in the Austrian Tyrol, I have eaten bread made from chestnuts. The Cherokee method, when they have corn also, is to use the chestnuts whole, mixing them with enough corn-meal dough to hold them together, and then baking cakes of this material enclosed in corn husks, like tamales. The peasants of southern Europe make bread from the meal of chestnuts alone—the large European chestnut, of course, being used. Such bread is palatable and nutritious, but lies heavily on one's stomach until he becomes accustomed to it.

Our Indians also have made bread from the kernels of buckeyes. These, in a raw state, are poisonous, but when dried, powdered, and freed from their poison by filtration, like acorns, they yield an edible and nutritious flour. The method is to first roast the nuts, then hull and peel them, mash them in a basket with a billet, and then leach them. The resulting paste may be baked, or eaten cold.

Hazel nuts, beech nuts, pecans, and wankapins may be used like chestnuts. The oil expressed from beech nuts is little inferior to the best olive oil for table use, and will keep sweet for ten years. The oil from butternuts and black walnuts used to be highly esteemed by the eastern Indians, either to mix with their food, or as a frying fat. They pounded the ripe kernels, boiled them in water, and skimmed off the oil, using the remaining paste as bread. Hickory nut oil was easily obtained by crushing the whole nuts, precipitating the broken shells in water, and skimming off the oily "milk," which was used as we use cream or butter. The nut of the ironwood (blue beech) is edible.

The kernel of the long-leaved pine cone is edible and of an agreeable taste. Many western pines have edible "nuts." The acridity of pine seeds can be removed by roasting.

All nuts are more digestible when roasted than when eaten raw.

ARROWHEAD, BROAD-LEAVED. Swan or Swamp Potato. *Sagittaria latifolia* (*S. variabilis*). In shallow water; ditches. Throughout North America, except extreme north, to Mexico. *July–Sep.*

Tuberous roots as large as hens' eggs, were an important article of food among Indians. Roots bitter when raw, but rendered sweet and palatable by boiling. Excellent when cooked with meat. Indians gather them by wading and loosening roots with their feet, when the tubers float up and are gathered. Leaves acrid.

ARUM, GREEN ARROW. *Peltandra Virginica* (*P. undulata, Arum Virginicum*). Swamps or shallow water. Me. and Ont. to Mich., south to Fla. and La. *May–June.*

Rootstock used by eastern Indians for food, under the name of *Taw-ho.* Roots very large; acrid when fresh. The method of cooking this root, and that of the Golden Club, is thus described by Captain John Smith in his *Historie of Virginia* (1624), p. 87: "The chiefe root they haue for food is called *Tockawhoughe.* It groweth like a flagge in Marishes. In one day a Salvage will gather sufficient for a week. These roots are much of the greatnesse and taste of Potatoes. They vse to cover a great many of them with Oke leaues and Ferne, and then cover all with earth in the manner of a Cole-pit [charcoal pit]; over it, on each side, they continue a great fire 24 houres before they dare eat it. Raw it is no better than poyson, and being roasted, except it be tender and the heat abated, or sliced and dryed in the Sunne, mixed with sorrell and meale or such like, it will prickle and torment the throat extreamely, and yet in sommer they vse this ordinarily for bread."

ARUM, WATER. Wild Calla. (*Calla pallustris.*) Cold bogs. Nova Scotia to Minn., south to Va., Wis., Iowa. *May–June.*

Missen bread is made in Lapland from the roots of this plant, which are acrid when raw. They are taken up in spring when the leaves come forth, are extremely well washed, and then dried. The fibrous parts are removed, and the remainder dried in an oven. This is then bruised and chopped into pieces as small as peas or oatmeal, and then ground. The meal is boiled slowly, and continually stirred like mush. It is then left standing for three or four days, when the acridity disappears. (Lankester.)

BROOM-RAPE, LOUISIANA. *Orobanche Ludoviciana* (*Aphyllon L.*). Sandy soil. Ill. to N. W. Ty., south to Texas, Ariz., Cal. *June–Aug.*

"All the plant except the bloom grows under ground, and consequently nearly all is very white and succulent. The Pah Utes consume great numbers of them in summer. . . . Being succulent, they answer for food and drink on these sandy plains, and, indeed, are often called sand-food." (Palmer.)

BULRUSH, GREAT. Mat-rush. Tule-root. *Scirpus lacustris.* Ponds and swamps. Throughout North America; also in Old World. *June–Sep.*

Roots resemble artichokes, but are much larger. Eaten raw, they prevent thirst and afford nourishment. Flour made from the dried root is white, sweet, and very nutritious. A great favorite with the western Indians, who pound the roots and make bread of them. When the fresh roots are bruised, mixed with water, and boiled, they afford a good syrup.

CAMASS, EASTERN. Wild Hyacinth. *Quamasia hyacynthia* (*Camassia Fraseri*). In meadows and along streams. Pa. to Minn., south to Ala. and Texas. *Apr.–May.*

Root is very nutritious, with an agreeable mucilaginous taste.

GOLDEN CLUB. *Orontium aquaticum.* Swamps and ponds. Mass. to Pa., south to Fla. and La., mostly near coast. *Apr.–May.*

The *Taw-kee* of coast Indians, who liked the dried seeds when cooked like peas. The raw root is acrid, but becomes edible when cooked like arrow-arum.

GRASS, DROP-SEED. Sand Drop-seed. *Sporobolus cryptandrus.* Also Barnyard or Cockspur Grass (*Panicum Crusgalli*).

When the seeds, which are gathered in great quantities by western Indians, are parched, ground, mixed with water or milk and baked into bread or made into mush, they are of good flavor and nutritious. Also eaten dry.

GRASS, PANIC. *Panicum*, several species.

The ripe seeds are collected, like the above, cleaned by winnowing, ground into flour, water added, and the mass is kneaded into hard cakes, which, when dried in the sun are ready for use. Also made into gruel and mush.

GRASS, FLOATING MANNA. *Panicularia fluitans* (*Glyceria fl.*).

The seeds are of agreeable flavor and highly nutritious material for soups and gruels.

GREENBRIER, BRISTLY. Stretch-berry. *Smilax Bona-nox.*

Thickets. Mass. and Kansas, south to Fla. and Texas. *Apr.–July.*

The large, tuberous rootstocks are said to have been used by the Indians, who ground them into meal and made bread or gruel of it.

In the South a drink is made from them.

GREENBRIER, LONG-STALKED. *Smilax Pseudo-China.* Dry or sandy thickets. Md. to Neb., south to Fla. and Texas. *March–Aug.*

Bartram says that the Florida Indians prepared from this plant "a very agreeable, cooling sort of jelly, which they call *conte* [not to be confounded with coontie or wild sago]; this is prepared from the root of the China brier (*Smilax Pseudo-China*). . . . They chop the roots in pieces which are afterwards well pounded in a wooden mortar, then being mixed with clean water, in a tray or trough, they strain it through baskets. The sediment, which settles to the bottom of the second vessel, is afterwards dried in the open air, and is then a very fine reddish flour or meal. A small quantity of this, mixed with warm water and sweetened with honey, when cool, becomes a beautiful, delicious jelly, very nourishing and wholesome. They also mix it with fine corn flour, which being fried in fresh bear's oil makes very good hot cakes or fritters."

GROUND-NUT. Wild Bean. Indian Potato. *Apios Apios* (*A. tuberosa*). Moist ground. New Bruns. to Fla., west to Minn. and Kan., south to La. *July–Sep.*

This is the famous *hopniss* of New Jersey Indians, the *saagaban* of the Micmacs, *openauk* of Virginia tribes, *scherzo* of the Carolinas, *taux* of the Osages, and *modo* of the Sioux, under one or other of which names it is frequently met by students of our early annals. "In 1654 the town laws of Southampton, Mass., ordained that if an Indian dug ground-nuts on land occupied by the English, he was to be set in the stocks, and for a second offence, to be whipped." The Pilgrims, during their first winter, lived on these roots.

The tubers vary from the size of cherries to that of a hen's egg, or larger. They grow in strings of perhaps 40 together, resembling common potatoes in shape, taste, and odor. When boiled they are quite palatable and wholesome. The seeds in the pod can be prepared like common peas.

INDIAN TURNIP. Jack-in-the-Pulpit. *Arisæma triphyllum* (*Arum triphyllum*). Moist woods and thickets. Nova Scotia to Florida, west to Minn., Kan., La. *April–June.* Fruit ripe, *June–July.*

The root of this plant is so acrid when raw that, if one but touch the tip of his tongue to it, in a few seconds that unlucky member will sting as if touched to a nettle. Yet it was a favorite bread-root of the Indians. I have found bulbs as much as 11 inches in circumference and weighing half a pound.

Some writers state that the acridity of the root is destroyed by boiling, while others recommend baking. Neither alone will do. The bulb may be boiled for two hours, or baked as long, and, while the outer portion will have a characteristically pleasant flavor, half potato, half chestnut, the inner part will still be as uneatable as a spoonful of red pepper. The root should either be roasted or boiled, then peeled, dried, and pounded in a mortar, or otherwise reduced to flour. Then if it is heated again, or let stand for a day or two, it becomes bland and wholesome, having been reduced to a starchy substance resembling arrowroot. Even if the fresh root is only grated finely and let stand exposed to air until it is thoroughly dry, the acridity will have evaporated with the juice.

The roots may be preserved for a year by storing in damp sand.

It is said that the Indians also cooked and ate the berries.

LILY, TURK'S-CAP. *Lilium superbum.* Meadows and marshes. Me. to Minn., south to N. C. and Tenn. *July–Aug.*

LILY, WILD YELLOW. Canada Lily. *Lilium Canadense.* Swamps, meadows and fields. Nova Scotia to Minn., south to Ga., Ala., Mo. *June–July.*

Both of these lilies have fleshy, edible bulbs. When green they look and taste somewhat like raw green corn on the ear. The Indians use them, instead of flour, to thicken stews, etc. (Thoreau.)

LILY, YELLOW POND. Spatter-dock. *Nymphæa advena (Nuphar ad.).* Ponds and slow streams. Nova Scotia to Rocky Mts., south to Fla., Texas, Utah. *Apr.–Sep.*

The roots, which are one or two feet long, grow four or five feet under water, and Indian women dive for them. They are very porous, slightly sweet, and glutinous. Generally boiled with wild fowl, but often roasted separately. Muskrats store large quantities for winter use, and their houses are frequently robbed by the Indians. The pulverized seeds of the plant are made into bread or gruel, or parched and eaten like popcorn.

NELUMBO, AMERICAN. Wankapin or Yoncopin. Water Chinquapin. *Nelumbo lutea.* Ponds and swamps. Locally east from Ontario to Fla., abundant west to Mich., Ind. Ty., La. *July–Aug.*

Tubers of root somewhat resemble sweet potatoes, and are little inferior to them when well boiled. A highly prized food of the Indians. The green and succulent half-ripe seed-pods are delicate and nutritious. From the sweet, mealy seeds, which resemble hazel nuts, the Indians made bread, soups, etc. The "nuts" were first steeped in water, and then parched in sand, to easily extricate the kernels. These were mixed with fat and made into a palatable soup, or were ground into flour and baked. Frequently they were parched without steeping, and the kernels eaten thus.

ORCHIS, SHOWY. *Orchis spectabilis.* Rich woods. New Brunsw. to Minn., south to Ga., Ky., Neb. *Apr.–June.*

"One of the orchids that springs from a tuberous root, and as such finds favor with the country people [of the South] in the preparation of a highly nourishing food for children." (Lounsberry.)

PEANUT, HOG. Wild peanut. *Falcata comosa* (*Glycine comosa*). Moist thickets. New Brunsw. to Fla., west to Lake Superior, Neb., La. *Aug.–Sep.*

The underground pod has been cultivated as a vegetable. (Porcher.)

POTATO, PRAIRIE. Prairie turnip. Indian or Missouri Breadroot. The *pomme blanche* of the voyageurs. *Psoralea esculenta.* Prairies. Manitoba and N. Dak. to Texas. *June.*

The farinaceous tuber, generally the size of a hen's egg, has a thick, leathery envelope, easily separable from the smoothe internal parts, which become friable when dry and are readily pulverized, affording a light, starchy flour, with sweetish, turnip-like taste. Often sliced and dried by the Indians for winter use. Palatable in any form.

RICE, WILD. *Zizania aquatica.* Swamps. New Brunsw. to Manitoba, south to Fla., La., Texas. *June–Oct.*

The chief farinaceous food of probably 30,000 of our northern Indians, and now on the market as a breakfast food. The harvesting is usually done by two persons working together, one propelling the canoe, and the one in the stern gently pulling the plants over the canoe and beating off the ripe seed with two sticks. The seed, when gathered, is spread out for a few hours to dry, and is then parched in a kettle over a slow fire for half an hour to an hour, meanwhile being evenly and constantly stirred. It is then spread out to cool. After this it is hulled by putting about a bushel of the seed into a hole in the ground, lined with staves or burnt clay, and beating or punching it with heavy sticks. The grains and hulls are separated by tossing the mixture into the wind from baskets. The grain will keep indefinitely.

Before cooking, it should have several washings in cold water, to remove the smoky taste. It is cooked with game, or as gruel, or made into bread, or merely eaten dry. Its food value is equal to that of our common cereals. "An acre of rice is nearly or quite equal to an acre of wheat in nutriment." (For details see *Bulletin No.* 50 of the Bureau of Plant Industry, U. S. Dep't. of Agriculture.)

SILVERWEED. Wild or Goose Tansy. Goose-grass. *Potentilla Anserina.* Shores and salt meadows, marshes and river banks. Greenland to N. J., west to Neb.; Alaska, south along Rocky Mts. to N. Mex. and Cal. *May–Sep.*

Roots gathered in spring and eaten either raw or roasted. Starchy and wholesome. When roasted or boiled their taste resembles chestnuts.

SUNFLOWER. *Helianthus,* many species. Prairies, etc. *July–Sep.* "The seeds of these plants form one of the staple articles of food for many Indians, and they gather them in great quantities. The agreeable oily nature of the seeds renders them very palatable. When parched and ground they are highly prized, and are eaten on hunting excursions. The meal or flour is also made into thin cakes and baked in hot ashes. These cakes are of a gray color, rather coarse looking, but palatable and very nutritious. Having eaten of the bread made from sunflowers, I must say that it is as good as much of the corn bread eaten by whites." (Palmer.)

The oil expressed from sunflower seeds is a good substitute for olive oil.

VALERIAN, EDIBLE. Tobacco-root. *Valeriana edulis.* Wet open places. Ontario to B. C., south to O., Wis., and in Rocky Mts. to N. Mex. and Ariz. *May–Aug.*

"I ate here, for the first time, the *kooyah* or tobacco-root (*valeriana edulis*), the principal edible root among the Indians who inhabit the upper waters of the streams on the western side of the [Rocky] mountains. It has a very strong and remarkably peculiar taste and odor, which I can compare to no other vegetable that I am acquainted with, and which to some persons is extremely offensive. . . . To others, however, the taste is rather an agreeable one, and I was afterwards always glad when it formed an addition to our scanty meals. It is full of nutriment. In its unprepared state it is said by the Indians to have very strong poisonous qualities, of which it is deprived by a peculiar process, being baked in the ground for about two days." (Fremont, *Exploring Expedition*, 1845, p. 135.)

POT-HERBS AND SALADS

All of the plants hitherto mentioned are native to the regions described. In the following list will be found many that are introduced weeds; but a considerable proportion of these foundlings may now be seen in clearings and old burnt tracts in the woods, far from regular settlements. Directions for cooking greens are given in the chapter on *Camp Cookery.*

ADDER'S-TONGUE, YELLOW. Dog's-tooth, Violet. *Erythronium Americanum.* Moist woods and thickets. Nova Scotia to Minn., south to Fla., Mo., Ark. *Mar.–May.*

Sometimes used for greens.

BEAN, WILD KIDNEY. *Phaseolus polystachyus* (*P. perennis*). Thickets. Canada to Fla., west to Minn., Neb., La. *July–Sep.*

Was used as food by the Indians; the Apaches eat it either green or dried.

BELLWORT. *Uvularia perfoliata.* Moist woods and thickets. Quebec and Ont. to Fla. and Miss. *May–June.*

The roots of this and other species of *Uvularia* are edible when cooked, and the young shoots are a good substitute for asparagus. (Porcher.)

BROOKLIME, AMERICAN. *Veronica Americana.* Brooks and swamps. Anticosti to Alaska, south to Pa., Neb., N. Mex., Cal. *Apr.–Sep.*

"A salad plant equal to the watercress. Delightful in flavor, healthful, anti-scorbutic." (*Sci. Amer.*)

BURDOCK, GREAT. Cockle-bur. *Arctium Lappa.* Waste places. New Brunsw. to southern N. Y., and locally in the interior. Not nearly so widely distributed as the smaller common burdock (*A. minus*). *July–Oct.*

A naturalized weed, so rank in appearance and odor that nothing but stark necessity could have driven people to experiment with it as a vegetable. Yet, like the skunk cabbage, it is capable of being turned to good account. In spring, the tender shoots, when peeled, can be eaten raw like radishes, or, with vinegar, can be used as a salad. The stalks cut before the flowers open, and stripped of their rind, form a delicate vegetable when boiled, similar in flavor to asparagus. The raw root has medicinal properties, but the Japanese eat the cooked root, preparing it as follows: The skin is scraped or peeled off, and the roots sliced in long strips, or cut into pieces about two inches long, and boiled with salt and pepper, or with soy, to impart flavor; or the boiled root is mashed, made into cakes, and fried like oyster plant.

CHARLOCK. Wild Mustard. *Brassica arvensis* (*B. Sinapistrum*). Fields and waste places. Naturalized everywhere. *May–Nov.*

Extensively used as a pot-herb; aids digestion.

CHICKWEED. *Alsine media* (*Stellaria m.*). Waste places, meadows, and woods. Naturalized; common everywhere. *Jan–Dec.*

Used like spinach, and quite as good.

CHICORY. Wild Succory. *Chichorium Intybus.* Roadsides, fields, and waste places. Nova Scotia to Minn., south to N. C. and Mo. *July–Oct.*

All parts of the plant are wholesome. The young leaves make a good salad, or may be cooked as a pot-herb like dandelion. The root, ground and roasted, is used as an adulterant of coffee.

CLOVER. *Trifolium*, many species.

The coast Indians of California use clover as a food. The fresh leaves and stems are used, before flowering. "Deserves test as a salad herb, with vinegar and salt."

COMFREY. *Symphytum officinale.* Waste places. Newf. to Minn., south to Md. Naturalized. *June–Aug.*

Makes good greens when gathered young.

COW PEA. China Bean. *Vigna Sinensis.* Escaped from cultivation. Mo. to Texas and Ga. *July–Sep.*

The seeds are edible.

Cress, Rocket. Yellow Rocket. Bitter Cress. *Barbarea Barbarea* (*B. vulgaris*). Fields and waste places. Naturalized. Labrador to Va., and locally in interior; also on Pacific coast. *Apr.–June.*

The young, tender leaves make a fair salad, but inferior to the winter cress.

Cress, Water. *Roripa Nasturtium* (*Nasturtium officinale*). Brooks and other streams, Nova Scotia to Manitoba, south to Va. and Mo. Naturalized from Europe. *Apr.–Nov.*

A well-known salad herb. The leaves and stems are eaten raw with salt, as a relish, or mixed as a salad.

Cress, Winter. Scurvy Grass. *Barbarea praecox.* Waste places, naturalized. Southern N. Y., Pa., and southward. *Apr.–June.*

Highly esteemed as a winter salad and pot-herb; sometimes cultivated.

Crinkle-Root. Two-leaved Toothwort. *Dentaria diphylla.* Rich woods and meadows. Nova Scotia to Minn., south to S. Car. and Ky. *May.*

The rootstocks are crisp and fleshy, with a spicy flavor like watercress. Eaten with salt, like celery.

Crowfoot, Celery-Leaved or Ditch. *Ranunculus sceleratus.* Swamps and wet ditches, New Brunsw. to Fla., abundant along the coast, and locally westward to Minn. *Apr.–Aug.*

Porcher cites this as a good example of the destruction of acrid and poisonous juices by heating. The fresh juice is so caustic that it will raise a blister, and two drops taken internally may excite fatal inflammation. Yet the boiled or baked root, he says, is edible. When cleansed, scraped and pounded, and the pulp soaked in a considerable quantity of water, a white sediment is deposited, which, when washed and dried, is a real starch.

Cuckoo-Flower. Meadow Bitter-cress. *Cardamine pratensis.* Wet meadows and swamps. Labrador to northern N. J., west to Minn. and B. C. *Apr.–May.*

Has a pungent savor and is used like water cress; occasionally cultivated as a salad plant.

Dandelion. *Taraxacum Taraxacum* (*T. officinale*). Fields and waste places everywhere; naturalized. *Jan.–Dec.*

Common pot-herb; also blanched for salad. In boiling, change the water two or three times.

Dock, Curled. *Rumex Crispus.* Fields and waste places, everywhere; naturalized. *June–Aug.*

The young leaves make good pot-herbs. The plant produces an abundance of seeds, which Indians grind into flour for bread or mush.

Ferns. Many species.

The young stems of ferns, gathered before they are covered with down, and before the leaves have uncurled, are tender, and when boiled like asparagus are delicious.

The rootstocks of ferns are starchy, and after being baked resemble the dough of wheat; their flavor is not very pleasant, but they are by no means to be despised by a hungry man.

FETTICUS. Corn Salad. *Valerianella Locusta.* Waste places. N. Y. to Va. and La. Naturalized. *Apr.–July.*

Cultivated for salad and as a pot-herb. The young leaves are very tender.

FLAG, CAT-TAIL. *Typha latifolia.* Marshes. Throughout North America except in extreme north. *June–July.*

The flowering ends are very tender in the spring, and are eaten raw, or when boiled in water make a good soup. The root is eaten as a salad. "The Cossacks of the Don peel off the outer cuticle of the stalk and eat raw the tender white part of the stem extending about 18 inches from the root. It has a somewhat insipid, but pleasant and cooling taste."

GARLIC, WILD OR MEADOW. *Allium Canadense.* Moist meadows and thickets. Me. to Minn., south to Fla., La., Ark. *May–June.*

A good substitute for garlic. "The top bulbs are superior to the common onion for pickling."

GINSENG, DWARF. Ground-nut. *Panax trifolium* (*Aralia trifolia*). Moist woods and thickets. Nova Scotia to Ga., west to Minn., Iowa, Ill. *Apr.–June.*

The tubers are edible and pungent.

HONEWORT. *Deringa Canadensis* (*Cryptotænia C.*). Woods. New Brunsw. to Minn., south to Ga. and Texas. *June–July.*

In the spring this is a wholesome green, used in soups, etc., like chervil.

HOP. *Cannabis sativa.* Waste places. New Brunsw. to Minn., south to N. C., Tenn., Kansas. Naturalized. *July–Sep.*

Used for yeast. "In Belgium the young shoots of the plant just as they emerge from the ground, are used as asparagus."

INDIAN CUCUMBER. *Medeola Virginiana.* Rich, damp woods and thickets. Nova Scotia to Minn., south to Fla. and Tenn. *May–June.*

"The common name alludes to the succulent, horizontal, white tuberous root, which tastes like cucumber, and was in all probability relished by the Indians." (Mathews.)

JERUSALEM ARTICHOKE. Canada Potato. Girasole. Topinambour. *Helianthus tuberosus.* Moist soil. New Brunsw. to N. W. Ty., south to Ga. and Ark. "Often occurs along roadsides in the east, a relic of cultivation by the aborigines."

Now cultivated and for sale in our markets. The tubers are large, and edible either raw or cooked, tasting somewhat like celery root. They are eaten as vegetables, and are also pickled.

LADY'S THUMB. English Smartweed. *Polygonum Persicaria.* Waste places throughout the continent, except extreme north. Naturalized; often an abundant weed. *June-Sep.*

Used as an early salad plant in the southern mountains.

LAMB'S QUARTERS. White Pigweed. *Chenopodium album.* Waste places, range universal, like the above. Naturalized. *June–Sep.*

A fine summer green and pot-herb, tender and succulent. Should be boiled about 20 minutes, the first water being thrown away, owing to its bad taste. The small seeds, which are not unpleasant when eaten raw, may be dried, ground, and made into cakes or gruel. They resemble buckwheat in color and taste, and are equally nutritious.

LETTUCE, SPANISH. Indian or Miner's Lettuce. *Claytonia perfoliata.* Native of Pacific coast, but spreading eastward. *Apr.–May.*

The whole plant is eaten by western Indians and by whites. In a raw state makes an excellent salad; also cooked with salt and pepper, as greens.

LUPINE, WILD. Wild Pea. *Lupinus perennis.* Dry, sandy soil. Me. to Minn., south to Fla., Mo., La. *May–June.*

Edible; cooked like domestic peas.

MALLOW, MARSH. *Althœa officinalis.* Salt marshes. Mass. to N. J. *Summer.*

The thick, very mucilaginous root, has familiar use as a confection; also used in medicine as a demulcent. May be eaten raw.

MALLOW, WHORLED OR CURLED. *Malva aerticillata (M. crispa).* Waste places. Vermont. Naturalized. *Summer.*

A good pot-herb.

MARIGOLD, MARSH. Meadow-gowan. Cowslip. *Caltha palustris.* Swamps and meadows. Newfoundland to S. C., west through Canada to Rocky Mts., and south to Iowa. *Apr.–June.*

Used as a spring vegetable, the young plant being thoroughly boiled for greens. The flower buds are sometimes pickled as a substitute for capers.

Beware of mistaking for this plant the poisonous white hellebore (*Veratrum viride*).

MEADOW BEAUTY. Deer Grass. *Rhexia Virginica.* Sandy swamps. Me. to Fla., west to north N. Y., Ill., Mo., La. *July–Sep.*

The leaves have a sweetish, yet acidulous taste. Make a good addition to a salad, and may be eaten with impunity.

MILKWEED. *Asclepias Syriaca (A. Cornuti).* Fields and waste places generally. *June–Aug.* Also other species.

The young shoots, in spring, are a good substitute for asparagus. Kalm says that a good brown sugar has been made by gathering the flowers while the dew was on them, expressing the dew, and boiling it down.

MUSHROOMS. The number of edible species is legion. It

is not difficult to distinguish the poisonous ones, when one has studied a good text-book; but no one should take chances with fungi until he has made such study, for a few of the common species are deadly, and for some of them no remedy is known. A beginner would do well, perhaps, to avoid all of the genus *Amanita*. All mushrooms on the following list are of delicious flavor.

Coprinus comatus.
Hypholoma appendiculatum.
Tricholoma personatum.
Boletus subaureus.
" *bovinus.*
" *subsanguineous.*
Clavaria botrytes.
" *cinerea.*
" *inæqualis.*
" *vermicularis.*
" *pistillaris.*
Lactarius volemus.
" *deliciosus.*
Russula alutacea.
" *virescens.*
Cantharellus cibarius.
Marasmius oreades.
Hydnum repandum.
" *caput-Medusæ.*
Morchella esculenta.
" *deliciosa.*

It would be well for every outer to learn the easily distinguishable beefsteak fungus (*Fistulina hepatica*) and sulphur mushroom (*Polyporus sulphureus*) that grow from the trunks of old trees and stumps, as they are very common, very large, and very "filling."

MUSTARD. *Brassica*, several species. Fields and waste places. Naturalized.

The young leaves are used for greens.

NETTLE. *Urtica dioica*, and other species; also the Sow Thistle, *Sonchus oleraceus*. Fields and waste places.

Should be gathered, with gloves, when the leaves are quite young and tender. A pleasant, nourishing and mildly aperient pot-herb, used with soups, salt meat, or as spinach; adds a piquant taste to other greens. Largely used for such purposes in Europe.

NIGHTSHADE, BLACK OR GARDEN. *Solanum nigrum*. Waste places, commonly in cultivated soil. Nova Scotia to N. W. Ty., south to Fla. and Texas. *July–Oct.*

This plant is reputed to be poisonous, though not to the same degree as its relative from Europe, the Woody Nightshade or Bittersweet (*S. Dulcamara*). It is, however, used as a pot-herb, like spinach, in some countries, and in China the young shoots and berries are eaten. Bessey reports that in the Mississippi Valley the little black berries are made into pies.

ONION, WILD. *Allium*, many species. Rich woods, moist meadows and thickets, banks and hillsides.

Used like the domestic onions.

PARSNIP, COW. Masterwort. *Heracleum lanatum*. Moist ground. Labrador to N. C. and Mo., Alaska to Cal. *June–July.*

"The tender leaf and flower stalks are sweet and very agreeably aromatic, and are therefore much sought after [by coast Indians] for green food in spring and early summer, before the flowers have expanded. In eating these, the outer skin is rejected."

PEPPERGRASS, WILD. *Lepidium Virginicum.* Fields and along roadsides. Quebec to Minn., south to Fla. and Mexico. *May–Nov.*

Like the cultivated peppergrass, this is sometimes used as a winter or early spring salad, but it is much inferior to other cresses. The spicy pods are good seasoning for salads, soups, etc.

PIGWEED, ROUGH. Beet-root. *Amaranthus retroflexus.* Fields and waste places. Throughout the continent, except extreme north. Naturalized. *Aug.–Oct.*

Related to the beet and spinach, and may be used for greens.

PIGWEED, SLENDER. Keerless. *Amaranthus hybridus* (*A. chlorostachys*). A weed of the same wide range as the preceding. Naturalized. *Aug.–Oct.*

Extensively used in the South, in early spring, as a salad plant, under the name of "keerless."

PLANTAIN, COMMON. *Plantago major.* A naturalized weed of general range, like the preceding. *May–Sep.*

Used as early spring greens.

PLEURISY-ROOT. *Asclepias Tuberosa.* Dry fields. Me. to Minn., south to Fla., Texas, Ariz. *June-Sep.*

The tender young shoots may be used like asparagus. The raw tuber is medicinal; but when boiled or baked it is edible.

POKEWEED. *Phytolacca decandra.* A common weed east of the Mississippi and west of Texas. Now cultivated in France, and the wild shoots are sold in our eastern markets.

In early spring the young shoots and leaves make an excellent substitute for asparagus.

The root is poisonous (this is destroyed by heat), and the raw juice of the old plant is an acrid purgative. The berries are harmless.

PRICKLY PEAR. *Opuntia.* Several species. Dry, sandy soil. Along eastern coast, and on western prairies and plains.

The ripe fruit is eaten raw. The unripe fruit, if boiled ten or twelve hours, becomes soft and resembles apple-sauce. When the leaves are roasted in hot ashes, the outer skin, with its thorns, is easily removed, leaving a slimy but sweet and succulent pulp which sustains life. Should be gathered with tongs, which can be extemporized by bending a green stick in the middle and beathing it over the fire.

PRIMROSE, EVENING. *Onagra biennis* (*Oenothera b.*). Usually in dry soil. Labrador to Fla., west to Rocky Mts. *June-Oct.*

Young sprigs are mucilaginous and can be eaten as salad. Roots have a nutty flavor, and are used in Europe either raw or stewed, like celery.

PURSLANE. Pussley. *Portulaca oleracea.* Fields and waste places. A weed of almost world-wide distribution. *Summer.*

This weed was used as a pot-herb by the Greeks and Romans, and is still so used in Europe. The young shoots should be gathered when from 2 to 5 inches long. May also be used as a salad, or pickled. Taste somewhat like string beans, with a slight acid flavor. The seeds, ground to flour, have been used by Indians in the form of mush.

RED-BUD. *Cercis Canadensis.*

French-Canadians use the acid flowers of this tree in salads. The buds and tender pods are pickled in vinegar. All may be fried in butter, or made into fritters.

SAXIFRAGE, LETTUCE. *Saxifraga micranthidifolia.* In cold brooks. Appalachian Mts. from Pa. to N. C. *May–June.*

Eaten by Carolina mountaineers as a salad, under the name of "lettuce."

SHEPHERD'S PURSE. *Bursa Bursa-pastoris* (*Capsella B.*). Fields and waste places everywhere. Naturalized. *Jan.–Dec.*

A good substitute for spinach. Delicious when blanched and served as a salad. Tastes somewhat like cabbage, but is much more delicate.

SKUNK CABBAGE. *Spathyema fœtida* (*Symplocarpus f.*). Swamps and wet soil. Throughout the east, and west to Minn. and Iowa. *Feb.–April.*

The root of this foul-smelling plant was baked or roasted by eastern Indians, to extract the juice, and used as a bread-root. Doubtless they got the hint from the bear, who is very fond of this, one of the first green things to appear in spring.

SOLOMON'S SEAL. *Polygonatum biflorum.* Woods and thickets. New Brunsw. to Mich., south to Fla. and W. Va. *April–July.*

Indians boiled the young shoots in spring and ate them; also dried the mature roots in fall, ground or pounded them, and baked them into bread. The raw plant is medicinal.

SORREL, MOUNTAIN. *Oxyria digyna.* Greenland to Alaska, south to White Mts. of N. H. and in Rocky Mts. to Colo. *July–Sep.*

A pleasant addition to salads.

SORREL, SHEEP. *Rumex Acetosella.* Dry fields and hillsides. Throughout the continent, except in extreme north. *May–Sep.*

The leaves are very acid. Young shoots may be eaten as a salad. Also used as a seasoning for soups, etc.

The European sorrels cultivated as salad plants are *R. Acetosa*, *R. scutatus*, and sometimes *R. Patientia.*

SORREL, WHITE WOOD. *Oxalis Acetosella.* Cold, damp woods. Nova Scotia to Manitoba, mts. of N. C., and north shore of Lake Superior. *May–July.*

Not related to the above. "The pleasant acid taste of the

leaves, when mixed with salads, imparts an agreeable, refreshing flavor." The fresh plant, or a "lemonade" made from it, is very useful in scurvy, and makes a cooling drink for fevers. Should be used in moderation, as it contains binoxalate of potash, which is poisonous. Yields the druggist's "salt of lemons."

STORKSBILL. Pin-clover. *Erodium cicutarium.* Waste places and fields. Locally in the east, abundant in the west. *April–Sep.* Naturalized.

The young plant is gathered by western Indians and eaten raw or cooked.

STRAWBERRY BLITE. *Blitum capitatum* (*Chenopodium c.*). Dry soil. Nova Scotia to Alaska, south to N. J., Ill., Colo., Utah, Nev. *June–Aug.*

Sometimes cultivated for greens. Used like spinach.

TRILLIUM. Wake-robin. Beth-root. *Trillium erectum;* also *T. undulatum* and *T. grandiflorum.* Woods. Nova Scotia to Minn., and south to Fla. *April–June.*

The popular notion that these plants are poisonous is incorrect. They make good greens when cooked.

TUCKAHOE. *Pachyma cocos.* A subterranean fungus which grows on decaying vegetable matter, such as old roots. It is found in light, loamy soils and in dry waste places, but not in very old fields or in woodlands. Outwardly it is woody, resembling a cocoanut or the bark of a hickory tree. The inside is a compact, white, fleshy mass, moist and yielding when fresh, but in drying it becomes very hard, cracking from within. It contains no starch, but is composed largely of pectose. The Indians made bread of it, and it is sometimes called Indian Bread. (For details, see an article by Prof. J. H. Gore in *Smithsonian Report*, 1881, pp. 687–701.)

UNICORN PLANT. *Martynia Louisiana* (*M. proboscidea*). Waste places. Me. to N. J. and N. C. Native in Mississippi Valley from Iowa and Ill. southward. *July–Sep.*

Cultivated in some places. The seed-pods, while yet tender, make excellent pickles. The Apaches gather the half-ripe pods of a related species and use them for food.

VETCH, MILK. *Astragalus,* several species. Prairies. *May–Aug.*

Used as food by the Indians. The pea is hulled and boiled.

VIOLET, EARLY BLUE. *Viola palmata.* Dry soil, mostly in woods. Me. to Minn., south to Ga. and Ark. *April–May.*

The plant is very mucilaginous, and is employed by negroes for thickening soup, under the name of "wild okra." (Porcher.)

WATERLEAF. *Hydrophyllum Virginicum.* Woods. Quebec to Alaska, south to S. C., Kan., Wash. *May–Aug.*

"Furnishes good greens. Reappears after being picked off, and does not become woody for a long time."

WILD FRUITS

It would extend this chapter beyond reasonable limits if I were to give details of all the wild fruits native to the region here considered. As fruits may be eaten raw, or require no special treatment in cooking, a mere list of them, with the time of ripening, must suffice:

Carolina Buckthorn. *Rhamnus Caroliniana. Sep.*
Woolly-leaved Buckthorn. *Bumelia languinosa. June–July.*
Buffalo-berry. *Lepargyræa argentea. July–Aug.*
American Barberry. *Berberis Canadensis. Aug.–Sep.*
Common Barberry. *Berberis vulgaris. Sep.* Naturalized.
Bailey's Blackberry. *Rubus Baileyanus.*
Bristly Blackberry. *R. setosus.*
Dewberry. *R. Canadensis. June–July.*
High Bush Blackberry. *R. villosus. July–Aug.*
Hispid Blackberry. *R. hispidus. Aug.*
Low Bush Blackberry. *R. trivialis.*
Millspaugh's Blackberry. *R. Millspaughii. Aug.–Sep.*
Mountain Blackberry. *R. Alleghaniensis. Aug.–Sep.*
Sand Blackberry. *R. Cuneifolius. July–Aug.*
Dwarf Bilberry. *Vaccinium caespitosum. Aug.*
Great Bilberry. *V. uliginosum. July–Aug.*
Oval-leaved Bilberry. *V. ovalifolium. July–Aug.*
Thin-leaved Bilberry. *V. membranaceum. July–Aug.*
Black Blueberry. *V. atrococcum. July–Aug.*
Canada Blueberry. *V. Canadense. July–Aug.*
Dwarf Blueberry. *V. Pennsylvanicum. June–July.*
High Bush Blueberry. *V. corymbosum. July–Aug.*
Low Blueberry. *V. vacillans. July–Aug.*
Low Black Blueberry. *V. nigrum. July.*
Mountain Blueberry. *V. pallidum. July–Aug.*
Southern Black Huckleberry. *V. virgatum. July.*
Mountain Cranberry. Windberry. *V. Vitis-Idaea. Aug.–Sep.*
Black Huckleberry. *Gaylussacia resinosa. July–Aug.*
Box Huckleberry. *G. brachycera.*
Dwarf Huckleberry. *G. dumosa. July–Aug.*
Tangleberry. *G. frondosa. July–Aug.*
Appalachian Cherry. *Prunus cuneata.*
Choke Cherry. *P. Virginiana. July–Aug.* (Edible later.)
Sand Cherry. *P. pumila. Aug.*
Sour Cherry. Egriot. *P. Cerasus. June–July.* Naturalized.
Western Wild Cherry. *P. demissa. Aug.*
Western Sand Cherry. *P. Besseyi.*

Wild Cherry. Crab Cherry. *P. Avium.* Naturalized.
Wild Black Cherry. *P. serotina. Aug.–Sep.*
Wild Red Cherry. *P. Pennsylvanica. Aug.*
American Crab-Apple. Sweet-scented C. *Malus coronaria. Sep.–Oct.*
Narrow-leaved Crab-Apple. *M. angustifolia.*
Soulard Crab-Apple. *M. Soulardi.*
Western Crab-Apple. *M. Ioensis.*
American Cranberry. *Oxycoccus macrocarpus. Sep.–Oct.*
Small Cranberry. Bog C. *O. Oxycoccus. Aug.–Sep.*
Southern Mountain Cranberry. *O. erythrocarpus. July–Sep.*
Cranberry Tree. *Viburnum Opulus. Aug.–Sep.*
Crowberry. Curlew-berry. *Empetrum nigrum. Summer.*
Golden Currant. Buffalo or Missouri C. *Ribes aureum.*
Northern Black Currant. *R. Hudsonianum.*
Red Currant. *R. rubrum.*
Wild Black Currant. *R. floridum. July–Aug.*
Elderberry. *Sambucus Canadensis. Aug.*
Wild Gooseberry. Dogberry. *Ribes Cynosbati. Aug.*
Missouri Gooseberry. *R. gracile.*
Northern Gooseberry. *R. oxyacanthoides. July–Aug.*
Round-leaved Gooseberry. *R. rotundifolium. July–Aug.*
Swamp Gooseberry. *R. lacustre. July–Aug.*
Bailey's Grape. *Vitis Baileyana.*
Blue Grape. Winter G. *V. bicolor.*
Downy Grape. *V. cinerea.*
Frost Grape. *V. cordifolia. Oct.–Nov.*
Missouri Grape. *V. palmata. Oct.*
Northern Fox Grape. *V. Labrusca. Aug.–Sep.*
Riverside Grape. Sweet-scented G. *V. vulpina. July–Oct.*
Sand Grape. Sugar G. *V. rupestris. Aug.*
Southern Fox Grape. *V. rotundifolia. Aug.–Sep.*
Summer Grape. *V. æstivalis. Sep.–Oct.*
Ground Cherry. *Physalis*, several species.
Hackberry. *Celtis occidentalis. Sep.–Oct.* Berries dry but edible.
Black Haw. *Viburnum prunifolium. Sep.–Oct.*
Scarlet Haw. Red H. *Crataegus mollis. Sep.–Oct.*
May Apple. Mandrake. *Podophyllum peltatum. July.*
Passion-flower. *Passiflora incarnata.* Also *P. lutea.* Fruit known as Maypops.
Pawpaw. *Asimina triloba.* Fruit edible when frost-bitten.
Persimmon. *Diospyros Virginiana.* Fruit edible after frost.
Beach Plum. *Prunus maritima. Sep.–Oct.*
Canada Plum. *P. nigra. Aug.*
Chickasaw Plum. *P. angustifolia. May–July.*
Low Plum. *P. gracilis.*
Porter's Plum. *P. Alleghaniensis. Aug.*

Watson's Plum. *P. Watsoni.*

Wild Goose Plum. *P. hortulana. Sep.–Oct.*

Wild Red Plum. Yellow P. *P. Americana. Aug.–Oct.*

Ground Plum. *Astragalus crassicarpus;* also *A. Mexicanus.* Unripe fruit resembles green plums, and is eaten raw or cooked.

Black Raspberry. Thimble-berry. *Rubus occidentalis. July.*

Cloudberry. *R. Chamaemorus.*

Dwarf Raspberry. *R. Americanus. July–Aug.*

Purple Wild Raspberry. *R. neglectus. July–Aug.*

Purple-flowering Raspberry. *R. odoratus. July–Sep.*

Salmon-berry. *R. parviflorus. July–Sep.*

Wild Red Raspberry. *R. strigosus. July–Sep.*

Service-berry. June-berry. *Amelanchier Canadensis. June–July.*

Low June-berry. *A. spicata.*

Northwestern June-berry. *A. alnifolia.*

Round-leaved June-berry. *A. rotundifolia. Aug.*

Shad-bush. *A. Botryapium. June–July.*

Silver berry. *Elæagnus argentea. July–Aug.*

Creeping Snowberry. *Chiogenes hispidula. Aug.–Sep.* Berries have flavor of sweet birch.

American Wood Strawberry. *Fragaria Americana.*

Northern Wild Strawberry. *F. Canadensis.*

Virginia Strawberry. Scarlet S. *F. Virginiana.*

Black Thorn. Pear Haw. *Cratægus tomentosa. Oct.*

Large-fruited Thorn. *C. punctata. Sep.–Oct.*

Scarlet Thorn. *C. coccinea. Sep.–Oct.*

MISCELLANEOUS

All substitutes for coffee are unsatisfying. In the South during the Civil War many pitiful expedients were tried, such as parched meal, dried sweet potatoes, wheat, chicory, cotton-seed, persimmon-seed, dandelion-seed, and the seeds of the Kentucky coffee-tree; but the best were found to be rye, the seeds of the coffee senna (*Cassia occidentalis*) called "Magdad coffee," and the parched and ground seeds of okra. None of our wild plants contain principles that act upon the nerves like caffein or thein.

Teas, so-called, of very good flavor can be made from the dried root-bark of sassafras, or from its early buds, from the bark and leaves of spicewood, from the leaves of chicory, ginseng, the sweet goldenrod (*Solidago odora*), and cinquefoil. Other plants used for the purpose are Labrador tea, Oswego tea, and (inferior) New Jersey tea. Our pioneers also made decoctions of chips of the arbor-vitæ (white cedar), the dried leaves of black birch, and the tips of hemlock boughs, sweetening them with maple sugar. The list of medicinal teas is unending.

Agreeable summer drinks can be made by infusing the sour fruit of the mountain ash (*Pyrus Americana*), from sumac berries (dwarf and staghorn), and from the fruit of the red mulberry. The sweet sap of both hard and soft maples, box elder, and the birches (except red birch) is potable. Small beer can be made from the sap of black birch, from the pulp of honey locust pods, the fruit of the persimmon, the shoots and root-bark of sassafras, and the twigs of black and red spruce. Cider has been made from the fruit of crab-apples and service-berries.

Sugar or syrup is made by boiling down the sap, not only of sugar maple, but of red and silver maples, box elder, the birches, butternut, and hickory, and from honey locust pods. Vinegar also can be made from these saps, as well as from fruit juices, by diluting with water and adding a little yeast. The very sour berries of sumac turn cider into vinegar, or they may be used alone.

IN EXTREMIS

The Far North is Famine Land, the world over, and to it we must look for examples of what men can subsist on when driven to the last extremity.

In all northern countries, within the tree limit, it is customary, in starving times, to mix with the scanty hoard of flour the ground bark of trees. It is possible to support life even with bark alone. The Jesuit missionary Nicollet reported, more than two centuries ago, that an acquaintance of his, a French Indian-agent, lived seven weeks on bark alone, and the *Relations* of the order, in Canada, contain many instances of a like expedient. Those were hard times in New France! Such an experience as this was dismissed with a single sentence, quite as a matter of course: "An eelskin was deemed a sumptuous supper; I had used one for mending a robe, but hunger obliged me to unstitch and eat it." Another brother says: "The bark of the oak, birch, linden, and that of other trees, when well cooked and pounded, and then put into the water in which fish had been boiled, or else mixed with fish-oil, made some excellent stews." Again: "they [the Indians] dried by a fire the bark of green oak, then they pounded it and made it into a porridge." It seems that the human stomach can stand a lot of tannin, if it has to do so.

The young shoots of spruce and tamarack, the inner bark (in spring) of pine, spruce, and hemlock, young leaf-stems of beech, hickory and other trees, and wild rose buds, are nutritious; but these can be had only, of course in spring. Far better than oak bark are the inner barks of alder, quaking aspen, basswood, birch, sweet bay, cottonwood, slippery elm (this especially is nutritious), white elm, pignut hickory, yellow locust, striped maple, and sassafras. The Chippewas boil the thick, sweetish bark of the shrubby bittersweet or staff-tree (*Celastrus scandens*) and use it for food.

The following entry in the diary of Sir John Franklin sounds naïve, when stripped of its context, but there is a world of grim pathos back of it: "There was no *tripe de roche*, so we drank tea and ate some of our shoes for supper." The rock tripe here referred to (*Umbilicaria arctica* or *Dillenii*) is one of several edible lichens that grow on rocks and are extensively used as human food in lands beyond the arctic tree limit. Reindeer moss (*Cladonia rangiferina*) and the well-known Iceland moss (*Cetraris Icelandica*) are other examples. These are starchy, and, after being boiled for two or three hours, form a gelatinous mass that is digestible, though repulsive in appearance, one of the early Jesuits likening it to the slime of snails, and another admitting that "it is necessary to close one's eyes to eat it."

It is pleasanter to turn, now, to the wild condiments that our fields and forests afford. Sassafras, oil of birch, wintergreen, peppermint and spearmint will occur to every one. Balm, sweet marjoram, summer savory and tansy are sometimes found in wild places, where they have escaped from cultivation. The rootstock of sweet cicely has a spicy taste, with a strong odor of anise, and is edible. Sweet gale gives a pleasant flavor to soups and dressings. The seeds of tansy mustard were used by the Indians in flavoring dishes. Wild garlic, wild onions, peppergrass, snowberry and spicewood may also be used for similar purposes.

Flavoring.

CHAPTER XVIII

AXEMANSHIP—QUALITIES OF WOOD AND BARK

BEFORE starting to fell a tree, clear away all underbrush and vines that are within reach of the extended axe, overhead as well as around you. Neglect of this precaution may cripple a man for life. Next decide in which direction you wish the tree to fall. This will be governed partly by the lay of the ground

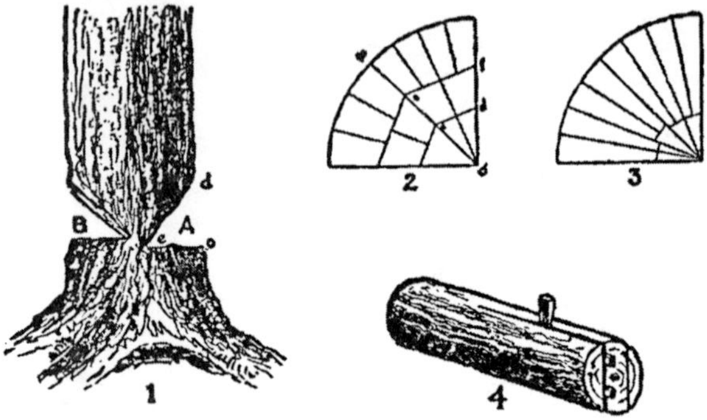

FIG 15. Illustrating how to Cut a Tree and Split a Log.

and the obstacles on it. The tree should fall where it will be easy to log-up. A matter of more consequence, however, in thick forest, is to throw the tree in such direction that it will not catch and hang on one of its neighbors, obliging you to fell the latter also.

Felling a Tree.

Now, suppose that you decide to throw the tree to the south. Cut a kerf or notch on the south side of the tree, half way through the trunk, as shown at *A* in Fig. 1. In making this cut you should not start it so narrow that you will soon find yourself wedging your axe. Make a nick at *c* as a guide, then another at *d*, which should be as far above *c* as the intended depth of the cut *ce*. Then chop out your kerf, making as big chips as you can. To do this, chop alternately at the notches *d* and *c*, and split out the block between with a downward blow of the axe. A green axeman is known by the finely minced chips and haggled stump that he leaves.

Beginners invariably over-exert themselves in chopping, and are soon blown. An accurate stroke counts for much more than a heavy but blundering one. A good chopper lands one blow exactly on top of the other with the precision and regularity of a machine; he chops slowly but rhythmically, and puts little more effort into striking than he does into lifting his axe for the blow. Trying to sink the axe deeply at every stroke is about the hardest work that a man can do, and it spoils accuracy.

If the tree is of such wood as is easy to cut, make the cut *ce* as nearly square across the butt as you can. To do this keep the hand that holds the hilt of the axe-helve well down. But if the tree is hard and stubborn to fell, or if you are rustling firewood in a hurry, it is easier to make this cut in a slanting direction, so as not to chop squarely across the grain.

Having finished this south kerf (which is two-thirds the labor of felling the tree), now begin the opposite one, *B*, at a point three or four inches *higher* than the other. By studying the diagram, and taking into account the tree's great weight, you can see why this method will infallibly throw the tree to the south, if it stands anywhere near perpendicular, and if there is not a strong wind blowing. Comparatively few blows are needed here. When the tree begins to crack, step to one side. Never jump in a direction opposite that in which the tree falls. Many a man has been killed in that way. Sometimes a falling tree, striking against one of its neighbors, shoots backward from the stump like lightning. Look out, too, for shattered limbs.

If a tree leans in the wrong direction for your purpose, insert a billet of wood in the kerf *B*, and drive a wedge or two above it in the direction of the kerf. A tree weighing many tons can be forced to fall in any desired direction by the proper use of wedges; and a good axeman, in open woods, can throw a tree with such accuracy as to drive a stake previously stuck in the ground at an agreed position. He can even do this when a considerable wind is blowing, by watching the sway of the tree and striking his final blow at the right moment.

When the tree is down and you go to log it up, make the outside chip not less in length than the diameter of the log. This will seem absurdly long, until you have cut a log in two. With a narrow cut you would be wedging your axe before you were nearly half through; and your work would be harder, anyway, because you would be cutting more nearly across the grain of the wood, instead of diagonally with it. In making these side cuts, be sure to make them perpendicular to the ground; otherwise you will soon find that the upper side of the log is cut away, but that you have no way of getting at the under side. When cutting close to the ground, look out for pebbles. A nick in the axe will make your work doubly hard. Before felling a tree on stony ground it is well worth while to place a small log across the way for the butt of the tree to fall on, so as to keep it off the ground. This will also make it easier to log-up. Speaking of nicks in the axe, beware how you cut into hemlock knots; in trimming limbs close to a hemlock trunk, you can ruin the best steel that ever was made.

Logging-Up.

In logging-up a large tree it is necessary for the axeman to stand on the prostrate trunk, with his legs well apart, and to cut down between his feet. This, to a beginner, looks like a risky performance; but I have seen one of my woodland neighbors, who professes to be "only a triflin' hand with an axe," stand on a slender tree-trunk that was balanced about ten feet over a gulch, whack away between his feet, with the trunk swaying several inches at every stroke, nor did he step over on the main trunk until two or three light blows sufficed to cut the end log free. But such a performance is tame compared with the feats of axemanship that regular choppers and river drivers do every day as a mere matter of course.

Certain woods, such as cedar, can be riven into serviceable boards with no other tool than an axe; but in general, if one has much splitting to do, he should make a maul and some gluts, steel wedges being, presumably, unobtainable. When one has no augur with which to bore a hole for the handle, a serviceable maul can be made in club shape. Beech, oak, and hickory are good materials, but any hardwood that does not splinter easily will do. Choose a sapling about five inches thick at the butt, not counting the bark. Dig a little below the surface of the ground and cut the sapling off where the stools of the roots begin. (The wood is very tough here, and this is to be used for the large end of the maul, which should be about ten inches long.) From this, forward, shave down the handle, which should be twenty inches long. Thus balanced, the maul will not jar one's hands.

Splitting Timber.

Gluts are simply wooden wedges. The best woods for them are dogwood and hornbeam or ironwood, as they are very hard and tough, even when green. Chop a sapling of suitable thickness, and make one end wedge-shaped; then cut it off square at the top; and so continue until you have all the gluts you want. It takes no mean skill to chop and shave a glut to a true wedge shape, and much depends upon getting the angles and surfaces correctly proportioned. A novice is apt to make a glut too short and thick. The gluts may well be fire-hardened, by placing them in hot ashes until the sap has been driven out, but leaving the surface only slightly charred.

To split a log, start the wedges in the smaller or top end of the log. If there is a crack or large check at the right place, drive two wedges into it, as the log will probably split best that way. If not, then with the axe in one hand and maul in the other, make a crack across the end of the log. Drive the wedges home, and others into the crack along the side of the log. The general rule in riving rails is to split a stick through the middle, then quarter it, then split the quarters through the middle, and so on until the required dimensions are reached. Figure 2 shows, for example, the method of splitting rails from a large log. The quarter of log is first halved along the line *ab;* then the rail *bcd* is split off; the remaining section is then halved as before; the rails are split off in the direction *ef*, and others are split from the remaining segments; or the method shown in the lower eighth is used, according to the dimensions required.

Figure 3 shows how clapboards, or the rough shingles called shakes, are riven. For splitting such wide, thin pieces a tool called a froe is used, it being a heavy steel blade, with a wooden handle set at right angles. A cut of the desired length is sawed from the log and stood on end. It may then be quartered, and from each quarter the shakes may be split off by placing the edge of the froe on the end of the billet and striking it with a mallet. The usual way, however, is to split around, but not through the core, detaching the latter now and then by the axe at right angles to the splits. The heart of oak, for example, is so tough that it would be impracticable to continue the split through the core.

In splitting puncheons the log is merely halved, and the round side left as it is, being turned under in flooring. With some woods, however, it is not difficult to rive out slabs that are flat on both sides, by working after the method shown in Figure 4.

Much depends upon the right selection of wood for the purpose in hand. For instance, it would be worse than useless to try to split shingles from cherry, because it splits irregularly; or from hemlock, for it splits spirally; or from sour gum, tupelo, or winged elm, because they cannot be split at all. Much depends, though, upon the individual tree. A timberman can tell whether a tree will split well or not by merely scanning the bark; if the ridges and furrows of the bark run straight up and down, in the main, the wood will have a corresponding straight grain, but if they are spiral, the wood will split waney, or not at all. Peculiarities of soil and climate also affect the riving qualities of wood. In the southern mountains, for example, one may see thousands of shingles and palings or clapboards split from hemlock, even up to the length of four or five feet.

To make a puncheon out of a log that will not split straight: cut deep notches along one side, one after the other, and of uniform depth, like saw teeth; then split or hew off the remaining blocks until the log is flattened as desired.

Qualities of Woods.

The working qualities of common woods ought to be known by every one who has occasion to use timber, and especially by a woodsman, who may at any time be driven to shifts in which a mistake in choosing material may have disagreeable consequences. A few simple tables are here given, which, it is hoped, may be of assistance. Only common native trees are included. The data refer to the seasoned wood only, except where green is specified. Such tables might easily be extended, but mine are confined to the qualities of most account to campers and explorers, and to trees native to the region north of Georgia and east of the Rocky Mountains.

Very Hard Woods

Osage Orange (hardest),
Dogwood,
Black Haw,
Yellow Locust,
Post Oak,
Overcup Oak,
Sugar Maple,
Crab-Apple,
Persimmon,
Hickory,
Service-berry,
Black Jack Oak,
Chestnut Oak,
Mountain Laurel,
Winged Elm.

Hard Woods

Other Oaks,
Hornbeam,
Ash,
Elm,
Cherry,
Beech,
Tupelo,
Red-bud,
Red Maple,
Holly,
Sycamore,
Yellow Pine,
Pecan,
Black Birch,
Hackberry,
Plum,
Sourwood,
Sour Gum,
Walnut,
Silver Maple,
Mulberry,
Honey Locust,
Yellow Birch.

Very Soft Woods

Spruce,
Balsam Poplar,
White Pine,
Pawpaw,
Aspen,
Balsam Fir,
Catalpa,
Buckeye,
Basswood,
Arbor-vitæ (softest).

(Common woods not mentioned above are of medium softness.)

Very Strong Woods

Yellow Locust,
Yellow Birch,
Shingle Oak,
Shellbark Hickory
Yellow Pine,
Hornbeam,
Service-berry,
Big-bud Hickory,
Basket Oak,
Pignut Hickory,
Chestnut Oak,
Black Birch,
Spanish Oak,
Sugar Maple,
Beech,
Osage Orange,
Bitternut Hickory.

Strong Woods

Other Oaks,
Paper Birch,
Silver Maple,
Red Birch,
Dogwood,
Ash,
Persimmon,
Plum,
White Elm,
Cherry,
Red Pine,
Rock Elm,
Water Locust,
Chinquapin,
Honey Locust,
Tamarack,
Loblolly Pine,
Slippery Elm,
Black Walnut,
Sour Gum,
Red Maple.

Very Stiff Woods

Yellow Birch,
Sugar Maple,
Spanish Oak,
Hornbeam,
Paper Birch,
Tamarack,
Yellow Pine,
Black Birch,
Shellbark Hickory,
Overcup Oak,
Yellow Locust,
Beech.

Very Tough Woods

Beech,
Osage Orange,
Water Oak,
Tupelo.

Tough Woods

Black Ash,
Basswood,
Yellow Birch,
Dogwood,
Sour Gum,
White Ash,
Paper Birch,
Cottonwood,
Elm,
Hickory,

Hornbeam,
Basket Oak,
Overcup Oak,
Yellow Pine,
Black Walnut,
Liquidambar,
Bur Oak,
Swamp White Oak,
Tamarack.

Woods that Split Easily

Arbor-vitæ,
Basswood,
Cedar,
Chestnut,
Slippery Elm (green),
Hackberry,
Red Oak,
The Soft Pines,
Spruce,
Ash,
Beech (when green),
White Birch,
Black Birch (green),
Dogwood (green),
Balsam Fir,
Basket Oak,
White Oak.

Woods Difficult to Split

Blue Ash (seasoned),
Buckeye,
White Elm,
Sour Gum,
Liquidambar,
Sugar Maple (seasoned),
Tupelo (unwedgeable),
Box Elder,
Wild Cherry,
Winged Elm (unwedgeable),
Hemlock,
Honey Locust (seasoned),
Sycamore.

Woods that Separate Easily into Thin Layers

Black Ash,
Basket Oak.

Flexible, Pliable Woods

Basswood,
Hackberry,
Red-bud,
Witch Hazel,
Elm,
Big-bud Hickory,
Yellow Poplar.

Springy Woods

Black Ash,
Hickory,
Honey Locust,
White Oak,
Service-berry,
White Ash,
Hornbeam,
Yellow Locust,
Osage Orange,
Spruce.

Woods Easily Wrought

Basswood,
Paper Birch,
Buckeye,
Catalpa,
Cherry,
Cottonwood,
Hackberry,
Silver Maple,
Yellow Poplar
Black Birch,
Red Birch,
Butternut,
Cedar,
Chestnut,
Cypress,
Red Maple,
White Pine,
Black Walnut.

Woods Liable to Check in Seasoning

Beech,
Chestnut,
Dogwood,
Hickory (except Shellbark),
Yellow Locust,
Sassafras,
Black Walnut,
White Birch,
Crab-Apple,
Sour Gum,
Hornbeam,
Most Oaks,
Sycamore.

Woods Liable to Shrink and Warp

Chestnut,
White Elm,
Hemlock,
Liquidambar,
Loblolly Pine,
Yellow Poplar,
Cottonwood,
Sour Gum,
Shellbark Hickory,
Pin Oak,
Sycamore.

Woods Difficult to Season

Beech,
Sour Gum,
Red Oak,
Water Oak,
Cottonwood,
Sugar Maple,
Rock Chestnut Oak,
Osage Orange.

Woods that Can Be Obtained in Wide Boards Free from Knots

Basswood,
Cypress,
Cottonwood,
Yellow Poplar.

Woods Durable in Soil, Water and Weather

Arbor-vitæ,
Catalpa,
Cherry,
Cucumber,
Slippery Elm,
Juniper,
Honey Locust,
Mulberry,
Chestnut Oak,
Post Oak,
Swamp White Oak,
Osage Orange,
Pitch Pine,
Tamarack,
Butternut,
Cedar,
Chestnut,
Cypress,
Hop Hornbeam,
Kentucky Coffee Tree,
Yellow Locust,
Bur Oak,
Overcup Oak,
Rock Chestnut Oak,
White Oak,
Yellow Pine (long leaved),
Sassafras,
Black Walnut.

Perishable Woods

White Birch,
Hackberry,
Black Jack Oak,
Spanish Oak,
Loblolly Pine,
Service-berry,
Box Elder,
Silver Maple,
Pin Oak,
Water Oak,
The Poplars,
Sycamore.

(Sapwood is more liable to decay than heart-wood.)

Naturally, these are only general guides. Trees have their individual peculiarities, just as people have.

Woods for Special Purposes.

The best woods for dugouts are butternut, cedar, chestnut, cucumber, cypress, sassafras, yellow poplar, and black walnut. Those best for the ribs and frames of canoes and boats are arbor-vitæ, white cedar, elm, sour gum, oak, gray pine, spruce, and tamarack, depending on locality and available species; for sheathing, arbor-vitæ, paper birch (bark), cedar, cypress, slippery elm (bark), pignut hickory (bark), mulberry, white pine, sassafras, spruce (bark), tamarack(for bottoms); for oars or paddles, ash and spruce. One will choose, of course, according to what is available on the spot. For snowshoe bows, black ash is best; for ski, birch; for toboggans, oak, ash, beech, birch; for axe-helves, hickory, or (if from green wood) hornbeam; for handspikes, (green) hornbeam, dogwood, hickory, service-berry, birch, maple; for wooden bowls or trenchers, black ash, cucumber, yellow poplar, sassafras, maple, sycamore; for treenails, yellow locust, bur oak, mulberry; for gunstocks, black walnut, cherry, sugar maple, red maple, yellow wood; for fishing rods, Osage orange, ash, service-berry; for sledge frames, etc., ash, yellow birch, slippery elm, hickory, oak; for runners, sourwood; for any such purpose as a wheel-hub, requiring toughness, and strength, yellow birch, dogwood, rock elm, winged elm, sour gum, liquidambar, honey locust, yellow locust, post oak, Osage orange, large tupelo; for anything requiring a very hard and close-grained wood, beech, birch, dogwood, rock elm, slippery elm, winged elm, hickory, holly, hornbeam, laurel, locust, maple, Osage orange, persimmon, plum, service-berry, thorn.

In building a log cabin, choose timber that is not only straight but light in weight, and, for the first course of logs, at least, pick out wood that will not rot easily when in contact with the ground; such are easily determined by using the tables here given; similarly, proper wood for shingles may be selected by consulting the tables for a wood that is both easy to split and durable. For a raft, pick out, if you can find them, dry logs of any very light wood; some timbers, such as black walnut and sour gum will not float at all when green. The weight of seasoned wood is no criterion of the weight of the green wood: for example, the dry wood of the sequoia or big tree of California is lighter than white pine, but a freshly cut log of it, full of sap, will scarcely float in water.

Quick Seasoning.

Green wood can quickly be seasoned by heating it in the embers of the camp-fire till the sap sizzles out. The old English word for such treatment of wood was "beathing." This also makes the wood, for the time being, so pliable that it can be bent into any required shape, or it can be straightened by hanging a weight from one end, or by fastening it to a straight form. The application of heat, without deeply charring, also hardens green wood, and makes it more durable.

Bending Wood.

Ordinarily, small pieces of green wood can be bent to a required form by merely soaking the pieces for two or three days in water; but if it is desired that they should retain their new shape, they should be steamed. Small pieces can be merely immersed in a kettle of hot water; large ones may be steamed in a trench partly filled with water, by throwing red-hot stones into it. Then drive stout stakes into the ground in the outline desired, and bend the suppled wood over these stakes, with small sticks underneath to keep the wood from contact with the ground, that it may dry more readily. If a simple bow-shape is all that is wanted, it can be secured by merely sticking the two ends of the wood into the ground and letting the bow stand upright to dry.

Wedging.

To wedge a wooden pin in an auger-hole, as in building a raft, split the top of the pin before driving, then seat it, and drive in a small wedge. This is called by raftsmen "witch-wedging." By the way, a wedge of soft wood will hold better, in an axe-helve, for instance, than one of hard wood.

When one has no auger, he can readily drive hardwood pins (sharpened at the point, or wedge-shaped) into softwood logs, in the same way that he would drive iron spikes.

Barking Trees.

The bark of the following trees makes good roofs and temporary shelters, and is useful for many other purposes: paper birch, basswood, buckeye, elm, hickory, spruce, hemlock, chestnut, balsam fir, white ash, cottonwood. Cedar bark may do, but it is very inflammable.

It is only when the sap is up (spring and summer) that bark will peel freely, although elm peels through eight months of the year, and some basswood trees can be found that will peel even in winter. But, as a rule, if one wishes to strip bark in cold weather, he will have to roast a log carefully without burning the outside. Remember that barking a tree generally kills it, and that it is illegal in some regions, as in the Adirondacks.

In the real wilderness, however, bark has so many uses, that a knowledge of how to select and manipulate it is one of the essentials of a woodsman's education.

Before stripping bark, select a large tree with smoothe and faultless trunk. If it is birch, choose one with bark that is thick and with few and small "eyes." For a temporary roof it will be enough merely to skin the bark off in long strips eight or ten inches wide, and lay them overlapping, with alternately the convex and concave sides out. But for nicer jobs the bark must be flattened, and the rough outer bark (except in case of birch) must be removed, only the tough, fibrous, soft inner bark being used. For rough work the outer bark may simply be "rossed" off with a hatchet, but for nice jobs the bark should be treated as described below.

If only a moderate sized sheet is needed, the tree may not have to be felled. First girdle the tree just above the swell of the butt, by cutting through into the sapwood. Then girdle it again as high up as you can reach. Connect these two rings by a vertical slit through the bark. Now cut into wedge-shape the larger end of a four-foot length of sapling; this is your "spud" or barking tool. With it gently work the bark free along one edge of the upright slit, and thus proceed around the tree till the whole sheet falls off. If the girdles are 5 feet apart, a tree 2 feet in diameter will thus yield a sheet about 5x6½ feet, and a 3-foot

FIG. 16.

tree will afford one 5x9½ feet. The bark is laid on the ground for a few days to dry in the sun, and is then soaked in water, which supples it and makes the inner bark easy to remove from the outer.

I have no space in which to describe all the utensils, etc., that can be made from bark. One or two simple examples must suffice. A tray or trough that will hold liquids is quickly made by rossing off the outer bark from the ends of a sheet of suitable size, but leaving it on the middle part to stiffen the vessel. The rossed ends are

Bark Utensils.

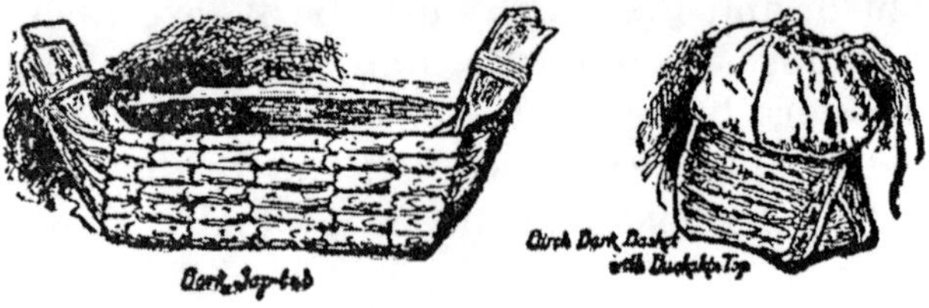

FIG. 17.

then folded over in several overlaying laps, gathered up somewhat in the shape of a canoe's bow and stern, and tied with bark straps. To make a dipper: take a forked stick of green wood, heat the fork, bend and bind it into bow form, and sew a bark bowl to it with

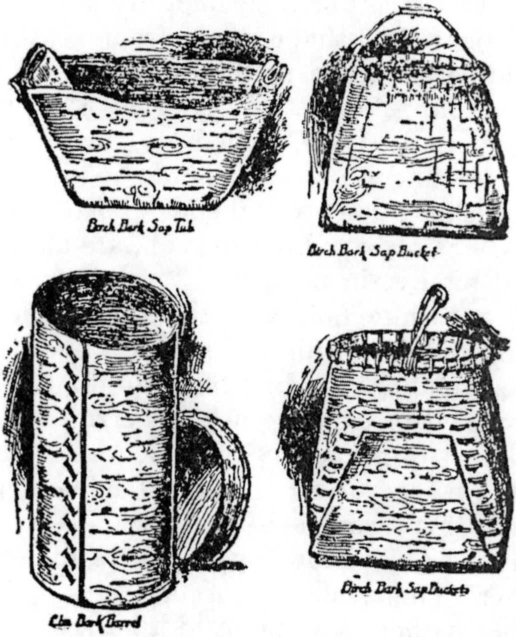

FIG. 18.

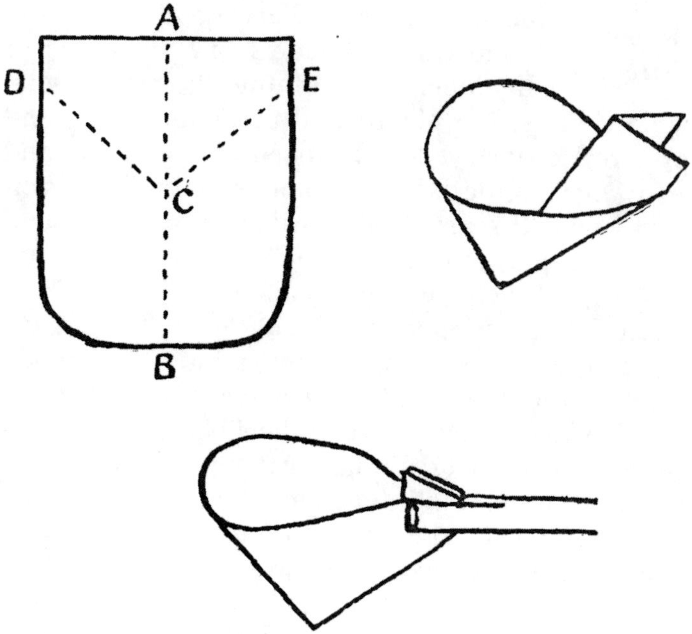

FIG. 19. Bark Dipper.

rootlets or bark twine; or a slender straight stick can similarly be bent into shape for a frame. A rough-and-ready dipper is made in three minutes as shown in the illustration. A sheet of bark, say 8x10 inches, is trimmed to spade-shape, folded lengthwise, opened out, the second finger placed behind *A*, the fold upward made as shown, and a split stick added as handle. The sewed seams of bark buckets, etc., are closed with a mixture of pine resin or spruce "gum" and grease or oil, laid on while hot, and the upper edges are stiffened with hoops or withes of pliable wood. Birch, elm, and basswood are the best barks to use.

A bark bucket for carrying fish or berries is quickly made by taking from a young poplar, for example, a sheet of bark twice as long as the intended depth of bucket. Fold this through the middle. Pass a bark-strap through slits at four upper corners to hold the sides together. The concavity of the bark holds the edges together without sewing. Add a bark sling-strap.

Straps, fish-stringers, etc., are made from the whole bark of pawpaw, leatherwood (remarkably strong), and hickory shoots.

Bast Ropes and Twine.

Very good ropes and twine can be made from the fibers of the inner bark of the slippery, white, and winged elms, the pignut and other hickories, and buckeye, red cedar, yellow locust, red mulberry, and Osage orange. One who has not examined the finished work would scarce believe what strong, soft, and durable cordage, matting, braided tumplines, and even thread, fish-nets, and garments can be made from such materials by proper manipulation. The Indians first separate the bark in long strips, remove the woody outer layer, and then boil it in a lye of sifted wood ashes and water, which softens the fiber so it can be manipulated without breaking. After it is dried it can be separated into small filaments by pounding, the strings running with the grain for several feet. Slippery elm especially makes a pliable rope, soft to the touch; it can be closely braided, and is very durable. If the woody splinters and hard fragments have not been entirely removed by pounding, the shoulder blade of a deer is fastened to an upright post, an inch hole is drilled through it, and bunches of the boiled bark are pulled backward and forward through the hole. The filaments are then put up in hanks and hung aside for use, being boiled to supple them when needed.

Bark twine is made by holding in the left hand one end of the fiber as it is pulled from the hank, and separating it into two parts, which are laid across the thigh. The palm of the right hand is then rolled forward over both, so as tightly to twist the pair of strands, when they are permitted to unite and twist into a cord, the left hand drawing it away as completed. Other strands are twisted in to make the length of cord desired. Twine and thread are made from the bark of young sprouts.

The bast or inner rind of basswood (linden) makes good rope. More than a century ago, two Indians whose canoe had drifted, while they were in a drunken sleep, upon Goat Island, between the American and Canadian falls of Niagara, let themselves down over the face of the cliff by a rope that they made from basswood bark, and thus escaped from what seemed to the on-lookers as certain death by starvation.

Mulberry and Osage orange bast yield a fine, white, flax-like fiber, that used to be spun by squaws to the thickness of packthread and then woven into garments. The inner bark of Indian hemp (*Apocynum cannabinum*), collected in the fall, is soft, silky, and exceedingly strong. The woody stems are first soaked in water; then the bast, with bark adhering, is easily removed; after which the bark is washed off, leaving the yellowish-brown fiber ready to be picked apart and used. A rope made from it is stronger, and keeps longer in water, than one made from common hemp. It was formerly used by the Indians, almost all over the continent, not only for ropes, but for nets, threads, and garments. The fibers of the nettle were also similarly used.

In the southern Appalachians, it is not many years since the mountain white women used to make bed-cords (perhaps you know how strong such cords must be) by twisting or plaiting together long, slender splits of hickory wood (preferably mocker-nut) that they suppled by soaking. Such bed-cords are in use to this day.

Root and Vine Cordage.

The remarkably tough and pliable rootlets of white spruce, about the size of a quill, when barked, split, and suppled in water, are used by Indians to stitch together the bark plates of their birch canoes, the seams being smeared with the resin that exudes from the tree; also for sewing up bark tents, and utensils that will hold water. The finely divided roots are called by northern Indians *watab* or *watape.*

Twine and stout cords are also made of this material, strands for fish-nets being sometimes made as much as fifty yards in length. The old-time Indians used to say that bark cords were better than hemp ropes, as they did not rot so quickly from alternate wetting and drying, nor were they so harsh and kinky, but, when damped, became as supple as leather. "Our bast cords," they said, "are always rather greasy in the water, and slip more easily through our hands. Nor do they cut the skin, like your ropes, when anything has to be pulled. Lastly, they feel rather warmer in winter."

The fibers of tamarack roots, and of hemlock, cedar, and cottonwood, are similarly used.

Grapevine rope is made in a manner similar to bark rope. The American wistaria (*Kraunhia frutescens*) is so tenacious and supple that it was formerly used along the lower Mississippi for boats' cables; it can be knotted with ease.

The long, tough rootstocks of sedge or saw-grass are much used by our Indians as substitutes for twine. Baskets made of them are the strongest, most durable and costliest of all the ingenious products of the aboriginal basket-maker. The fiber is strongest when well moistened.

A favorite basket plant of the Apaches and Navajos is the ill-scented sumac or skunk-bush (*Rhus trilobata*), which is common from Illinois westward. The twigs are soaked in water, scraped, and then split. Baskets of this material are so made that they will hold water, and they are often used to cook in, by dropping hot stones in the water.

Withes.

A southern shrub, the supple-jack (*Berchemia scandens*), makes good withes. The fibers of the red-bud tree are said by basket-makers to equal in strength those of palm or bamboo. For such purpose as basket-making, withes should be gathered in spring or early summer, when the wood is full of sap and pliable. If the material is to be kept for some time before weaving, it should be buried in the ground to keep it fresh. In any case, a good soaking is necessary, and the work should be done while the withes are still wet and soft. Other good woods for withes are leatherwood, liquid-ambar, willow, and witch hazel. Large withes for binding rails, raft logs, etc., are made from tall shoots of hickory or other tough wood, by twisting at one end with the hands until the fiber separates into strands, making the withe pliable so that it can be knotted. A sapling as thick as one's wrist can be twisted in this way. To fasten a withe to a log, chop a notch in the log, making it a little wider at the bottom than at the top, trim the butt of the sapling to fit loosely, and drive a wedge in alongside of it, then twist.

The best hoops are made from hickory, white or black ash, birch, alder, arbor-vitæ, cedar, dogwood.

Splints.

Splints are easily made from slippery elm, for instance, by taking saplings or limbs three or four inches in diameter, and hammering them with a wooden mallet until the individual layers of wood are detached from those underneath, then cutting these into thin, narrow strips. The strips are kept in coils until wanted for use, and then are soaked.

Black ash and basket oak, when green, separate easily into thin sheets or ribbons along the line of each annual ring of growth, when beaten with mallets. The Indians, in making splint baskets, cut the wood into sticks as wide along the rings as the splints are to be, and perhaps two inches thick. These are then bent sharply in the plane of the radius of the rings, when they part into thin strips, nearly or quite as many of them as there are rings of growth.

Fitting Axe-Helves.

A broken axe-helve is a not uncommon accident in the woods, and a very serious one until a new helve is made and fitted. Now it often happens that the stub of old handle cannot be removed by ordinary means: it must be burnt out. To do this without drawing the temper of the steel might seem impracticable; but the thing is as simple as rolling off a log, when you see it done. Pick out a spot where the earth is free from stones and pebbles, and drive the blade of the axe into the ground up to the eye. Then build a fire around the axe-head—that is all. If the axe is double-bitted, dig a little trench about six inches deep and the width of the axe-eye, or a little more. Lay the axe flat over it, cover both blades with two inches of earth, and build a small fire on top.

In making a new axe-helve, do not bother to make a crooked one like the store pattern. Thousands of expert axemen use, from preference, straight handles in their axes—single-bitted axes at that. I have seen such handles full four feet long, to be used chiefly in logging-up big trees. Two feet eight inches is a good length for ordinary chopping.

To smoothe any article made of wood, when you have no sandpaper, use loose sand in a piece of buckskin.

A Vise.

To make a vise: cut a good-sized hardwood sapling, leaving a square-topped stump of convenient height. Split the stump through the middle as far as necessary. Trim the upper part, if needful for the purpose. Then, about eighteen inches from the top, lash the stump firmly with a rope, and twist it tight with a stick, like a tourniquet. Open the split with wedges, insert the article to be held, knock out the wedges, and—there you are.

For a cold-weather camp, a log hut is more comfortable than any tent, and it is much more secure at all times. The saving in firewood, over an open camp, is immense, for it takes a good-sized tree to keep up a good all-night fire before a lean-to. If you intend to build a cabin, take along either a cross-cut saw and a froe for splitting shingles, or a roll of roofing paper. A bark roof is only fit for a temporary lodge, as it soon gets leaky, tatterdemalion, and inflammable. To hold a shingled roof in place, if you have no nails, overlap the shakes like ordinary shingles, but with several inches more "to the weather," and fasten them down with "binders" or "weight-logs." These are poles laid over the butts of the shakes and immediately over the stringers of the roof, the ends of binders and stringers being withed tightly together. For details in the construction of log cabins, and many designs from the rudest to large club-houses, see Wicks's book *Log Cabins and Cottages* (Forest & Stream Pub. Co., New York).

Cabins.

A cabin without a window is a cheerless, fusty den, and there is seldom good excuse for such shiftlessness. If you cannot carry window panes and a knock-down sash into the woods, take along some oiled paper or translucent parchment. A recipe for the latter is given in the next chapter.

For chinking between logs, moss mixed with clay or tenacious mud is sufficient, but this should not be used in a chimney. For such purpose, mix thoroughly blue clay and wet sand; this makes a particularly hard and durable cement, but yellow clay will do. A tenacious mortar may be made from the slime of a swamp mixed with deer's hair, feathers, etc. Better, however, is one made by pounding mussel shells to a fine powder, mixing this with clay freed from pebbles, pouring water over the mass, kneading, and then letting the fire do the rest.

Mortar.

This may be as good a place as any in which to describe some rough-and-ready but effective ways of procuring charcoal and lime. For the former, dig a pit 5 feet square by 3 feet deep and build a fire in it. Keep adding fuel as the fire burns down, until the pit is almost full of embers. Then pile on split sticks of uniform size until the pile

Charcoal.

stands a foot above the ground, whereupon shovel over it the earth that was dug out of the pit. After letting the pit cool for twenty-four hours, it will be found nearly full of charcoal.

Lime.

Lime can be made, without much trouble, wherever there is limestone, by a process similar to that of burning charcoal. If you want enough of it to mix mortar for a cabin chimney, inclose a circular space of 5 feet diameter by a rude stone wall 3 feet high; cover the bottom of this inclosure with brush to facilitate kindling the kiln; then fill with alternate layers of dry hardwood and limestone broken into moderate-sized pieces, piling the top into conical form. Light the pile and when it is well going cover the top with sods to make the calcination slow and regular. Keep it going for two days and nights.

CHAPTER XIX

TROPHIES, BUCKSKIN, AND RAWHIDE

IN skinning the head of any animal of the deer tribe, if it is to be given to a taxidermist for mounting, the slit should be made up the back of the neck, instead of the throat, so that no seam may show in the finished trophy. After cutting around the neck, *close to the shoulders and brisket*, make an opening cut from the center of the top of the skull, just back of the antlers, and slit the skin along the top of the neck, back to the end of the neck skin. Then make a straight cut to the base of each antler, the result being a Y-shaped incision as shown in the figure. Then work off the skin of the neck, being careful not to rupture any of the large blood-vessels in doing so.

Skinning a Head.

Now, turn the head to one side and insert the knife between the base of the skull and the first or atlas vertebra, severing the muscles and tendons; then turn the head in the opposite direction and perform a similar operation there; give a wrench, and the skull is detached. Cut off the cartilage of the ears close to the skull, and cut and pry the skin away from the base of each antler, inserting under the skin a wedge-shaped stick and pounding a little on it. Peel off the skin until the eye sockets are reached. Be careful here not to cut the eyelids; use the small blade of your pocket-knife and work deliberately. Then peel the skin off as far as the lips, taking pains not to cut the skin where it sinks into the pit below the eye. When the lips are reached, cut close to the bone all around, so as to leave the cartilage attached to the skin. Sever the cartilage of the nose well back of the nostrils. The skin is now free from the skull. If the head is that of a moose, split the bell all the way down on the back side. Pare off all the flesh, especially from the butts of ears, lips and nose, but do not trim away the cartilage. Split the lips on the inside to allow the salt to penetrate. Detach the skin of the back of the ears from the cartilage, and skin them clear to the tips if you can, but at

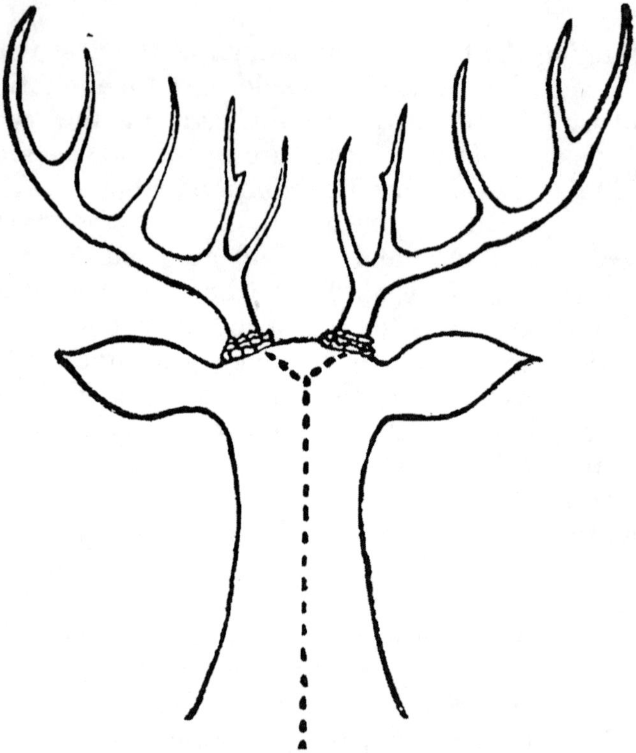

FIG. 20. How to Skin a Deer's Head.

any rate skin up the back side as far as you can do so; then the salt will get in its work and keep the hair of the ears from slipping. Having carefully trimmed off all flesh that adheres to the skin, wash the latter clean of blood and wring it dry. Then cut and scrape all flesh from the skull. Disarticulate the lower jaw so that you can work better, and clean it. Now get a stiff stick small enough to enter the hole in the base of the skull, splinter one end of it by beating it, and work this end around inside the skull so as to break up and remove the brain, using water to assist you; wash out the inside of the skull and tie the lower jaw in place; turn the skin inside out while it is still damp and soft.

Curing the Skin.

On arriving at camp, rub *plenty* of fine salt over every inch of the inner surface of the skin; then roll the skin up and let it lie until morning; do not stretch it nor hang it up by the nose. The next morning examine it carefully for soft spots where the salt has not struck in and hardened the tissues; shave these down and rub salt into them. All told, it may take fifteen pounds of salt for a moose head. Do not use any alum, for it would shrink the skin. Now hang up the skin and skull in a shady place, well out of reach of dogs and vermin. Never dry a skin by the fire nor in the sun. When all is dry, pack the skin in a sack, if you have one. If salt and blood once get into caribou hair they cause a rust that cannot be eradicated.

Bear Skin

A bear is skinned in the same manner as a deer, save that the opening slit is made by extending the belly cut up along the throat between the angles of the jaws. The bottoms of the feet must be opened. Remove the skin with the bones of the feet still in position. Remove the skull and clean it; split the lips from the inside, turn the ears wrong side out and wash the skin well to remove blood stains. To cure the skin, spread is out on the ground, rub salt into it and roll it up, flesh to flesh. Next morning fix up a sapling for a "beam" (as described below), throw the skin over it, flesh side up, rub some corn-meal or ashes on it and thoroughly scrape off the fat; then salt the skin again and roll it up.

Preserving Pelts.

Pelts of any kind can be preserved indefinitely in a soft state, without any slipping of the hair, by keeping them immersed in a liquor prepared by boiling some water, dissolving salt in it, in the proportion of one quart of salt to the gallon, and adding to each gallon one ounce by measure of sulphuric acid. Let the liquor cool before immersing the skins.

Hides should not be salted if it is intended to make

buckskin from them. The latter is a hard job; but it is well for every big game hunter to understand the process, if for no other reason than to avoid being humbugged. Much of the so-called buckskin used by glovers and others is a base imitation. Genuine Indian-tanned buckskin is, properly speaking, not tanned at all. Tanned leather has undergone a chemical change, from the tannin or other chemicals used in converting it from the raw hide to leather. Buckskin, on the contrary, is still a raw skin that has been made supple and soft by breaking up the fibers mechanically and has then merely been treated with brains and smoke to preserve its softness. In color and pliability it is somewhat like what is called chamois skin, but it is far stronger and has the singular property that, although it shrinks some after wetting and gets stiff in drying, it can easily be made as soft as ever by merely rubbing it in the hands. For some purposes buckskin is superior to any leather. It was used by our frontiersmen, as well as by the Indians, for moccasins, leggings, hunting shirts, gun covers and numerous other purposes. It is warmer than cloth, pliable as kid, noiseless against bushes, proof against thorns, collects no burs, wears like iron and its soft neutral color renders the wearer inconspicuous amid any surroundings. When of good quality it can be washed like a piece of cloth. Its only fault is that it is very unpleasant to wear in wet weather; but against this is the consideration that buckskin can be prepared in the wilderness, with no materials save those furnished on the spot by the forest, the stream, and the animal itself. Not even salt is used in its manufacture. Neither tannin nor any substitute for it has touched a piece of buckskin; its fibers have been loosened and rendered permanently soft and flexible, its pores have been closed up, but there has been little or no chemical change from the raw state of the skin and consequently it has no tendency to rot.

Buckskin.

Different Indian tribes have different methods of making buckskin, but the essential processes are the same, namely: (1) soaking, (2) depilating and fleshing, (3) stretching and treating with brains, with repeated soaking and drying, (4) smoking. The skin of a deer, for example, is first soaked in water from three to five days, depending upon temperature. Elk or buffalo hides were immersed in a lye of wood ashes and water or rolled up in ashes moistened with warm water. After soaking, the hide is taken to a graining log, which is simply a piece of sapling or small tree about 8 feet long and 6 or 8 inches thick at the butt. The bark is removed from the thick end and the other end is stuck under a root or otherwise fastened in the ground at an angle, leaving the smoothe end about waist high, like a tanner's beam. Or, a short log may be used—one that will reach to a man's chin when stood on end; in which case a notch is cut in the butt by which the stick is braced against the limb of a small tree, with smoothe surface facing the operator, and the small end sticking in the ground about two feet from the tree.

"Indian Tan."

A graining-knife is now required. It was formerly made of hardwood, of flint, of the sharpened rib or scapula of an animal, or of the attached bones of a deer's foreleg with the front end of the ulna scraped sharp, the latter instrument being used like a spokeshave. Sometimes a large, strong mussel shell was used. A favorite instrument was an adze or hoe-shaped tool made from the fork of an elk antler. After they could get iron, the squaws made skin-scrapers shaped as in the accompanying illustration, the handle being about a foot long. Dealers in taxidermists' supplies sell scrapers made specially for this purpose. The back of a thin butcher-knife does well enough, if the point of the blade be driven into a stick so as to give a handle at each end. In fact, almost anything with a scraping rather than a cutting edge will answer the purpose. The skin is placed on the graining log with the neck drawn over the upper end of the log about six or eight inches; the operator places a flat stick between the neck and his body, to prevent slipping, and presses his weight against it. If the short notched log is used, the neck is caught between the notch and the limb. The hair and grain (black epidermis) are scraped off by working the knife down the skin the way the hair runs. If the hair is stubborn, a little ashes rubbed into such spots will offer resistance to the knife and will make the grain slip. The hide is now turned over and fleshed with a sharp knife, by removing all superfluous tissue and working the skin down to an even thickness throughout. This operation must be performed with extreme care or the buckskin will have thick and stiff spots which make it comparatively worthless—a point to be considered in buying buckskin. In olden times, when a squaw wanted to make something particularly nice, she would patiently work

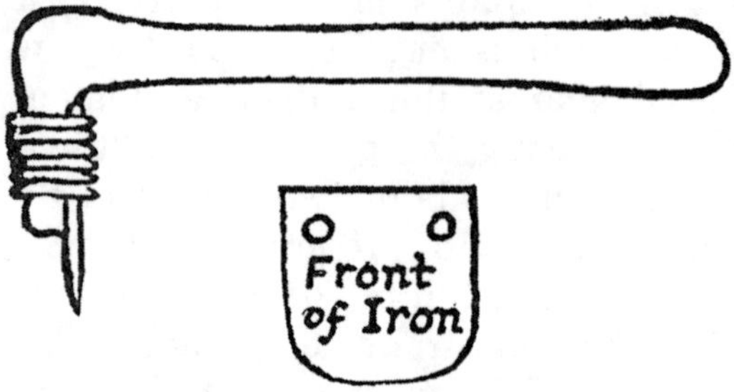

Fig. 21. Indian Skin-Scraper.

down a deerskin until it was almost as thin and pliable as a piece of cotton cloth. After cleaning in this manner the skin is allowed to dry and then is re-soaked over night.

Softening the Skin.

Now comes the job of stretching and softening the hide. There is only one recipe for this: elbow-grease and plenty of it. The skin is pulled, twisted, and worked in every direction until it becomes white and soft, after which the operator rubs into it the brains of the animal, which have been removed by splitting the skull lengthwise half in two. Sometimes the brains are first dissolved in tepid water, being allowed to simmer over a slow fire while the lumps are rolled between the fingers till they form a paste which will dissolve more freely. This solution is then rubbed into the hide on the hair side, which is coarser than the flesh side.

The brains act as a sort of dubbing; if there is not likely to be enough for the job, the macerated liver of the animal is added to the brains. Deer brains may be preserved by mixing them with moss so as to make the mass adhere enough to be formed into a cake, which is hung by the fire to dry. Such a cake will keep for years. When wanted for dressing a hide, it is dissolved in hot water and the moss is removed. A skin may be treated by soaking it in the solution, wringing out, drying and re-soaking till it is thoroughly penetrated. After this process the skin must again be pulled, stretched, kneaded, and rubbed, until the fiber is thoroughly loosened and every part becomes as pliable as chamois skin. If two men are available they saw the hide back and forth over the sharpened edge of a plank or over a taut rope, lariat, or a twisted sinew as thick as one's finger. Large and refractory hides may be softened by stretching them firmly on elevated frames and dancing on them. It is a hard job for one man to soften a large hide, but he can accomplish it by throwing the wet skin over a convenient limb, forming a loop at the other end, passing a stout stick through it, and twisting into a hard knot—leaving it to dry; then he re-soaks it and repeats the operation as often as necessary. The oftener a skin is wet and softened, the more pliable it becomes.

Smoking the Skin.

The final process is smoking, which closes the pores, toughens the skin, gives it the desired color, and insures its drying soft after a wetting. Ordinarily the skin is made its own smoke-house. A small hole is dug in the ground and a smudge started in it. The best smudge is made from "dozed" wood, that is, from wood affected with dry rot until it is spongy; this, when dried, gives out a pale blue smoke without flame. If a particular shade of yellow or brown is desired, some discrimination must be used in selecting the fuel. Above all things, the smudge must not be allowed to break out in flame, for heating would ruin the skin. Several small poles are stuck around the hole and the skin is wrapped around them somewhat like a teepee cover, the edges being sewed or skewered together; it is best, when practicable, to smoke two or more skins at once, so as to have plenty of room around and above the smudge. When two skins of about equal size are ready, a good way to smoke them is to loosely baste their edges together in the form of a bag, the outside of the skins forming the inside of the bag and the after part of the skins forming its bottom, the neck end being left open; to the edges of the open end sew a cloth continuation, leaving it open. Suspend this bag from its bottom to a tree or pole. Bend a small green stick into a hoop and place it within the bottom of the bag; under the mouth of the bag place a pan containing the smouldering wood (the cloth mouth is to prevent the skin from heating). Inspect the inside of the skins from time to time and when they are smoked to a deep yellow or light brown the process is finished; sometimes both sides of the skins are smoked; otherwise, fold the skins with the smoked side within and lay them away for a few days to season. This sets the color, making it permanent. The skins of antelope or any of the deer tribe are treated in the same way. Antelope, deer, moose and caribou hides make good buckskin, but elk hides are comparatively weak and inferior material.

Rawhide.

Rawhide is often useful in camp and is easily prepared. Soak the fresh hide in water, or in a weak lye made by adding wood ashes to water, until the hair will slip. The alkali is not necessary for deerskins. Then remove the hair and stretch the hide with great force on a frame or on the side of a building, extending it in all directions as tightly as possible, so that when it dries it will be as taut as a drumhead. Dry it in the shade; use no salt or other preservative. This is all, unless you wish to make the rawhide supple, in which case rub into it thoroughly a mixture of oil and tallow. A convenient way of making a stretching frame in the woods is to go where two trees grow at the right distance apart; notch them at the proper height to receive a strong, stiff sapling that has been cut to fit the notches, the deep cut of the latter being at the lower side so that no force can pull the pole down; similarly fit another pole into reversed notches just above the ground; cut slits in the edges of the hide and from them stretch thongs or very strong cords to the trees and poles, twisting them up tightly.

Parflèche. The plains Indians used to make rawhide trunks or boxes which would stand any amount of abuse in packing and travel. These were called by the voyageurs *parflèche*. (Our dictionaries surmise that this is a French adaptation of some Indian word, but it is simply Canadian-French, meaning an arrow-fender, because it was from rawhide that the Indians made their almost impenetrable shields. The word is commonly pronounced by Americans "par-flesh," with the accent on the last syllable.) In making these rawhide receptacles the thickest hides of buffalo bulls were dehaired, cut into the required shapes and stretched on wooden forms to dry; they then retained their shapes and were almost as hard as iron. A hide bucket can be made by cutting off from the rawhide some thin strips for lacing, soaking the skin until it is quite soft, shaping from it a bag, sewing this up with the lace-leather, fitting to it a handle of twisted or plaited hide, then filling the bucket with dry sand or earth and letting it stand till dry.

Whang-leather. Woodchuck skins are proverbially tough, and are good for shoestrings and whangs. Squirrel skins can be used for thinner ones. An old summer coon's skin is very good for this purpose; wildcat's skin is best of all. To prepare a hide for whang-leather: soak it until the hair will slip. Do not use wood ashes unless you must, for lye will weaken the hide. Remove the hair, and then take a large tablespoonful of alum, and not quite half as much salt, and rub this into the flesh side. Roll up the skin, cover with a cloth to keep moist, and let it stand about two days and a night. Then pull and work it until dry. Soften by rubbing over the edge of a plank or shake. Some use soap in tanning such skins, but it makes the strings too slippery thereafter, and makes them draw dampness till they rot.

Lace-leather is cut of uniform width by the following means. With a pair of compasses (a forked stick with pencil or metal scoring point attached to one leg will serve) draw a circle on a piece of hide; cut out this round piece with a keen knife; make a starting cut of the desired width on the edge of the circular piece of hide. Drive an awl or a slender round nail into a board and alongside of it; at precisely the width of the lace, stick the knife, edge foremost, and inclining a little to the rear; then lay the round bit of hide in front of the knife, draw the cut strip between the awl and the knife and steadily pull away; the round leather will revolve as the knife cuts its way, and the awl, acting as a gauge, will insure a uniform width of lacing.

A Riata.

To make a rawhide riata: select carefully skinned hides that have no false cuts in them. A 30-foot riata will require two large cowhides if it is to be made three-stranded, or four small ones if four-stranded. Having removed the hair, stake the hides out on level ground, keeping them well stretched and constantly wetted so as not to harden; keep them pegged out two days. Cut up the hide in the manner of laces, the width of the strip not exceeding one-half inch; wet each strip, when cut, and wrap it around a stick; then fasten the strips to a tree and plait them to a uniform circumference and tightness of twist. Keep the strands and plaited portion wet; a Mexican fills his mouth with water which he squirts slowly over the work and materials. When the rope is finished, stretch it thoroughly, and then grease it. To preserve its pliability, keep it continually greased.

Catgut.

The catgut of commerce is never made from cats, any more than chamois skin is made from chamois; but it can be made from the intestines of almost any good-sized animal. Thoroughly cleanse the intestine from all impurities, inside and out; this is more easily done while the gut is still warm from the animal. Wash it and then scrape it with a blunt knife to remove slime and grease; then steep it in running water for a day or two, so as to loosen both the inner and outer membranes, which are then removed by scraping. To turn the gut inside out, double back a few inches of one end, invert this, take the bag thus formed between finger and thumb and dip water up into it till the double fold is nearly full, when the weight of the water will cause the gut to become inverted. The fibrous inner membrane is then soaked three or four hours in water to which wood ashes have been added. It is then washed free from lye and can either be split into thin fibers when it has dried or may be twisted into a bowstring or similar cord. To twist it, plant two stout stakes in the ground, a little wider apart than the length of the gut; make a saw-cut in the top of each stake; cut two narrow, flat pieces of wood into the shape of knife-blades, thin enough to enter the saw-cuts, and notch one end of each; firmly lash each end of the gut to one of these notched ends. By alternately twisting these and fixing them in the saw-cuts, to prevent their running back, the gut may be evenly and smoothly twisted like a single-strand cord. Let it dry and then rub it smoothe with a woollen rag and a little grease.

Membranes.

Bladders only need cleaning, inflation with air and drying to preserve them. They may then be made pliable by oiling. The paunches of animals, after cleaning, can be expanded with grass until dried. Such receptacles have many uses in wilderness camps, where bottles and cans are unobtainable; for example, to hold bear's oil, wild honey, and other fluid or semi-fluid substances.

Sinew.

A very strong, pliable and durable sewing thread is made from sinew. It splits into even threads, is easy to work with when damp, and, on drying, it shrinks tightly and becomes almost as hard as horn; hence it is a better material than any vegetable fiber for certain kinds of sewing, particularly in sewing leather or buckskin, and for binding together any two parts, such as a tool and its handle, where the former has no eye. For bowstrings and heavy sewing, the Indians preferred the sinews of the buffalo or the moose, and then the elk, these being coarse in texture; for finer work they chose those of the deer, antelope, and bighorn. The sinew of the panther or mountain-lion was esteemed as the finest and most durable. The ligaments that extend from the head backwards along each side of the spinal process were preferred to those of the legs. The aboriginal method of preparing and using sinew is thus described by Isham G. Allen: "The sinew is prepared for use by first removing all adhering flesh with the back of a knife; it is then stretched on a board or lodge-pole and left to dry for an hour or so, preparatory to the separation of the fibers or threads by twisting in the hands. By the same or similar twisting motion, and by pulling, the fiber can be extended to a reasonable length. [Dried sinews may readily be shredded by wetting, and, if necessary, by gentle hammering.] Cords or small ropes are made by twisting many fibers together between two forked sticks fastened in the ground, and, during the process, rubbing with thin skins of the elk or deer to soften them; the largest cord I have seen made in this manner was one-fourth of an inch in diameter. To prepare it for sewing, the sinew is wet, and, at the needle end, rolled on the knee with the palm of the hand to a fine, hard point, like that of a shoemaker's bristle. As suggested, the sinews are made sufficiently fine for use in fixing the guiding feathers, and fastening the iron or flint heads of arrows, and in wrapping of clubs, etc. Formerly the awl used in sewing was of bone taken from the leg of the eagle; this has been displaced by the common sailor's needle; the overstitch is that most commonly employed in aboriginal sewing."

Parchment.

It may sometime happen that one wishes to prepare a sheet of parchment on which to write an important document; this can be done in the wilderness, if one can kill some animal that has a gall-bladder. Make the parchment like ordinary rawhide, from the thin skin of a medium-sized animal, say a fawn or a wildcat. Rub it down with a flat piece of sandstone or pumice-stone. Then get a smoothe, water-worn pebble and with it rub every part of one surface (hair side) of the skin, making it firm and smoothe. Then give this a coat of gall diluted with water. The old-fashioned way of making ox-gall was as follows: take the gall of a newly killed ox and after having allowed it to settle twelve or fifteen hours in a basin, pour the floating liquor off the sediment into a small pan or cup, put the latter in a larger vessel that has a little boiling water in the bottom, and keep up a boiling heat until the liquor is somewhat thick; then spread this substance on a dish and place it before a fire till it becomes nearly dry. In this state it can be kept for years in a pot covered with paper, without undergoing any alteration. To use it, dissolve a piece the size of a pea in a tablespoonful of water. It makes ink or watercolors spead evenly on parchment, paper, or ivory. A coating of it sets lead-pencil or crayon marks so that they cannot be removed. It is also used for taking out spots of grease or oil.

Translucent Parchment.

To make parchment translucent, as for a window: take a raw skin, curried, and dried on a stretcher without any preservative; steep it in an infusion of water, boiled honey, and the white of eggs.

Another method is to soak a thin skin of parchment in a strong lye of wood ashes, often wringing it out, until you find that it is partly transparent; then stretch it on a frame and let it dry. This will be improved and made rain-proof if, after it is dry, you coat it on both sides with a clear mastic varnish, made as directed below.

Unsized paper or a thin skin is made waterproof and translucent by applying lightly to both sides a varnish made by putting $\frac{1}{4}$ ounce gum mastic in 6 ounces best spirits of turpentine, and shaking it up thoroughly, day by day, until dissolved. The bottle should be kept in a warm place while contents are dissolving.

Or, use equal parts Canada balsam (fir balsam) and turpentine: this dries slowly, but is flexible like map varnish.

Or, dissolve $\frac{1}{2}$ ounce beeswax in $\frac{1}{2}$ pint turpentine

CHAPTER XX

TANNING PELTS—OTHER ANIMAL PRODUCTS

Tanning a Robe with the Fur on.

WHILE the methods used by regular furriers in tanning pelts with the fur on are complicated and beyond the resources of men in the woods, at the same time very good results may be obtained by the simpler means described below.

The best work is done with skins fresh from the animal. Cleanse all blood and dirt from the pelt by soaking it in running water from one to four hours, depending upon temperature of water and quality of fur; or, if the skinning has been carefully done, the fur can be cleaned by sponging. Soaking is necessary to relax a dried skin. If a skin be immersed too long, the hair or fur will slip—particularly if the water be warm. Next thoroughly rub into the flesh side plenty of table salt. Double the skin, fur side out, roll it up, and let it lie over night. Then work it over a beam with the scraper, carefully removing all flesh and fat. A greasy skin will not take the tan. Hot corn-meal, hot sand, or sawdust, will help to remove grease; but be particular not to get it on the fur, for it may be hard to remove. If benzin were to be had, the skin could be immersed in it for an hour and then dried.

The pelt is now ready for tanning. The easiest way to do this is to soak it at least two days in the tan liquor described in the preceding chapter. (One quart of salt boiled in a gallon of water, then 1 ounce of sulphuric acid added.) If you prefer to keep the fur dry through the process, simply sponge the tan liquor on the flesh side from time to time, keeping it moistened thus for a couple of days; then rinse out the superfluous salt with clear water. Let the skin become partially dry and then work it over the edge of a plank or a tightly stretched rope, until the fiber is broken up.

To stretch a dressed skin so that it will lie flat on the floor, moisten the flesh side with water, and, when it is relaxed, tack it, fur side out, on a board or the side of a building in a shady place. If the skin has hardened when dry again, work it once more over the plank. After a skin has thoroughly dried it may be worked down as thin and soft as desired by rubbing with a piece of sandpaper folded over a block of wood.

To tan a pelt with alum, first cleanse it and rub salt into it, as described above, then rub into it a good sprinkling of powdered alum, but keep this out of the fur, for alum makes it hard to wash afterwards. Roll the skin up and let it lie at least two days—preferably longer; then place it in a stretcher and draw it tightly in every direction, so that there will be no wrinkles, but not tightly enough to make the fur thin. Smear the flesh side with a paste of flour, oatmeal, and water, and let it dry thoroughly in the shade; now work off the paste with a dull knife. Afterwards place the stretched skin in a damp place, until the superfluous salt comes out in beads of brine on the flesh side; wash this off, or the skin will turn damp thereafter in moist weather; then dry the skin again thoroughly. After this, wash and scour it with yellow soap and water, to which a little ammonia has been added (the water should be as hot as the hand can bear). Thoroughly rinse all soap from the fur, but let as little water get on it as possible. Give the pelt a hard shaking and hang it fur side out, to dry. When it is about half dry, work it over the edge of a plank or a square bar of iron, to draw out and soften every part of the skin; then work it with a knife, finish off with sandpaper or pumice-stone, and comb out the fur.

In preparing a rug on which the animal's head is to be mounted—as, for example, a bear's head with the mouth open—the skin of the head should *not* be tanned, but merely salted.

It is possible to make a soft and pliable robe without tanning, after the Indian method, but it is hard work. The method employed on buffalo robes has been described by Col. Dodge as follows: "The skin of even the youngest and fattest cow is, in its natural condition, much too thick for use, being unwieldy and lacking pliability. This thickness must be reduced at least one-half and the skin at the same time made soft and pliable. When the stretched skin has become dry and hard from the action of the sun, the woman goes to work with a small implement shaped somewhat like a carpenter's adze; it has a short handle of wood or elkhorn, tied on with rawhide, and is used with one hand [this was before iron or steel tools were obtainable]. With this tool the woman chips at the hardened skin, cutting off a thin shaving at every blow. The skill in the whole process consists in so directing and tempering the blows as to cut the skin, yet not cut too deep, and in finally obtaining a uniform thickness and perfectly smoothe and even inner surface. To render the skin soft and pliable the chipping is stopped every little while and the chipped surface smeared with brains of buffalo, which are thoroughly rubbed in with a smoothe stone. When very great care and delicacy are required the skin is stretched vertically on a frame of poles. It is claimed that the chipping process can be much more perfectly performed on a skin stretched in this way than on one stretched on the uneven and unyielding ground, but the latter is used for all common robes, because it is the easiest. When the thinning and softening process is completed, the robe is taken out of its frame, trimmed, and sometimes smoked. It is now ready for use. This is a long and tedious process and no one but an Indian would go through it." Sometimes, after the fleshing of the hide was completed, a mixture of boiled brains, marrow grease, and pounded roast liver was thickly spread on the flesh side and allowed to dry in; then the hide was rubbed with fat, dampened with warm water, rolled up and laid away for a day. After this the hide was slowly dried in the

Robes "Indian-tanned."

sun or very carefully before a fire, being frequently and thoroughly rubbed over a riata while drying.

Furs that one intends to sell to a furrier should be stretched and dried without any preservative, not even salt.

Tanning a Snake's Skin.

A snake's skin is easily tanned, either with the tan liquor or with alum. All foreign matter is scraped from it; the skin is then re-soaked and washed clean with soap and water. If a smoothe board be procurable, the skin can be "squee-geed" to the planed surface and it will cling to the board naturally. A tack on each side every eight or ten inches will keep it in place while drying. After two or three days the skin can be removed, softened with oil, and rolled up until wanted.

Glue.

The Indian method of making and using glue may come in handy at times when one is far in the wilderness. The glue is made from the hoofs of deer, or any other hoofed animals, by boiling. A stick is then cut about six inches long and as thick as one's little finger; one end of this is dipped in the melted glue, which is allowed to harden; this process is then repeated until there is a considerable bulb of glue on the end of the stick. To use it, the stick is dipped in hot water and then rubbed on the object to be glued.

Working in Horn.

Horn is easily manipulated by soaking it in boiling water. The western Indians used to make superior bows of buffalo horns, and from those of the mountain sheep, by leaving the horns in hot springs until they were perfectly malleable, then straightening them and cutting them into strips of suitable width. Two buffalo horns were pieced in the center and riveted; then bound strongly at the splice with sinew.

To make a horn cup: Select a large horn with a sharp bend in it; trim the butt end smoothe and even for the bottom of the cup; then, back from this, at a distance equal to the proposed height of the cup, saw through the greater part of the horn, as shown in the diagram, but leave enough of the top for a handle, the latter strip being about 6 inches long and $\frac{3}{4}$ inch wide. Scrape the handle gradually down to $\frac{1}{8}$ inch thickness at the end. Then soak the handle in a strong boiling solution of lime until it is soft, bend it backward around a stick and bind the end fast to base of handle at top, until it has cooled and hardened; then fit a wooden bottom in it, and tack and lute it in place. A powerful cement or lute for such purpose, as well as for mending broken vessels, is made by kneading with a stick a strong solution of newly slaked lime into a doughlike mass with glue or blood or white of egg. Before putting in the bottom, scrape and sandpaper the cup inside and out. Such a cup is light, it stands the hard knocks of travel better than a metal one, and it is pleasanter to

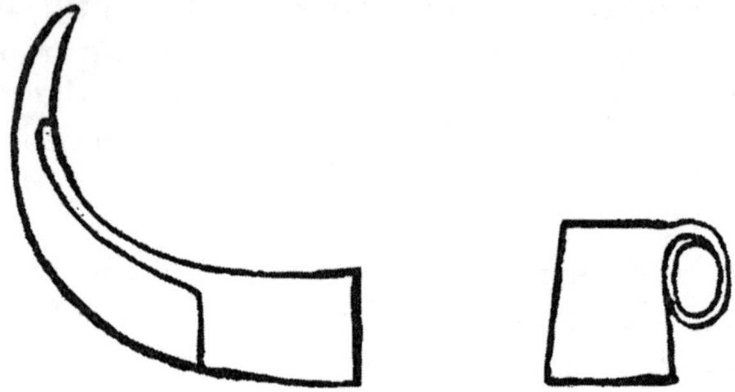

Fig. 22. Horn Cup.

drink hot coffee from. It can be ornamented with scrimshaw carvings.

A Huntsman's Horn.

The following description of how to make a huntsman's horn is condensed from one given some years ago by D. M. Morris: Select a cow's horn 14 to 16 inches long; 12 inches will do. With a limber stick determine how far the hollow extends and saw off the tip about an inch above that point. With a gimlet bore down to the hollow, taking care to hit it fairly. Ream out the hole from $\frac{1}{4}$ to 5-16 inch diameter. Dress the horn down with a half-round file but do not scrape it. Be careful to get a fair and even surface. To avoid working the horn too thin, press with thumb on doubtful places to see if there is any spring. Work down the neck as much as it will safely bear. A brass ferrule should now be fitted tighly around the neck to prevent the stem of the mouthpiece from splitting it. Now, to polish the horn: take a piece of sandpaper 2 or 3 inches square, and a little finer than the file, in the palm of the right hand; then, grasping the horn with the left hand, twist it round and round from end to end, occasionally rubbing it lengthwise. Continue this process with finer grades of sandpaper till the very finest has been used and complete the polishing with pumice or rotten stone and water. Then get from any dealer in musical instruments an E flat or cornet mouthpiece, fit it perfectly, drive it in tightly and your horn is complete. Or take the small end of another horn, or the piece sawed off, and with a sharp and round-pointed pocket-knife work out a conical cavity at the large end, and make a hole through the small end for the stem. Work off the outside, shaping it in the form of a cone the sides of which are concaved near the base and convexed toward the stem. This shape will look well, and the top will be thick enough to rest easily against the lips. The hole should be about the size of a rye straw. The shape of the mouthpiece and the size of the hole—provided it be large enough—do not materially affect the horn. The stem of the mouthpiece should be $\frac{3}{4}$ to 1 inch long. If shorter, the sound will be too harsh; if longer, too soft and not far-sounding. Long horns produce flat sounds, shorter ones sharp sounds. A good horn may be heard three to three and a half miles. The best horns have a double curve (crooks in two directions), gradually tapering from butt to tip, highly colored, or with black or dark points. A part of the butt must always be removed, as it is thin and brittle.

Gun Oil.

It is easy to make excellent gun oil from the fat of almost any animal. Never use a vegetable oil on a firearm—it is sure to gum. Rattlesnake oil has more body than almost any other animal oil; but that of woodchucks, squirrels, 'coons, etc., is good. A fine oil can also be made from the fat of the ruffed grouse, or from the marrow of a deer's leg bones. Put the fat on a board and with a sharp knife cut it up fine; then put it out in the hot sunlight, or warm it gently (do not let it get hot) before the fire; now force the oil through a strong cloth bag by squeezing it. To clarify it so that it will never become viscid, put it in a bottle with a charge of shot, or some shavings of lead, and stand the bottle where the sun's rays will strike it. A heavy deposit will fall. Repeat, and you will then have an oil equal to that of watchmakers, but with enough body to stay where it is put, rather than running down into the chamber of the gun so as to leave unprotected spots in the barrel. A large squirrel will yield over an ounce of tried oil, a fat woodchuck nearly a pint, and a bear several gallons—eight gallons of grease have been procured from a big grizzly.

Bear's Oil.

Bear's oil, by the way, is better than lard for shortening biscuit and for frying, and, when mixed with sugar and spread on bread, is not a bad substitute for butter and syrup. It is rendered by cooking in a pot hung high over a slow fire, so as not to scorch the fat, which would give off an acrid smell and make the oil less bland. No salt is added; the oil will keep sweet without it, unless in very hot weather (when it should be kept in a cool room, or in a spring, or in a pot sunk in the earth). The Indians, who were very fond of bear's grease, used to preserve it so that it would not turn rancid even when they were traveling in summer, by adding the inner bark of the slippery elm (1 drachm to a pound of grease), keeping them heated together for a few minutes, and then straining off. They also used sassafras bark and wild cinnamon for the same purpose. Bear's oil is superior to olive oil for the table, and can be used with impunity by people whose stomachs will not endure pork fat. I happen to be rendering some bear's grease at the time of this writing. The yield is a gallon of oil to ten pounds of fat.

Rattlesnake Oil.

Rattlesnake oil is solemnly regarded by the old-fashioned Pennsylvania Dutch as a specific for rheumatism, ringworm, sties, sore eyes generally, and even for hydrophobia. A large, fat snake yields from two to two and a half ounces of oil. A piece of muslin is stretched over a glass jar, and the fat, which resembles that of a chicken, is spread on this. The hot summer sun renders it, and the muslin strains it. The Dutch are reported to have a curious way of telling whether the snake has bitten itself and thereby poisoned its fat. They drop a little of the oil into a glass of milk. If the oil floats as a film on top it is good; but if it separates into small beads and the milk gathers in thick white flakes, as though soured, it is a sign that the snake bit itself.

While I am on the subject of animal fats and oils, I may as well say something about extemporized lights for a fixed camp that is far in the wilderness. A slush-lamp is made by taking a tin can, half filling it with sand or earth, sticking in it a thin rod of pine or other inflammable wood, wrapping around this a strip of soft cotton cloth, and filling the can with melted fat which contains no salt. Grease can be freed from salt by boiling it in water. This is a much better arrangement than to use a shallow dish, or, as some have done, a mussel shell, and letting the end of the immersed wick project over one side, where it will drip grease. But such a light, although it was the best that many of our pioneers had in the olden days, is at best a smoky and stinking affair. The estimation in which it was held by those who had to use it may be judged from the fact that in English-speaking countries it has universally been known as a "slut," except in the Klondike, where they call it a "bitch."

Slush-Lamps.

A rush-light is made by soaking the pith of rushes in melted tallow. When dry, a length of the rush is then placed in a split stick, or any kind of clip, and lighted.

Wherever deer, elk, or other animals whose fat is tallow, are procurable, there is no excuse but laziness for such vile illumination. Very satisfactory candles can be made by the following process, which is called "dipping." For wicking, use cotton cord loosely unwound, or dry

Candles.

shredded bark. Put your tallow in a kettle with some boiling water. One part of hog's lard to three of tallow may improve the product. Scald and skim twice. Lay two poles sidewise and about a foot apart on supports, so that they shall be about as high from the ground as the top of an ordinary chair; cut some sticks about 15 or 18 inches long for candle rods; twist your wicking one way, then double it; slip the loop over the candle rod and twist the other way, making a firm wick; put about six wicks on each rod, a couple of inches apart. Dip a row of wicks into the melted tallow, place the rod across the two long poles, and thus dip each row of wicks in turn. Each will have time to cool and harden between the dips. If allowed to cool too fast they will crack: so work slowly. When the first dipping has hardened, repeat the process, and so on until the candles are of desired thickness. Replenish the tallow as needed, taking it off the fire, of course, for each dip. This is the way our foremothers made candles before they got candle molds. For a candlestick, split the end of a stick for several inches, then again crosswise; open these segments by pushing a flat, thin stick down each; insert candle, and remove wedges; sharpen the other end of the stick, and jab it into the ground wherever wanted. Or, put a loop of bark in the cleft end of a stick, the loop projecting at one side. Or, cut the end of a large potato square off, and gouge a hole for the candle in the opposite end.

Soap-Making.

Soap can be made wherever there is wood and grease. A rough-and-ready way is to boil wood ashes from the camp-fire in a little water and allow them to settle, the clear liquid being decanted off; this can be done from day to day until the required quantity of weak lye has accumulated. Evaporate this by boiling until it is strong enough to float an egg. Then melt down any kind of animal fat (do not have the kettle more than half full), and, while it is hot, add it to the boiling lye. Continue boiling and stirring until the mixture is of about the consistency of thick porridge; then pour it into any flat vessel and let it cool. The result is soft soap. To make hard soap, you have merely to stir into the above, as soon as it is poured out, some salt, in the proportion of two or three pints to five gallons of soap. A little powdered rosin added gradually to the melted tallow, before mixing with the lye, will make the soap firmer. Soap can be made without boiling, but it takes longer.

Only the ashes of hardwoods are good for lye; those of resinous woods will not mix with the fat in boiling.

Lye-Running. The woods richest in potash are hickory, sugar maple, ash, beech and buckeye. The poisonous kernels of buckeye are soapy and can be used to cleanse fine fabrics. As lye is often useful to a backwoods tanner, and for other purposes, it may be worth while to put up an ash-hopper at a permanent camp. Take a section of hollow tree, or a barrel with both heads knocked out. Stand it on a wide board that is elevated high enough for a bucket to stand below it. Cut a groove in the board around the bottom of the barrel and out to one end of the board. Tilt the board a little and fasten it so that the liquor from the barrel will follow the grooved channel to the end of the board and thus trickle into a pail set below it. Now put two or three layers of small round sticks in the bottom of the barrel, laying each course crosswise of the one below, cob-house fashion, and on top of this lay a couple of inches of straw or coarse grass; now put your ashes in the barrel, tamping them down firmly as they are shoveled in; make a funnel-shaped depression in the top and pour a bucket of water into it. It will be from half a day to a day before the leach will run. Thereafter keep some water standing in the depression, adding only when the other water has disappeared. If the ashes have been firmly tamped, the leach will only trickle through, and that is what you want. The first run will be strong enough to cut grease; later runs should be put through twice. Such lye needs no boiling down.

CHAPTER XXI

ACCIDENTS—THEIR BACKWOODS TREATMENT

THE present chapter is boiled down for the use of men of no surgical experience, who may suddenly find themselves wounded, or with an injured companion on their hands, when far from any physician, and with no special surgical appliances.

In operating upon a comrade, the main things are to keep cool, act promptly, and make him feel that you have no doubt that you can pull him through all right. Place him in a comfortable position, and expose the wound. If you cannot otherwise remove the clothing quickly and without hurting him, rip it up the seam. First stop the bleeding, if there is any; then cleanse the wound; then close it, if a cut or torn wound; then apply a *sterilized* dressing; then bandage it in place. Of course, if the injury is serious, you will immediately send a messenger hot-footed for a surgeon, provided there is any chance of getting one.

As for the patient himself, let him never say die. Pluck has carried many a man triumphantly through what seemed the forlornest hope. Let me take space for an example or two.

Kit Carson once helped to amputate a comrade's limb when the only instruments available were a razor, a handsaw, and the kingbolt of a wagon. Not a man in the party knew how to take up an artery. Fine teeth were filed in the back of the saw, the iron was made white-hot, the arm was removed, the stump seared so as to close the blood-vessels, and—the patient recovered.

Charles F. Lummis, having fractured his right arm so badly that the bone protruded, and being alone in the desert, gave his canteen strap two flat turns about the wrist, buckled it around a cedar tree, mounted a nearby rock, set his heels upon the edge, and threw himself backward. He fainted; but the bone was set. Then, having rigged splints to the injured member with his left hand and teeth, he walked fifty-two miles without resting, before he could get food, and finished the 700-mile tramp to Los Angeles with the broken arm slung in a bandanna.

Richardson tells of a Montana trapper who, having his leg shattered in an Indian fight, and finding that gangrene was setting in, whetted one edge of his big hunting knife, filed the other into a saw, and with his own hands cut the flesh, sawed the bone, and seared the arteries with a hot iron. He survived.

To Check Bleeding.

Stop the flow of blood temporarily by raising the injured part as high as you can above the heart, and pressing very firmly with thumb or finger either on or into the wound. The patient can do this for himself, and can control the bleeding until his hand gives out. There is record of an Austrian soldier who stopped bleeding from the great artery of the thigh for four hours by plugging the wound with his thumb; if he had let go for a minute he would have bled to death.

Observe whether the bleeding is arterial or venous. If it comes from a vein, the blood will be dark red or purplish, and will flow in a steady stream. Press upon the vein *below* the wound; then prepare a clean pad (compress) and bind it upon the wound firmly enough to stop the bleeding permanently.

If an artery is cut, the blood will be bright red, and it will probably spurt in jets. Try to locate the artery *above* the wound (between it and the heart) by pressing very hard where you think the artery may pass close to a bone, and watch if this checks the flow. When you find the artery, then, if the wound be in leg, arm, head, or any other place where a tourniquet can be applied, proceed as follows:

Tie a strong bandage (handkerchief, belt, suspender, rope, strip of clothing) around the wounded member, and between the wound and the heart. Under it, and directly over the artery, place a smoothe pebble, a cartridge, piece of stick, or other hard lump. Then thrust a stout stick under the bandage, and twist until the wound stops bleeding. The lump serves two purposes: it brings the most pressure where it will do the most good, and it allows passage of enough blood on either side to keep the limb from being strangled to death.

If the position of the artery above the wound cannot be determined, then, in case of a gaping wound that would be hard to plug, apply the tourniquet without any lump, and twist it very tight indeed. This can only be done for a short time, while you are preparing to ligate the artery; if prolonged, it will kill the limb, and gangrene will ensue. In case of a punctured wound, such as a bullet hole, it is better to push a plug hard down in the wound itself, leaving the outer end projecting so that a bandage will hold the plug firmly on the artery. This must be done, anyway, wherever a tourniquet cannot be used.

The above expedients are only temporary; for a cut artery, if of any considerable size, must be ligated—that is to say, permanently closed by tying one or both of the severed ends. To do this you must have at least a pair of sharp-pointed forceps or strong tweezers. Perhaps you may have to extemporize them—if you have no iron, make a little pair of tongs by heating the middle of a green hardwood stick, bending over, and then shaping and fire-hardening the ends. Get hold of the end of the artery with this, draw it out, and have some one hold it. Then take a piece of strong thread that has been sterilized in boiling salt water, make a loop in it as for a common knot, but pass the right hand end of the thread *twice* around the other, instead of once (surgeon's knot—it will never slip). Slip this loop down over the forceps and around the end of the artery, and draw tight. If the vessel bleeds from both ends, ligate both. When an artery is merely ruptured, not severed, cut it clean in two before operating; it will close better.

Powdered alum, tamped hard into a wound will stop

bleeding from all but a large artery. So will substances rich in tannin, such as powdered sumac leaves (dried over the fire, if green) and pulverized oak or hemlock bark. Do not use cobwebs, nor the woolly inside of puffballs—these old-fashioned styptics are likely to infect a wound with micro-organisms, and thus do more harm than good.

If a finger or toe is cut off, as with an axe, clap it quickly into place and bind it there; it may grow on again.

Nosebleed is sometimes uncontrollable by ordinary means. Try lifting the arms above the head and snuffing up alum water or salt water. If this fails, make a plug by rolling up part of a half-inch strip of cloth, leaving one end dangling. Push this plug as far up the nose as it will go, pack the rest of the strip tightly into the nostril, and let the end protrude. If there is leakage backward into the mouth, pack the lower part of plug more tightly. Leave the plug in place several hours; then loosen with warm water or oil, and remove very gently.

After stopping the flow of blood, cleanse the wound of any foreign substances that may have entered it.

Cleansing Wounds.

To remove a splinter, slip the point of a small knife-blade under the protruding end and catch it with the thumb nail. A fish-hook imbedded in the flesh should be pushed on through; then nip or file off the barb, and withdraw. If a bullet is deeply imbedded, let it alone; the chances are that it will do no harm.

After picking out dirt, bits of cloth, or other matter that would make the wound sore and slow to heal, wash the injured part with perfectly clean water. If there be any doubt about the water, boil it. Do not mop the wound with a rag. Hold the water a few inches above it and let a small stream gently trickle down upon it. A clean cut needs no washing; simply draw the edges together and fasten them in place. Whenever it can be done, shave the skin for some distance around the wound. Hairs, no matter how small, are grease-coated and favor the growth of germs.

Shaving also scrapes off the surface dirt and dead scales of skin.

Closing Wounds.

Never cover a wound with court plaster. It prevents the free escape of suppuration, inflames the part, and makes the place difficult to cleanse thereafter. The only legitimate uses for sticking plaster are to hold dressings in place where bandaging is difficult (as on the buttock), or, in case of a cut, to keep the edges closed without sewing the skin. In the latter case the cut may be crossed with narrow strips of plaster, leaving spaces between; but a better way, if you have regular surgeon's plaster, is as follows: Lay a broad strip on each side of the cut, half an inch apart, and extending beyond the wound at each end. Stick these strips firmly in place, except about a quarter of an inch of the inner margins, which are left loose for the present. With needle and thread lace the strips (deep stitches, so they'll not pull out) so as to draw the edges of the wound together, and then stick the inner margins down, not covering the wound.

Sewing a wound should be avoided by inexperienced persons, unless it really is necessary, as in the case of a foot almost severed by an axe cut. If an ordinary needle and thread must be used, sterilize them by soaking in a boiling solution of salt and water. (It is here assumed that no better antiseptic agents are available. Sugar and water, or vinegar will do in a pinch.) Do not sew continuously over and over, but make a deep stitch and snip off the thread, leaving enough at each end to tie with by and by. Repeat this at proper intervals, until enough stitches have been taken; then, go back and tie them, one after another, with surgeon's knot. Such sewing is easy to remove when the proper time comes, say within about six days.

Dressing Wounds.

All inflammation of wounds, suppuration, and blood poisoning, are due to living germs, and to *nothing else.* These germs are not born in the wound, but enter from the outside. We may as well say that they are present everywhere. To prevent their entrance is much easier than to kill them once they have gained foothold. The only guarantee of a wound healing nicely is to make it antiseptic—that is to say, *surgically clean.* That means sterilize everything used about a wound (by heat, if you have no antiseptics), not trusting that anything is germ-free merely because it *looks* clean. The micro-organisms that cause inflammation of a wound, fever, putrefaction, cannot be seen with the eye, and they may lurk anywhere. The unparalleled medical and surgical record of the Japanese in their late war was chiefly due to unparalleled cleanliness in camp and field.

Do not use a mere bandage directly on an open wound. First, cover the injury with a compress (soft pad, made by folding a strip of cloth in several layers); then bandage. Unless you have a first-aid packet, or are otherwise provided with sterilized dressings or antiseptics, hold the material of the compress over a clear fire until it is fairly scorched; then let it cool. A little charring of the surface will do no harm; in fact, charcoal is itself a good application to the surface of a wound. Of course the compress is to be renewed every time that the wound is dressed.

Directions for bandaging cannot be given here from lack of space. The cuts printed on the triangular bandage in a soldier's first-aid packet show, at a glance, how to bandage any part of the body. I cannot too highly recommend that every woodsman carry one of these packets in his pouch or pocket. It costs but a quarter, is no larger than a purse, and weighs practically nothing.

Burns.

If clothing sticks to the burn, do not try to remove it, but cut around it and flood it with oil. Prick blisters at both ends with a perfectly clean needle, and remove the water by gentle pressure, being careful not to break the skin. A good application for a burn, including sunburn, is carron oil (equal parts linseed oil and limewater). Druggists supply an ointment known as "solidified carron oil" that is easier to carry. A three per cent. solution of carbolic acid, applied with absorbent cotton or a bandage, is an excellent application. Better still is the salve known as unguentine. Lacking these, the next best thing is common baking soda.* Dissolve some in as little water as is required to take it up; saturate a cloth with this, and apply. Another good application for burns is the scrapings of a raw potato, renewed when it feels hot. If you have none of these, use any kind of clean oil or unsalted grease, or dust flour over the burn, or use moist earth, preferably clay: then cover with cotton cloth. Do not remove the dead skin until new skin has formed underneath.

Bruises. Ordinary bruises are best treated with cold, wet cloths. Raw, lean meat applied to the part will prevent discoloration. Severe bruises, which are likely to form abscesses, should be covered with cloth wrung out in water as hot as can be borne, to be reheated as it cools; afterwards with hot poultices.

Poultices. Poultices may be needed not only for bruises but for felons, boils, carbuncles, etc. They are easily made from corn-meal or oatmeal. Mix by adding a little at a time to boiling water and stirring to a thick paste; then spread on cloth. Renew from time to time as it cools.

To prevent a poultice from sticking, cover the under surface with clean mosquito netting, or smear the bruise with oil. It is a good idea to dust some charcoal over a sore before putting the poultice on. The woods themselves afford plenty of materials for good poultices. Chief of these is slippery elm, the mucilaginous inner bark of which, boiled in water and kneaded into a poultice, is soothing to inflammation and softens the tissues. Good poultices can also be made from the soft rind of tamarack, the root bark of basswood or cottonwood, and many other trees or plants. Our frontiersmen, like the Indians, often treated wounds by merely applying the chewed fresh leaves of alder, striped maple (moosewood), or sassafras. You may remember Leatherstocking (he was "Hawkeye" then)

* Baking soda is the bicarbonate; washing soda, or plain soda, is the carbonate: do not confuse them.

advising a wounded companion that "a little bruised alder will work like a charm."

Balsam obtained by pricking the little blisters on the bark of balsam firs is a good application for a wound; so is the honey-like gum of the liquidambar or sweet gum tree, raw turpentine from any pine tree, and the resin procured by "boxing" (gashing) a cypress or hemlock tree, or by boiling a knot of the wood and skimming off the surface. All of these resins are antiseptic and soothing to a wound.

Salves.

The regular medical treatment is to plunge a sprained ankle, wrist, or finger, into water as hot as can be borne at the start, and to raise the heat gradually thereafter to the limit of endurance. Continue for half an hour, then put the joint in a hot, wet bandage, reheat from time to time, and support the limb in an elevated position, the leg being stretched as high as the hip, or the arm carried in a sling. In a day or two begin gently moving and kneading the joint, and rub with liniment, oil, or vaselin.

Sprains.

In case of necessity, a sprain of the ankle can be *walked off*. You may shudder, but the thing has been done more than once. Similarly I have overcome, in a few hours, an attack of lumbago, though I had to start almost on all-fours. It was better than lying around a damp camp for a week—decidedly better after I got limbered up.

As a soothing application for sprains, bruises, etc., the virtues of witch hazel are well known. A decoction (strong tea) of the bark is easily made, or a poultice can be made from it. The inner bark of kinnikinick, otherwise known as red willow or silky cornel, makes an excellent astringent poultice for sprains. The pain and inflammation of a sprained ankle are much relieved by dipping tobacco leaves in water and binding them around the injured part.

Dislocations.

A dislocation of the finger can generally be reduced by pulling strongly and at the same time pushing the tip of the finger backward.

If a shoulder is thrown out of joint, have the man lie down, place a pad in his armpit, remove your shoe, and seat yourself by his side, facing him; then put your foot in his armpit, grasp the dislocated arm in both hands, and simultaneously push with your foot, pull on his arm, and swing the arm toward his body till a snap is heard or felt.

For any other dislocation, if you can possibly get a surgeon, do not meddle with the joint, but surround it with flannel cloths, wrung out in hot water, and support with soft pads.

Broken Bones.

If a bone is broken, and a surgeon can be summoned within a couple of days, do not try to reduce the fracture, for unskilled handling may do more harm than good. Place the man in a comfortable position, the injured part resting on a pad, and keep him perfectly quiet.

It may be, however, that you must act the surgeon yourself. If the bone is broken in only one place, and it does not protrude, the injury is not serious. Get splints and bandages ready. Rip the clothing up the seam, and steadily pull the broken parts in opposite directions, without the slightest twisting. Begin gently, and gradually increase the strain. It may take a strong pull. When the two pieces are end to end, an assistant must gently work them till they fit. This will be announced by a slight thud. Then apply splints, and bandage them so as to hold the injured member immovable while the fracture heals.

Bark, when it can be peeled, makes the best splints for an arm or leg. Pick out a sapling (chestnut, basswood, elm, cedar, spruce) as near the size of the limb as possible. Remove the bark in two equal pieces by vertical slits. It is well, in some cases, to have these somewhat longer than the bone that is broken, so as to clamp the connecting joints as well. Cover the concave insides with cloth, dry moss, crumpled grass, or other soft padding, to cushion the limb and prevent irritation. The edges of splints should not quite meet around the limb. Then get a long bandage, about two inches wide. Having set the bone, apply the splints on each side, and bandage them firmly enough to hold in place, but by no means so tightly as to impede circulation.

In default of bark, almost anything will do for splints that is stiff enough to hold the parts in place—barrel staves, thin boards, sticks, bundles of rushes, etc.

If a bone is broken in more than one place, or if it protrude through the skin, and you cannot fetch a surgeon to the patient, then get him out of the woods at all hazards. The utmost pains must be taken in transporting him, lest the sharp edges of the bones saw off an artery or pierce an important organ. The best litter is a big trough of bark, padded, and attached to a frame swung between two poles. A two-horse litter is better than a travois; but if the latter must be used, then make one shaft a little shorter than the other, so that, in crossing uneven places, the shock will not all come at one jolt.

Fainting.

Lay the patient on his back, with feet higher than his head. Loosen tight clothing, and let him have plenty of fresh air. Sprinkle his face with cold water and rub his arms with it. When consciousness returns, give him a stimulant. For an attack of dizziness, bend the head down firmly between the knees.

Shock.

In case of collapse following an accident, operation, fright: treat first as for fainting. Then rub the limbs with flannel, stroking the extremities toward the heart. Apply hot plates, stones, or bottles of hot water, wrapped in towels, to the extremities and over the stomach. Then give hot tea or coffee, or, if there is no bleeding, a tablespoonful of whiskey and hot water, repeating three or four times an hour.

Stunning.

Concussion of the brain: Lay the man on his back, with head somewhat *raised*. Apply heat, as for shock, but keep the head cool with wet cloths. Do not give any stimulant—that would drive blood to the brain, where it is not wanted.

Lay the patient in a cool place, position same as for

stunning. **Sunstroke.** If the skin is hot, remove clothing, or at least loosen it. Hold a vessel or hatful of cold water four or five feet above him and pour a stream first on his head, then on his body, and last on his extremities. Continue until consciousness returns. Renew if symptoms recur.

If the skin is cool (a bad sign) apply warmth, and give stimulating drinks.

Excessive Fatigue. Take a stimulant or hot drink when you get to camp (but not until then), and immediately eat something. Then rest between blankets to avoid catching cold.

Famishing. Do not let a starved person eat much at a time. Prepare some broth, or a gruel of corn-meal or oatmeal *thoroughly cooked*, and feed but a small spoonful, repeating at intervals of a few minutes. Give very little the first day, or there will be bloating and nausea.

Thirst. Allow the sufferer only a spoonful of water at a time, but at frequent intervals. Bathe him, if possible.

Freezing. Keep away from heat. To toast frost-bitten fingers or toes before the fire would bring chilblains, and thawing out a badly frozen part would probably result in gangrene, making amputation necessary. Rub the frozen part with snow, or with ice-cold water, until the natural color of the skin is restored. Then treat as a burn.

Chilblains should be rubbed with whiskey or alum water.

Poisonous Plants. A specific for poison ivy or poison sumac is tincture of grindelia. I have cured cases two or three days old, where both eyes were swollen shut and other parts correspondingly affected. Prompt application of a saturated solution of baking soda will generally check the trouble at the start. Dissolve plenty of the soda in hot water, and let it stand until cool, when the excess will be precipitated, and the liquor will be a saturated solution. Weak ammonia water serves as well. A hot decoction of the green bark of witch hazel is useful; apply as hot as can be borne. Other woodland remedies are decoctions of sassafras root, or of the bark and berries of common spice bush, taken both internally and externally. The druggist's prescription is: add powdered sugar of lead (lead acetate) to weak alcohol (50 to 75%) until no more will dissolve; strain, and wash the affected parts with it several times a day. To render the skin proof against these irritant poisons, bathe face and hands freely, before going out, in salt water, or the baking soda solution, or weak ammonia water.

If one swallows a vegetable poison, the remedy is an emetic, followed by whiskey or strong coffee, and, if necessary, artificial respiration as for drowning. To make an emetic, add a tablespoonful of common salt, or powdered mustard, to a tumblerful of lukewarm water.

Insect Stings.

Extract the sting, if left in the wound, and apply a solution of baking soda, or a slice of raw onion, or a paste of clay, mixed with saliva, or a moist quid of tobacco. Ammonia is the common remedy, but oil of sassafras is better. A watch key or other small hollow tube pressed with force over the puncture and held there several minutes will expel a good deal of the poison.

Bite of Rabid Animal.

The bite of a mad dog, wolf, skunk, or other animal subject to rabies, requires instant and heroic treatment. Immediately twist a tourniquet very tight above the wound, and then cut out the whole wound with a knife, or cauterize it to the bottom with a hot iron; then drink enough whiskey to counteract the shock.*

* The notion that skunk-bite is very likely to cause hydrophobia is common in the Southwest, and is borne out by the reports of army surgeons. The facts seem to be, as explained by W. Wade in the *American Naturalist*, that men and other animals have occasionally been stricken mad by skunk-bite and have died therefrom; but this has only happened during an epidemic of rabies, in which skunks, being slow-moving and utterly fearless creatures, fell easy prey to rabid dogs or wolves. Becoming mad, in their turn, they would bite men sleeping in the open, and their bites would usually be inflicted upon the men's faces, hands and other exposed parts of their persons. In such cases, since none of the poisonous saliva was wiped off by clothing, the result was almost certain death. But rabies is very exceptional among skunks, and the bite of a healthy animal is a trifling matter.

Snakebite.

The only dangerous snakes in the United States are the *rattlesnake*, the *copperhead*, and the *cottonmouth moccasin*. The small coral snake (harlequin, bead snake) of the Gulf states, and the Sonoran coral snake of New Mexico and Arizona, are somewhat venomous, but their bite is not fatal to a healthy adult. The Gila monster of the Southwest is a dangerous lizard—the only one that is venomous—but can scarcely be provoked to bite.

All other reptiles of our country and Canada are *harmless*—their bite is no more to be feared than that of a mouse. The notion that the bite of a puff-adder

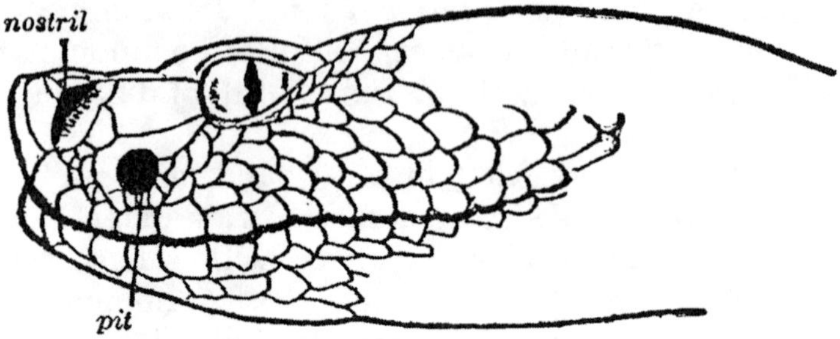

FIG. 23. Head of Rattlesnake. (After Stejneger.)

must be dangerous, because the snake puffs up its neck and hisses like a goose, or that the common water-snake is a moccasin and consequently venomous, is all moonshine, like the story of the hoop-snake and the snake with a poisonous sting in its tail.

However, that other notion that a rattlesnake's bite is not a serious matter is moonshine, too. Men who know nothing about other rattlers than the little prairie rattlesnake are not competent to express an opinion on the subject.

A bite from any venomous snake is dangerous, *in proportion to the size of the snake*, and to the *amount of venom that enters the circulation.* A bite that does not pierce an important blood vessel is seldom fatal, even if no treatment is given, unless the snake be quite large.

The rattlesnake, copperhead, and cottonmouth are easily distinguished from all other snakes, as all three of them bear a peculiar mark, or rather a pair of marks, that no other animal possesses. This mark is the *pit*, which is a deep cavity on each side of the face between the nostril and the eye, sinking into the upper jawbone. Its position is shown in the accompanying cut.

All venomous snakes have fangs, and no harmless ones have them. The fangs are in the upper jaw only. In the coral snakes they are permanently erect, but in the other venomous snakes here named they lie flat against the roof of the mouth, when not in use, pointing backward, and are erected by the reptile in striking. They are long, slender, sharply pointed, either grooved on the outside or perforated,* and connected by a duct with the venom glands which lie behind the eyes. Auxiliary fangs lie in a sac underneath the regular fang on each side, and, in case the latter is broken off or extracted, a new fang will be ready for business within a few days.

Here are a few characteristics of the pit vipers, as our three deadly snakes are collectively called:

1. *Copperhead* (also called deaf adder, upland moccasin, pilot snake, chunk head). A small snake, 2 to 3 ft. long, with moderately thick body, broad and triangular head quite distinct from the neck, tail short, dark colored, and pointed. Color of back, a bronze hazel or light reddish brown; with 15 to 20 darker bands, which are narrow on the back and expand to wide blotches on the flanks, the shape being somewhat like that of a dumb-bell with very short handle. Head, a bright copper-red, with two small dark-brown spots close together on the forehead at upper part of head-shield, and with a cream-colored band around the mouth.

The copperhead inhabits the mountainous and hilly regions from Massachusetts southward to the Gulf, and westward (south of Michigan, Wisconsin, Iowa, and Nebraska) to Kansas, Indian Ty., and Texas.

Its venom is as deadly as that of the rattlesnake, but it is not secreted in as large quantity as that of the larger rattlers; consequently the wound is not likely to be so serious. Still, the copperhead is a particularly dangerous creature, because

* High authorities have declared that the fang of the rattlesnake is not perforated, but only grooved. They are mistaken. I have examined many mature fangs of timber rattlesnakes killed by myself or by my companions within the past month, and every fang was perforated throughout, the front opening being exactly like that of a hypodermic needle. A fine wire can be run through, from base to point.

it gives no warning of its presence, nor, according to my observation, does it try to get out of the way, but holds its ground and springs at any intruder.

Only one species.

2. *Cottonmouth moccasin* (water moccasin). A larger snake, ordinarily about 3 ft., sometimes 4 ft. long. Stout body, head shaped like that of the copperhead and similarly distinct from the neck. Back brown, reddish, or olive, with 11 to 15 rather inconspicuous bars, or pairs of bars, of dark brown, with light centers on each flank. Tail short, pointed, and dark brown or banded. Belly brownish-yellow mottled with dark blotches.

Habitat, North Carolina southward to the Gulf, westward through Kentucky, southern Illinois, and Missouri, to Oklahoma and eastern Texas.

Not so poisonous as the larger kinds of rattlesnakes, but still dangerous to human life. Quite numerous in the southern states. More aggressive than the rattlesnake, striking at everything within reach; but usually rather deliberate about striking, first opening its mouth widely for some seconds, as if to intimidate, and showing the white interior (hence the name "cottonmouth"). Usually found near water, and often on low limbs overhanging the water.

Only one species. The other so-called "moccasins" are either the copperhead or harmless snakes.

3. *Rattlesnake*. Of rattlers we have no less than sixteen species, but only two of them, the massasauga and the banded or timber rattlesnake, are found in the eastern and central states. The little prairie rattlesnake, which is not very dangerous, is abundant on the plains west of the Missouri River. The great diamond rattlesnake of the South, which sometimes grows to a length of nearly nine feet, is the most formidable member of this group. The small ground rattlesnake of the southern states is aggressive, and gives only a faint warning, and on this account is more dreaded by the negroes than the larger species; but its bite is seldom fatal to grown people. The other species are confined to the southwest and the Pacific coast.

Rattlesnakes are easily identified by their rattles. These generally last only long enough to become 8 or 10 jointed. Rattles with as many as 15 or 18 joints are quite rare. The number of rattles does not indicate the snake's age. Their office is not clearly understood. Doctor Stejneger says: "They are a substitute for a voice."

When a rattlesnake sees a man approaching, it generally lies quiet to escape observation, so long as it thinks itself concealed. It does not strike unless provoked. If alarmed when it is wide-awake, it always springs its rattle before striking, the sound being very similar to that made by our common "locust" or cicada. If the reptile is trodden on when asleep, it strikes like lightning, and does its rattling afterward.

Unfortunately for us, the poisonous snakes sleep in the day time and hunt at night. They are prone to seek the warmth of bed-clothes, and will sometimes coil up alongside of a sleeping man. Mosquito netting is an effective bar against snakes. Snakes despise musk, tobacco, and turpentine.

A snake is not obliged to coil before striking, but can strike from any position; it will coil first, however, unless attacked very suddenly or taken at a disadvantage. A snake does not intentionally throw its venom; but, if it misses its mark, the act of hissing may throw the poison several feet. The blow is delivered with lightning rapidity, and the fangs are instantly sunk into the victim. No snake can leap entirely from the ground, nor can it strike more than two-thirds its own length, unless it has the advantage of striking downhill or from some purchase on a rock or bush. A snake does not expend all its venom at one blow. It is not rendered permanently harmless by extracting its fangs, for it will promptly grow new ones. A venomous snake is immune against its own poison, and probably against that of other poisonous reptiles, but non-poisonous snakes are not immune. The bite of even a newly-born snake of venomous species is serious.

The bite of a venomous reptile is intensely painful. The victim soon becomes dull and languid, breathing with difficulty. The venom first enfeebles the heart, then the breathing apparatus. If this early depression passes over, recovery is often sudden; but if the quantity of venom injected be large, death may follow, in man, within twenty minutes. The tendency of the poison is to spread very rapidly through the system, making the blood thin, and destroying its power to clot. At the same time it rots the blood-vessels, and, in fatal cases, causes a general seepage of blood throughout the system. In some cases a whole limb is soaked to the bone with decomposed blood. There is always inflammation around the wound, with great pain.

Much depends upon the part struck. Bites on the bare skin are more dangerous than those received through the clothing. A bite in the extremities is rarely fatal. In a large majority of cases the wound does not touch an important blood-vessel, and the patient will recover with no other treatment than a ligature promptly applied, and a free bleeding and sucking of the wound.

Many species of wild plants are popularly supposed to have the property of neutralizing the venom of serpents, but scientific research has failed to demonstrate that any of them have any effect on the poison at all. This, notwithstanding that probably all of the reputed "snake-masters" have been identified and their physiological action determined. However, I have received such positive and respectable testimony to the efficacy of the following three plants that I would like their properties thoroughly tested:

1. Common violet (*Viola Cucullata*).
2. Cedron seed (the fluid extract).
3. Sanicle (*Sanicula Marylandica*).

When a man is bitten he should instantly twist a tourniquet very tightly between the wound and the heart, to keep the poison, as far as possible, from entering the system. Then cut the wound wide open, so it may bleed freely, and suck the wound, if practicable (the poison is harmless, if swallowed, but not if it gets into the circulation through an abrasion in the mouth, or through a hollow tooth). Loosen the ligature before long to admit fresh blood to the injured part, but tighten it again very soon, and repeat this alternate tightening and loosening for a considerable time. The object is to admit only a little of the poison at a time into the general circulation. Meantime drink whiskey in moderate doses, but at frequent intervals. If a great quantity is guzzled all at once it will do more harm than good. Whiskey is not an antidote; it has no effect at all on the venom; its service is simply as a stimulant for the heart and lungs, thus helping the system itself to throw off the poison, and as a bracer to the victim's nerves, helping him over the crisis.

The only known positive antidotes for snake venom, in the form of drugs, are chromic acid, potassium permanganate, and strychnin, administered hypodermically. Of the former, a one per cent. solution is used. As for the permanganate, it is easy to carry in crystallized form, and I have frequently seen recommendations that it be carried in that way, to be dissolved in water before injecting, or to be merely rubbed into the opened wound. But a man may be struck when he is far from water. I do not believe that the crystals can be brought into close enough contact with the seat of the wound (bottom of puncture) with certainty, nor that they will dissolve quickly enough in blood, to do very much good. My own practice, when traveling in a "snake country," is to carry a solution of the permanganate in a glass-stoppered tube, together with a similar tube containing a solution of strychnin, and a hypodermic syringe. Promptitude with these remedies, after ligating, may be depended upon to cure the bite. Fresh permanganate solution should be made at intervals to avoid precipitation. Chronic acid does not precipitate.

As for the use of the hypodermic syringe, I here copy, by permission, a clear and concise article on this subject prepared expressly for explorers and other campers by Dr. H. Plympton, and published in Abercrombie & Fitch's catalogue:

THE USE OF THE HYPODERMIC SYRINGE

The following article gives directions for using the syringe and four remedies which are most likely to be needed.

These four remedies are:

First—Potassium permanganate in half-grain tablets.

Second—Cocain and morphin tablets composed of cocain, one-fifth grain; morphin, one-fortieth grain; soda chlor., one-fifth grain.

Third—Morphin in one-quarter-grain tablets.

Fourth—Strychnia in one-fortieth-grain tablets.

These four remedies are all that are absolutely necessary for emergencies, such as venomous insect, reptile or snake bite, exhaustion, shock, heart failure, minor surgical operations, and allaying intense pain.

The object of hypodermic medication is to get the remedy into the blood as quickly as possible and to introduce it as near as may be to the seat of injury or the pain. To insure its rapid assimilation by the blood, the medicine should be injected just between the skin and the muscles underneath; in other words, into the fat.

USE—Dissolve the tablet to be used in the proper amount

of water, or put any solution to be used into a teaspoon or what you may have that will hold it. A leaf properly folded will do; even the hollow of the hand in an emergency. You will find a fine wire run through the hollow needle to keep it clear. Remove this. Remove the cap from the end of the syringe and suck up the solution from the teaspoon by drawing out the piston of the syringe. Screw the needle firmly on the end of the syringe from which the cap was removed. Hold the syringe with the needle pointing upwards and press gently on the piston until the fluid begins to come out of the needle. This is to force all the air out of the syringe.

Now take up a fold or pinch of skin between the thumb and forefinger, insert the needle with a rotary motion of the syringe, as when boring a hole with an awl, being careful not to press on the piston while so doing. Keep the needle in a line with the line of the fold and it will be in correct position.

The needle will slip through the skin quickly and almost painlessly. Push it in its full length. Now press firmly on the piston and force it in slowly until the contents have been injected, being careful to keep the syringe in position. Withdraw the needle, and with the thumb press on the little hole made by the needle; with the first and second fingers rub the swelling made by the injected fluid for a few moments and it will disappear, leaving nothing but a tiny, red spot.

LOCATION—If the injection be made between the skin and the muscles, as described, it may be made anywhere on the body, although just over a bone that is close to the surface, as the shin bone, or on the back of the hand, are places to be avoided. Also in the bend of the elbows and knees and in the armpits are vessels that would be injured by the careless use of the syringe. The outside of the forearm or the upper arm, the calf of the leg, or the thigh, the big muscles of the buttocks, and the shoulder, and anywhere on the back are all places where the needle may be used without hesitation.

A short needle, three-eighths of an inch long, accompanies most outfits, and this may be used without taking up a fold of the skin; simply jabbed quickly and firmly as deep as it will go straight into any one of the big muscles.

The dangers in the use of the hypodermic are practically nothing. Exercise the same amount of care as in administering medicine by the mouth and no harm can be done; and as, in the case of a rattlesnake wound, the advantages are so immeasurably ahead of any treatment by the mouth, even if it were dangerous, it would be worth taking the chance.

PRECAUTIONS—Be sure that the tablet is thoroughly dissolved, or you may force a piece into the needle and spoil it. Ten drops of water will dissolve any one tablet, and fifteen will suffice for any two, especially if the water be warm. Do not use more tablets than this, unless by direction. After using the syringe, and before removing the needle, draw up some water and eject it to clear the needle. A little vaselin or gun grease on the wire will prevent the needle from rusting.

FIRST—For venomous insect and snake bite, tie a piece of small rope, a heavy handkerchief, or a bandage, loosely around the limb two and one-half inches from the wound and between the wound and the heart. (If the wound be on the face or the body, this is manifestly impossible.) Tighten this binder by twisting a stick in it till the binder sinks into the flesh and is quite painful. This is to stop circulation as much as possible. Prepare the syringe, using a short needle. Dissolve one one-half-grain tablet of potassium permanganate in two teaspoonfuls of water. Fill the syringe and inject at once half the contents directly into the swelling made by the bite. Inject the remainder about an inch nearer the body. Use deep injection if possible, otherwise just under the skin. Two more injections must now be made in the immediate neighborhood of the wound, each of them being about half a syringeful and all between the wound and the bandage. As the swelling of the limb increases, the binder may be gradually loosened, and after half an hour it may be removed entirely.

Immediately after giving the injection of potassium permanganate dissolve one tablet of strychnia sulph. (one-fortieth of a grain) in about fifteen drops of water and inject it into the outside surface of the upper arm, midway between the elbow and the shoulder and just under the skin. Dissolve another strychnia tablet and prepare it in the syringe. Note the symptoms. The first symptoms are excitement, quickened pulse and rapid breathing, followed by depression, shallow breathing and drowsiness. This condition must be treated by tablespoonful doses of brandy or whiskey at half-hour intervals. Three doses will be enough. Large amounts of whiskey will not cure snake-bite, *but will do much harm.*

The condition of the respiration must be carefully watched, and if there is a continuance or recurrence of "shallow" or quick breathing, the second syringeful of strychnia should be injected into the arm as before. This strychnia injection may be repeated at fifteen-minute intervals—one tablet at each injection until five tablets have been given, or the breathing becomes more nearly normal.

The patient should not be allowed to sleep for more than two hours continuously during the first twenty-four hours. The bowels should be made to move freely by means of cathartic pills, salts or oil. Cheerful and encouraging suggestions will do much to counteract the depression following the absorption of the poison.

Careful investigation and close observation of properly authenticated cases of rattlesnake poisoning have led to the positive conclusion that a man in good general health will stand an even chance of recovery from a rattlesnake strike without any treatment whatever. With a hypodermic syringe and proper remedies at hand, there is no danger of a serious result.

SECOND—For minor surgical operations the cocain and morphin tablet should be used as follows: Dissolve one tablet in one teaspoonful of water and take up a syringeful of the solution. Inject half the quantity under the skin, not deep, where the cut is to be made. Almost immediately the skin will become waxlike—this will indicate that the part is benumbed, so that an incision can be made without causing pain. Make a sufficient number of injections to cover the part to be cut. The surface benumbed by each injection will be about the size of a 25-cent piece.

THIRD—For allaying intense pain and physical suffering morphin should be used by dissolving one tablet (one-quarter grain) in about ten drops of water and injecting it under the skin as near the seat of the pain as possible. If the pain is caused by some injury, such as a broken bone or a severe burn, and is likely to last, a second tablet may be given in fifteen minutes and a third one twenty minutes later. Pain is the antidote for morphin, and as long as pain exists there is no danger from a much larger dose than the above. If, however, the pain arises from some cause, such as cramps, that is likely to end abruptly, the above dose is enough.

FOURTH—For exhaustion, shock, great fatigue, hunger, heart failure, strychnia should be used as follows: Dissolve the tablet in ten drops of water and inject into the outside of the arm, midway between the elbow and the shoulder. The condition of exhaustion, whether from great exertion, loss of blood, or hunger, has caused a marked depression of the heart's action and the nervous system is noticeably affected. The patient is pale, a cold perspiration covers the face, the breathing is shallow and quick, and the pulse is faint and very rapid. One injection will show a decided effect, but if a second is necessary fifteen minutes afterward do not hesitate to give it.

[A traveler should examine the syringe from time to time so as to ensure that it is in working order.]

Drowning. On this subject I can do no better than reprint the instructions issued by the U. S. Volunteer Life-Saving Corps, which are as follows:

RESCUING—Approach the drowning man from behind, seizing him by the coat collar, or a woman by the back hair, and tow him at arm's length to boat or shore. Do not let him cling around your neck or arms to endanger you. Duck him until unconscious if necessary to break a dangerous hold upon you: but do not strike to stun him.

RESUSCITATION—*First:* Immediately loosen the clothing about the neck and chest, exposing them to the wind, except in very severe weather, and *get the water out of the body.*

First try tickling in the throat by a straw or feather, or ammonia to the nose; try a severe slap with the open hand upon the chest and soles of feet; if no immediate result, proceed as follows:

Second—Lay the body with its weight on the stomach, across any convenient object, a keg, box, boat, timber or your knee, in the open air, with the head hanging down. Open the mouth quickly, drawing the tongue forward with handkerchief or cloth so as to let the water escape. Keep the mouth clear of liquid. Then roll the body gently from side to side so as to relieve the pressure on the stomach, then back to the stomach. Do this several times to force the water from the stomach and throat.

Third—Laying the body on the back, make a roll of coat or any garment, place it under the shoulders of patient, allowing the head to fall back. Then kneel at the head of the patient. Grasp the arms at the middle of the forearms, folded across the stomach, raise the arms over the head to a perpendicular position, drawing them backwards straight, then forward overhead to the sides again, pressing the arms on the lower part of the ribs and sides, so as to produce a bellows movement upon the lungs. Do this sixteen or eighteen times a minute. Smelling salts, camphor or ammonia may be applied to the nostrils to excite breathing. But give no spirits internally until after breathing and circulation are restored. The clothing should be removed, the body dried, and the legs rubbed briskly upwards, from foot to knee, occasionally slapping the soles of the feet with the open hand.

Fourth—On signs of life, or when breathing is restored, wrap in warm blanket or hot cloths. To encourage circulation, hot tea, brandy or any spirits may be given in small doses, with care to avoid strangulation, and brisk rubbing and warmth applied to the entire body.

Keep at work until recovery, or death is pronounced certain by a physician. Persons have revived after two hours' steady work, but most cases revive within thirty minutes.